This Green World

RUTHERFORD PLATT

This Green World

Foreword to this Edition by
Rutherford H. Platt, Jr.

Preface, New Material, and
Bibliography by Carl P. Swanson

The
Edwin Way Teale
Library of
Nature Classics

DODD, MEAD & COMPANY · NEW YORK

First paperback edition published in 1988 by Dodd, Mead & Company, Inc.
71 Fifth Avenue, New York, New York 10003.
Manufactured in the United States of America.
Second Edition

1 2 3 4 5 6 7 8 9 10

Library of Congress Cataloging-in-Publication Data

Platt, Rutherford Hayes, 1894–1975
This green world.

(The Edwin Way Teale library of nature classics)
Bibliography: p.
Includes index.
1. Botany—Popular works.   I. Platt, Rutherford H.
II. Swanson, Carl P.   III. Title.   IV. Series.
QK50.P55   1988   582.16   87-33142
ISBN 0-396-09189-X (pbk.)

Contents

CONTENTS

FLOWERS

SUPPLEMENTS

Acknowledgments

It is customary to acknowledge assistance in writing a book of this sort by mentioning a long list of names. This is apt to consist of prominent scientists who were kind enough to answer a question, to aid in finding a reference, or to send a pamphlet. For the friendship of botanists and what they have taught me, I am inexpressibly grateful. But to imply by naming them that they are directly interested in this book seems to me a little presumptuous.

One exception is the help given by Dr. Beulah Ennis Glasgow, Curator of the Geneva Nature Museum, Geneva, New York, and formerly head of the Biology Department of Lindenwood College, who generously read the manuscript. As I have never been fortunate enough to meet Dr. Glasgow, her criticisms may be all the more constructive because they are uninfluenced by personal acquaintance.

It is only fair, also, to acknowledge the generosity of Dr. R. P. Wodehouse and his publisher, McGraw-Hill Book Company, Inc., for permission to use the pictures of the pollen grains on page 140. They are from Dr. Wodehouse's remarkable book entitled *Pollen Grains*.

The Yale University Press kindly gave permission to use the diagrams of the maple leaf and the regular pentagon on page 43. These appeared originally in *Dynamic Symmetry: The Greek Vase*, by Jay Hambidge.

A number of the line diagrams showing leaf and flower forms were originally made by the author for *Patapar News*, and permission to use them in this book was granted by the Paterson Parchment Paper Company.

Foreword

Recently, a geography graduate student at the University of Massachusetts submitted a thesis on the use of remote sensing imagery to detect stress in oak forests (such as due to acid rain). Her research project involved computer analysis of wave length patterns of light reflected from oak leaves as detected by a Landsat camera orbiting some 150 miles above the earth.

At about this time, I happened to reread my father's *This Green World* to prepare this introductory note. This book looks at the same subject matter as my student's thesis but through the opposite end of the telescope. My father explored the details of trees with his Zeiss Contax from a distance of inches, a very different experience from sifting through computer data obtained from outer space. Ironically, the more advanced our technical capabilities, the more remote, literally and emotionally, we become from the stuff of nature. (My student admitted that the best part of the project for her was hiking in the Quabbin forest in central Massachusetts to collect "ground truth" leaf specimens.)

This Green World was the work of an amateur who had neither studied formally nor previously published in the field of natural science. It was first published in November 1942, when much of the world was anything but green. The book quickly gained popularity with the help of a series of photographic excerpts that appeared in *Life Magazine* amid accounts of World War II invasions, bombings, and cities in ruins. The book perhaps provided a needed literary and aesthetic oasis from the tumults of war.

This Green World was soon recognized to be not only timely but timeless. In 1945, it was awarded the John Burroughs Medal as the year's "foremost literary work" in the field of natural science. This was the first time the award had been made to a non-professional naturalist since its establishment in 1921. The book was reprinted several times by Dodd, Mead, eventually going out of print in the late 1950s. It marked the beginning of a tremendously productive phase of my father's life that lasted essentially until his death in 1975. Before considering his subsequent work, however, it is intriguing to review what led up to this seminal book.

My father was born August 11, 1894, as the second eldest son in a prominent, conventional late-Victorian household in Columbus, Ohio. His full name (as well as mine), Rutherford Hayes Platt, was derived from his great-uncle, the nineteenth U.S. President. The Hayes connection opened doors to my father; a 1911 diary entry records a casual visit to President Taft in the White House while visiting a Hayes cousin in Washington. He seems to have spent most of his youth commuting by train between Columbus and schools in New England, first Groton, then Hotchkiss, and finally Yale. His experience at Hotchkiss was apparently favorable since he and his second wife (my mother) purchased ten acres of wooded property in Lakeville, Connecticut, within sight of the school in 1937. But that is getting ahead of the story.

Yale to my father was William Lyon Phelps, the great professor of English literature. Phelps's thousand-page *Autobiography* was one of his most treasured books; his copy is profusely annotated. Under Phelps's tutelage, Dad emerged from Yale a writer. But as noted early in *This Green World*, he and his classmates knew nothing more of botany than the elms of the Yale campus, where their college days quickly passed.

In fact they passed more quickly than expected because much of the Yale Class of '18 spent their senior year in military camps. Dad was assigned to an Ohio artillery regiment that was shipped to France in June and to the front at Argonne in September. After six weeks of bitter combat, the armistice brought peace and converted my father into "mayor" of the occupied town of Dernbach. During the ensuing months, he co-authored a lively and high-spirited account of his unit's war experience: "A History of Battery F, 323rd Field Artillery," which was privately printed by its commanding officer. The war also inspired his first serious book, *Mr. Archer, U.S.A.*, published by Doubleday in 1924. This biography of a crusty career Army officer won no literary prizes but established its author (in the eyes of his family at least) as a serious writer.

During the 1920s, Dad worked for Doubleday and raised his first family nearby in Garden City, Long Island. During this period he wrote a strange assortment of articles whose eclecticism suggests indecision in the selection of genre and subject matter. These included, for instance, a piece on the uses of IQ tests ("A New Way with Dullards and Scapegoats," *The World's Work*, September 1920); a biographical essay on Joseph Conrad ("How Conrad Came to Write," *The Mentor*, March 1925); and a surprisingly good short story in the style of F. Scott Fitzgerald ("Puritan Sinners," *Woman's World*, July 1925). His writings encompassed both the sublime (editor of *The Lost Books of the Bible*, 1926) and the absurd (*You Can't Fail*, 1929—which proved to be his foremost flop). In the height of the Depression, he produced *The Book of Opportunities: A Dictionary of Jobs* (1933), which advised the unemployed how to become a "wig maker," "snout puller," "sandwich woman" ("Not required to pace street, wear placards, if sandwiches are succulent."), or "captain" ("Last man to leave ship . . . empowered to marry couples impatient of delay").

This crazyquilt of whimsy and pretense ended in the mid-1930s as Dad launched a serious career as a New York advertising executive. At about this time, he also launched a new marriage and family. He purchased the acreage in Connecticut previously mentioned and with my mother built a rustic cottage for weekend and summer getaways. Whether the Lakeville property was cause or effect of his discovery of the natural world is not clear, perhaps a little of both. But the halcyon surroundings obviously stimulated his scientific curiosity and his muse. He began to explore the natural world around him with hand lens and camera, and to broaden his technical information base through study of copious texts and treatises on botany. *This Green World* at last appeared, a rare blend of scientific description, photographic and literary artistry, and mischievous good humor. He had found his voice.

This Green World was in fact mistitled. It deals not with the macro-environment of the biosphere, but with the micro-elements of individual trees: leaves, bark, cambium, buds, tree flowers, pollen. It intentionally ignores the forest for the trees. This perspective was then reversed in the sequel published by Dodd, Mead in 1947, *Our Flowering World*. The latter book assumed the perspective of the yet unnamed science of ecology, tracing the evolution of the North American forest from the basic cell, to the carbon swamp, to the "seed revolution," to the ice ages and the advent and spread of modern forests. Now confident in his newfound style, Dad treated these cosmic matters with a combination of rapture, scientific detail, and whimsy. It was embellished by some of his best photographs. *Our Flowering World* was revised and reissued as *The Woods of Time*. A further reworking of the basic themes of all three books appeared in 1965 as *The Great American Forest*, his final and perhaps best tree book.

The influence of the Ice Age on forest development fascinated Dad. In the summer of 1947, he took leave of his wife and new brood of three children to sail north to the polar regions with Admiral Donald B. MacMillan aboard the famous arctic schooner "Bowdoin." During three months of rigorous sailing and exploring along the coasts of Labrador, Baffin Island, and Greenland, Dad took 4,000 botanical photographs and collected several thousand specimens of miniature arctic flora for the New York Botanical Garden. Besides having a whale of a good time, he established himself as a bona fide field researcher. He published his botanical findings from this and a second expedition with MacMillan in 1954 in a *Scientific American* cover article (February 1956), as well as in *The National Geographic* and elsewhere. Dad's two arctic odysseys were among the high points of his life; Donald and Miriam MacMillan became two of his closest friends. He later wrote a biographical tribute to "Mac" that appeared in *Reader's Digest* (February 1966).

Another good friend and influence upon Dad's work in the 1950s was Walt Disney, who invited him to serve as a science consultant in the production of several of the famous "True-Life Adventure" films, such as "Secrets of Life" and "Living Desert." These films were cinematographic equivalents to *This Green World* in the blending of exquisite photography and lively, entertaining narrative, with the further addition of musical background. (This art form has been superbly adapted for television by The National Geographic Society and the Nova series.) Dad also wrote two children's books for Disney: *Secrets of Life* (1957) and *Worlds of Nature* (1957).

Although my father maintained his toehold in the rapidly expanding and increasingly cut-throat New York advertising industry until the late 1950s, his heart was clearly in his writing. His *Pocket Guide to Trees* was first published by Pocket Books in 1952 and was subsequently revised and republished by Dodd, Mead in 1960 and 1968 as *Discover American Trees*.

The River of Life (Simon and Schuster, 1956) marked a bold departure from his previous genre. Its subject was the insect world, not trees, and it was illustrated not with Platt photographs, but with sixteen full-page line drawings by Bernarda Bryson. This was a richly descriptive work of prose with chapter titles worthy of Stephen King (e.g., "Curtains of Mystery" and "A Splash of Sun Fire"). It was published in England as *The Living World* and was also issued in both French and Flemish editions.

Dad went even further afield, so to speak, in his surprising book *Wilderness* (Dodd, Mead, 1961). This and a subsequent children's book, *Adventures in the Wilderness* (American Heritage Junior Library, 1963), dealt with the exploration and settlement of the North American continent. These were nonscientific excursions along the paths of anecdote and imagination in which forests served as backdrop rather than the cast of the drama. Soon thereafter, *The Great American Forest* (Prentice-Hall, 1965) appeared, which provided an elegant and eloquent coda to the tree books of Rutherford Platt.

His creative juices were still flowing vigorously. Beginning in 1961, at the age of sixty-seven, Dad started an entirely new type of science writing in the form of a series of original articles for *Reader's Digest*. This ultimately yielded ten articles with an eleventh in progress at the time of his death in 1975. With its readership of millions, *Reader's Digest* had special requirements that made demands beyond any of Dad's previous writing activities. Each article involved countless revisions with intense scrutiny of every word. For an old man with a bad back and ulcers this was a tough road. But the articles kept appearing on a wealth of subjects including DNA, extra-sensory perception, biorhythms, life on the ocean floor, the cell, trees, a MacMillan tribute, and a wistful, last look at Ohio. During this period he also produced a final book (*Water: The Wonder of Life*, Prentice-Hall, 1971), which was translated into German and Japanese.

Always restless, Dad found time and energy during his last decade for some rigorous travel—to the Shetlands and Orkneys, to Spitzbergen, and to the central desert of Australia. Thanks to the Disney influence, he made these trips not simply with the old Contax and light meter, but with a baggage train of his personal movie equipment. He converted our upstairs hall into a miniature Disney studio with terns divebombing to the strains of the "1812 Overture" or sandpipers parading solemnly to Debussy's "La Mer."

Dad ironically remained a New Yorker to the end, although he professed to despise city life. He served as a board member of both the New York and Brooklyn Botanical Gardens, and was a longtime member of the Yale Club.

In 1960, he was elected to the extraordinary status of "Lay Fellow" of the American Association for the Advancement of Science. But by and large, he was a maverick to scientific orthodoxy. He eschewed a rigid academic style, and wrote for a more general, albeit educated, audience. His writing exudes enthusiasm, which is anathema to the proper, credentialed scientist. Yet many an experienced botanist trained in the 1940s and 50s has expressed to me their admiration for his work. As an academician myself, I chafe under the constraints of writing for a strictly professional audience in a sober and disciplined style. (It has been said that the average refereed journal article has three readers: the writer, the writer's mother, and the plagiarist.)

It is therefore a joy to revive *This Green World*. In a world contemplating the ecosuicide of nuclear winter, this book speaks eternal truths.

Rutherford H. Platt, Jr.
Northampton, Massachusetts

Preface

A remarkable lineage of American naturalists and writers ac-
cepted the earth as they found it, saw that it was good, and led
others to share it with them. These were not conscious prophets
or media-oriented environmentalists with a messianic mission.
No, they were, or so it seems to me, writers of a finer breed.
They were freer in spirit, devoid of limiting ideologies; sensitive
to the beauty and diversity of natural things, both large and small;
rolling through the night skies with the Pleiades, or following
Orion, the hunter, in his chase; tuned to the wind in the grass,
and feeling the sting of salt spray from the breaking wave; and
having no need to conquer Nature, but only to observe and to
enjoy her in all of her varied moods, and to be constantly renewed by her changing aspects. And these writers carry us with
them by their words, each with a style peculiarly his own, but

each adding to a literature that is not diminished by being read time and again.

For me the lineage begins with the gentle curate of Selborne, Gilbert White, whose *Natural History and Antiquities of Selborne* (1798) has gone through more than two hundred editions. There were others who preceded him—Mark Catesby, for example—but there is only one Gilbert White. To name but two more in England, Charles Darwin, with his *Voyage of the Beagle*, was a worthy nineteenth-century successor to White, while W. H. Hudson's *A Shepherd's Life* and *Green Mansions* continued the lineage over into the beginnings of the twentieth century. In America the tradition of natural history writing begins with William Bartram's *Travels Through North and South Carolina, Georgia, East and West Florida* (1791), one of the earliest American volumes to be acclaimed in Europe, and an inspiration to the Romantic poets, especially Samuel Coleridge. The *Journals* of Lewis and Clark would follow in the early 1800's, then the works of the enigmatic Thoreau, and later the writings of John Muir and John Burroughs. The twentieth century would bring a galaxy of natural historians, more numerous perhaps because they are closer to me in time: Henry Beston, Donald Culross Peattie, Rachael Carson, Loren Eisley, Aldo Leopold and Edwin Way Teale. There are many others in this, and earlier, periods, but if I were to choose my favorite writings they would be Beston's *Outermost House* and Leopold's *Sand County Almanac*.

Amid this band of gifted writers and keen observers of the natural scene one would find Rutherford Platt. As with his contemporaries, he was an inheritor of a rich past, but an imitator of no one. He wore his earned mantle with the easy grace that typifies the outdoor man; in all seasons, he was at home in field and forest. No writer of purple prose, his style was simple and direct, the scientific fact was linked comfortably with easy description, and the reader is carried along as he shares his feelings of delight and respect for plants in a manner unassuming but evocative. Indeed, his writings in their totality can be thought of as a paean of botanical delight, and of his joyful awe in the presence of those amazing things we call plants.

But 1942, when *This Green World* appeared, was a long time ago, and the plant sciences have not stood still. The descriptive tenor of the first half of the century has given way to an analytical fervor that had its genesis in the discovery of the structure of DNA in 1953, and has continued at an accelerated pace. The plant of field and forest is now the plant of the laboratory: ground up, chemically analyzed in the test tube and minutely examined in the electron microscope, genetically altered to such an extent that we can justly think of the entire plant kingdom as one huge gene pool, and artificially manipulated in ways hardly dreamed of a few decades ago. Some of the areas of botany affected by this surge of advancing science are dealt with in the addenda to certain chapters, and the bibliography has been revised accordingly to lead the reader to sources of additional information, and so to enhance the original text. But this is not a revised edition; the original text has remained untouched so that the unaltered essence of Rutherford Platt is brought to you.

—Carl P. Swanson

CHAPTER ONE

Listen to Them Grow

You can hear the tattoo of rain on leaves; the burring of tree limbs as they rub together; the hiss of wind across a field of dry grass. But that is not listening to the plants of this green world grow. Behind the poetry of the landscape are mechanisms of dramatic events. Gay colors, fragrance, marvelous designs are outward expressions of never-ending activities. Listen again— not with your ears this time but with imagination. You may hear the wrenching of bark as it forms its patterns; the whirr of a studded pollen grain through the air; the report of a bursting seed; the tinkle of sap in the tubes of a tree trunk; the whisper of air and water being converted by chlorophyll; the twang of red rays ricochetting from the petal of a cardinal flower; the muffled sounds in roots expanding with the power of dynamite. The landscape is a vast system constantly in action.

Some of the actions of plants are so fast, such as the bursting of pollen sacs and the ejection of pollen, or so obscure, like the releasing of spring mechanisms that throw out seeds, that we hardly perceive that they happen at all. Other actions are so slow, such as the elongation of a twig or the turning of leaves to receive light, that we never think of them as motion. Yet if you poke your finger forward in a corkscrew spiral there is no difference, in space, between that motion and the motion of the tip end of a growing twig—but only a difference in time. The same is true with structures. Pollen is so small in our everyday perspective that it looks like dust, instead of billions of perfectly formed units, each one containing the essence for creating a fully equipped plant. On the other hand, the strides of evolution move on such a large scale that we regard the different kinds of flowers and trees as finally fixed types, instead of fluid, with new forms constantly in the making.

To see these realities of motion and change you must look at trees and flowers, not once, as most people do, but twice—the second time with an eye for their functional beauty and mechanical precision. Doing so, your attention is caught and held. You are filled with curiosity. You suddenly wonder why some flowers open in sunlight and fold up in the rain, how a root system gets inside hard ground, and where the leaves that a tree unfurls in the spring have been stored all winter.

This dynamic point of view offers the fascination of finding something unexpected at every turn. You may learn to call every flower you see by name, but you will never be able to know all the secrets about that flower. There is always something new to discover. Between here and the horizon there lies a world of beauty and brilliance, action and climax, but no finale. And beyond the horizon, there stretch more trees, more flowers—and fungi, ferns, clubmosses and horsetails.

Three hundred twenty-five of us were graduated one June not so many years ago with B.A. degrees from Yale. If any one of that group could call by name any native tree but the elm, I don't know who he was. The elm we all knew. Its deliquescent branches arched the campus and it was celebrated in a song

2

'Neath the Elms. But such recognition was hardly more complete than knowing the outside of a building which is a familiar presence but which you have never entered, and about which you feel no curiosity.

I am quite sure that few, if any, of us bachelors of art knew the following facts about the world around us: that there is an unbroken column of water in every living tree extending from the deepest rootlet to the topmost twig and that by a highly efficient mechanism the tree pulls on this as on a rope, lifting tons of water; that leaves are green because they throw away green light while absorbing and using blue and red light; that trees like oaks, elms and maples have flowers; that buds do not come out in the spring but are out and fully formed in the fall; that the flamboyant fall foliage is not just a dress parade, but a vital act of a tree and related to its preservation through the winter; that there is not *an* elm tree, but four kinds of elm; not *an* oak tree, but possibly a dozen separate and distinct kinds of oak in any one neighborhood; six kinds of maple; five kinds of hickory.

If we were ignorant, back there when we were given diplomas, of such basic, highly interesting facts about the trees of the world in which we live, we were even less aware of wild flowers and their dramatic performances. We knew by name more flowers than trees, thanks to some primary grade teacher years back. But for bachelors of art the subject of skunk cabbages and buttercups had about as much meaning and prestige as paper dolls.

Ours was the academic world of literature, history and language, of athletics, social life and to some extent of man-made mechanical things like cars and boats. No one knew . . . that the flower which is called a *daisy* in everyday life is actually a closely packed aggregation of several hundred flowers, that each dot in the yellow center is a separate and complete flower, and each white "petal" is a separate and complete flower . . . that roses and strawberries and apples are so closely related that they are members of the same family . . . that orchids grow not only in hothouses and equatorial jungles, but also abound all around us in woods and fields (there are forty native species of orchids in the State of Connecticut) . . . that wheat, oats, corn, rye and sugar cane are grass, even though aristocratic grass . . . that every flower advertises for the special kind of insect with which it wants to collaborate in its life cycle, and has ingenious ways of rejecting other kinds of insect . . . that the various stages of the scale of evolution from the simplest form of plant life (bacteria) to the highest form (the daisy and its kin) can actually be seen growing together like a diagram of the ages in almost any lush acre in its natural state.

This book contains a few hints of what is to be found and what goes on in our everyday outdoor environment. The point is that this natural world is thrilling in the way it works. I am not thinking so much of the poetry and melody, or of reflecting on a tree or flower as you might on a masterpiece in an art gallery. I am thinking of the mental stimulation, of the value of information, of accuracy of expression, of the feeling of freedom, and sheer entertainment—all around us and available at little expense and bother for anyone who will only take a look.

As a business man who has had the surprise of his life, I can assert that you will enjoy looking twice at trees and flowers because they are exciting, refreshing, reassuring. Maybe you will also feel as I do that they are part of the power and glory of America, part of the sweep and dignity of life.

CHAPTER TWO

World's Greatest Waterworks

When I was a boy in Columbus, Ohio, I took trees for granted, like the furniture in the house. I never thought of trees as changing. They were solid; they had no particular animation. Leaves came and went seasonally for no special reason, just as slip covers come and go on a sofa.

Nevertheless, a dozen trees in our yard were so much a part of a boy's world that I can see them today vividly and in every detail. I can see them and feel them: the texture and color of the bark, the angles of the limbs, the size and outline of the whole tree. So clear is this photograph of memory that today I can key out these trees in retrospect and call them by name. Yet, as a boy, I knew only the apple and the pear by name.

Of all trees, the apple is the most friendly. One grew behind our house and we lived with it and in it for years. Today every mature old-fashioned apple tree seems to me a copy of that one

. . . stocky and leaning, the blue-gray bark tinged with lavender. A boy wearing sneakers or barefoot can walk up an apple tree like that on all fours. The fluted trunk gives a toe hold. If you take a running start, you can usually reach a knothole on the right side which gives a good grip. Then you draw yourself up into the wide open crotch a dizzy five feet above the ground. There, at the top of the trunk, smooth muscular limbs curve outward. It's a perfect arrangement for nailing boards to make a platform and seats. Besides, this tree supplies apples in which you can get some delicious bites between worm tunnels.

Another of our trees was like a bully who forces you to do things that are cruelly hard to do. Its trunk was a perpendicular column, without lateral branches. Some ten feet above the ground, a great height from the boy's eye level, this unfriendly column separated into two equal parts that continued to pour upward at steep angles. The bark was rough and dingy gray. When you wrapped your arms around the tree to shinny up, your sweater was frayed, shirt dirtied, and buttons torn off. To win prestige among your fellows, you must reach the crotch but no relaxation could be found there. You had to hug one of the limbs and hold on for dear life, while the V-shaped vise caught your foot and tore off your sneaker. Many times since then I have seen this tree, the American elm, with up-pouring branches at steep angles, absence of low branches and twigs, and crown high in the sky. It's a fountain of seven million buds, but I still suffer at the thought of shinnying up!

The greatest tree of my boyhood stood in our baseball oval, near the street fence, just behind center field. It was as tall as the clouds with a broad billowing crown. The long strong trunk leaned toward the fellow at bat as though beckoning to him to wallop the ball. When he did, the tree would make it a home run by returning the ball to earth slowly. It dribbled down among the leaves and bounced erratically from branch to branch. I can see the heart-shaped leaves and gray bark, but above all, the tall, graceful, leaning trunk. In my memory picture, that tree keys out accurately to a *linden*. During the ball game years it was simply "the home run tree."

Another tree vivid from these early memories was as true to its own nature as it was a friend of boys. It stood several miles out beyond the city limits, but you could reach it on a bicycle on Saturday, if you had all day off. Sometimes a sneaker came off just as you reached the tree, because it was mushy and muddy around its base, and if you didn't look out you'd step into a cow pie. None of this mattered, though, because a boy could vanish inside the hollow trunk. It was deep and thick and leaned a good deal—our popular hollow tree. No question about it, that tree in memory has all the aspects of a *black willow*. It grows so fast in wet places that it never toughens up around a core of heartwood. Its whole interior may disintegrate to make a deep hollow tree.

A boy has his own way of knowing trees, bending them to his ends as he does ball bats and parents. But that sort of intimacy is different from *appreciation*. To enjoy their beauty and drama is more apt to be an adult faculty. After I moved away from the home preserve to boarding school and college there came a long hiatus in my relationship with trees. They were ignored at the seats of learning. In fact, after his boyhood experiences a man is apt to get along without trees for the rest of his life.

One winter afternoon, at the age of thirty-five, I went out for a walk with Dr. Graves of the Brooklyn Botanic Garden. He pointed out the buds on the trees. I was astonished, once my attention was drawn to them, to see that every tree was fully equipped with buds. I had never before seen buds in winter. It violated a rock-ribbed notion. I had always supposed that buds "came out" in spring, according to some first grade legend. We looked at the buds through Dr. Graves' hand lens. This dispelled another illusion. They were not standardized ovals, covered with overlapping scales. They were as varied as jewelry, in all sorts of exquisite shapes and bright colors. Some were covered with fur, some with glue, others were varnished.

7

This was my first look at the precision mechanism of trees. It stirred my curiosity. Here were marvels that I had never had the slightest inkling of, up to that moment. Yet they were not rare nor discovered in a remote place, but they were here all the time in the immediate surroundings of the everyday world.

I was surprised to see that each kind of tree produced its own individual type of bud. Instead of vague similarities between trees, here were specific, eloquent differences. My eyes were opened to other details, of bark, angles of branches, thickness and patterns of twigs. These interesting distinctions suddenly appeared as though they had not existed up to that time.

This winter morning I took an hour's walk in Gramercy Park in the heart of New York. Some fifty well-groomed trees are the asset of this park for the shade they cast in summer, and for raising rents when apartment windows look out on them. But I have never seen anybody look at the trees in winter; they receive no more attention than black dead sticks. People on the benches were working the cross-word puzzles in the Sunday paper. In an atmosphere of so much indifference one feels a little foolish staring at the trees, and reaching for a twig to pull it down and examine the end buds. But it makes a good hour's diversion.* The clues were all there—just as they are out in the country. The silver tam-o'-shanters of the dogwood buds; the long varnished pyramids of the poplar; the bright red tridents of the red maple; the fat buds of the magnolia as furry as a cat's paw; and the crumpled black wells of the locust in which the buds are hidden. One by one I told off their names, and checked the answer with the bark and twigs and branches. It's marvelous how the potencies packed in a tiny seed had imprinted each vast structure with the clear-cut resemblances of its kind, and equipped it perfectly to the minutest detail.

Every step I have taken along this path of discovery, since that afternoon when my complacency about trees was suddenly

---

*If you would play this game in winter or summer you will find the tree clues and instructions for using them toward the end of this book.

upset by discovering winter buds, has revealed unsuspected wonders and revised benighted notions. Roots are now something other than obstinate anchors; trunks are not merely solid wood; leaves are much more than green canopies.

Sometimes enthusiasts, carried away by a leaf-fringed legend, impart to trees faculties of love; a tree is faithful or it desires to be beautiful. Such pathetic fallacy only serves man's ego and obscures the unique and wonderful reality of a tree. For its beauty is functional, like the beauty of a great machine that performs swiftly and quietly. Or like the grandeur and dignity of a ship where every line is in harmony with the law of its being, and every accessory fits perfectly, as to shape and size, into the situation which demands exactly that thing.

We can justly admire man-made structures like a machine shop or milk pasteurizing plant or rolling mill. These are, after all, only adaptations of fundamental laws. But we can be astonished at a tree which is an original expression of those laws, mysteriously compounded out of the elements.

When man builds a structure, raw materials have to be converted into building materials, and then those materials have to be transported to their places. When a tree is built, the raw materials are air and water, with solutions of chemicals from the earth, and the building material is the cell. Then two miracles occur. One is that cells are never transported. No bricklayer ever places one on top of another. They simply occur in the right place and at the right moment by means of cell division. The other miracle is that, after cells have appeared at the right place, they are converted into specialized structural materials on the spot. It is as though bricks turned into plaster, roof, plumbing, and built-in cupboards.

We learn in school that the basic unit of a plant is a cell. But few of us realize what this means. A cell is so small that we can see it only through a microscope. That makes it remote to most of us. But the power of a cell to build a tree out of water and air is a tale worth hearing.

A living cell looks like a battered shoe box, filled with a fluid

9

called protoplasm. This flows spasmodically round and round with the impulse of life, carrying along little specks. These specks are important. Some are air bubbles that serve a purpose as we shall see. Others may be grains of starch that disappear when they dissolve and travel out of the cell by seeping through the wall. Some specks may be green chlorophyll, especially if the living cell is from a leaf. Most important of all, a spot called the "nucleus" is submerged in the protoplasm. Scientists who switch on the high power of their microscopes have discovered that this spot under certain conditions is composed of tiny bars called chromosomes, which animate the whole cell. Their number, shape and the way these chromosomes arrange themselves determine the kind of plant they are building and its characteristics.

One scientist I know has given up teaching and other activities for research among the chromosomes in corn plants. This scientist can predict from the number and arrangement of chromosome bars in a living cell of a corn plant taken from root, stalk, leaf or anywhere, whether that plant will produce, for example, red kernels or yellow kernels. Some day this sort of study will have great practical importance in our control over

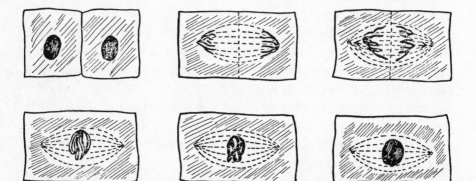

A CELL DIVIDES. Left to right: (1) Spindle forms around nucleus. (2) Chromosome ribbons appear in a bunch. (3) Ribbons split lengthwise. (4) Halves of ribbons travel in opposite directions. (5) They reach tips of spindle. (6) Spindle disappears, new cell wall divides halves, two complete cells are created where one existed before.

plants. All living cells are essentially the same, whether they belong to an Indian pipe or a sequoia, with cell wall, protoplasm and nucleus. The sort of tree or other plant they build is their own secret. Even more mysterious is the force which causes seemingly identical cells of the same plant to build a wide variety of structures. When a tree is built you have leaves, flowers, seeds, bark, wood, roots, and so on—all perfectly proportioned and fitted into the system.

A tree, for example, is built and grows by dividing its cells. This appears simple enough, but just what makes a cell divide is, of course, the unsolved mystery of life. There's nothing hit or miss about it. Cell division is an act of precision effected in a series of standardized steps. First, the contents take the form of a spindle with long strands coming to a point toward each end of the cell. The bars of the chromosomes then join together forming a ribbon at the center of the spindle. Next this ribbon splits lengthwise. The halves move to opposite ends of the cell pulled apart by the strands of the spindle, forming definite patterns as they go. After they have gathered into two groups at far ends of the cell a new cell wall appears, separating the two halves of the original cell. Finally the spindle disappears, and each half of the cell acquires a nucleus around its share of chromosomes. Then the halves grow as large as the first mother cell. Thus, with one cell becoming two, two cells becoming four, and so on, a plant grows with geometric progression. Countless billions of cells are created inside a tree by the same principle expressed in that old story about a checkerboard and grains of wheat. If you put one grain on the first square, two grains on the next, four on the next, and so on ... by the time you reach the last square the wheat will overflow a granary. In this way a unit, so infinitesimal you can't see it with the naked eye, will raise a prairie of grain, a forest of redwoods, fill your garden with flowers, or build a fine maple tree beside your house.

Although a tree is built entirely by the force of living cells, it does not follow that every cell in it is alive. Far from it. The bulk of a tree is "dead," although functioning like the frame, concrete, or plumbing system of a building. The living cells are a small percentage of the whole system but they are strategically located. They live at the tips of roots to absorb water; in a thin sheath just below the bark to keep food moving through the system and to enlarge the trunk; at tips of twigs to keep them elongating; and in leaves where they work as sun motors to keep the whole plant in operation. Considering the great size of a tree, this is a thin fringe of life. In a big tree perhaps less than one per cent of its body consists of living cells. The rest is mechanical structure.

In all parts of this fringe of life, in the right order and at exactly the right moment, certain cells which are no longer dividing are yielding up their lives and transforming their bodies into structural material. Manufacturers have a word for this, they would say that the cells are "processed." The succulent box with its protoplasm is converted into a unit of entirely different form and substance.

If a certain cell is located just below the bark where the blueprint of the tree calls for adding a unit of wood, the air bubbles in the protoplasm will combine. One big bubble is formed which finally fills the whole interior of the cell. The protoplasm disappears and the cell becomes hollow. While this is going on, the walls are thickening and lose their transparency. If sheer strength and reinforcing are needed at that spot, the walls may thicken so much that the cell becomes solid. Welded firmly to neighboring cells, it makes a fiber that functions like a steel reinforcement of a building. Or a cell may strengthen its walls with rings like barrel hoops or spiralling ridges, leaving the interior hollow. In this case the cells adjacent at each end do the same thing, the walls at their tips dissolve, and you have a tube. This makes a pipeline that ultimately may run from the roots to the topmost tips. That is the nature of what we call wood. If a cell happens to be located near the outer rim where a unit of bark is to be added, instead of turning into a fiber or a tube, it will fill up with corky substance, and become bark. Location exerts a mysterious effect.

Sometimes sap is compared with the life stream of the blood of an animal. But sap does not flow round and round in a tree, and there is no muscular pump like the heart to keep it circulating. Sap is mostly water. A great amount of it streams upward inside the trunk and limbs, and is dissipated into the air by the leaves. It doesn't return to the tree. It just goes up and out. A small amount of that water, perhaps two per cent, is used to dissolve plant food, and this concentrated solution will flow downward around the trunk through a thin layer of cells just beneath the bark.

From one point of view, the drama of a tree may be described by calling it the "world's greatest waterworks." Actually all plants are waterworks. Their capacity to lift water depends on the size of their leaf area, which is like saying the size of the nozzle. As the capacity of the stem or trunk is much greater than needed the leaves are the "bottleneck."

In proportion to size the grasses can be said to be the greatest of the water raisers because they have a relatively large leaf area. In fact, most of the visible plant body in the grasses is leaf. Corn is a grass, and one stalk will lift 440 pounds of water during its brief growing season. A farmer across the road from my house has a rich cornfield. If all the water which his corn collected under ground and raised up and expelled into the air stayed on top of the field where you could see it, the farmer would have a lake of water five feet deep by the end of August.

An acre of grass in a lush meadow will lift six and a half tons of water per day at the height of its power in late June. The amount lifted by one plant may be only a few drops, but the number of grass plants in an acre is legion.

Of course, trees operate on a grander scale. A well-spaced apple orchard will have forty trees to the acre. If they're healthy and mature they will be equipped with about a hundred thousand leaves each, and those forty trees will lift sixteen tons of water a day. That's at the rate of four gallons per tree per hour. And as trees go, apple trees are comparatively small!

It takes a good deal of imagination to think of water travelling up the long tapering cylinder of a tall tree and spraying out through the perforations of the leaves as from a fine nozzle. Yet every leaf of the several million of a great elm, or the 100 thousand of a squat apple tree, and every blade of grass of the myriads in an acre of pasture is, as we have seen, constantly performing like a nozzle. The spray is so fine that it is invisible, so that we say the water is evaporating out of the leaf as water vapor.

In this way a tree serves as a vital link in the rotation of water. In all the world 340 cubic miles of water fall every day. This averages about sixteen million tons of rain per second! In a world-wide sense there is no such thing, therefore, as a drought. It's only a question of *where* the water falls. When the reservoirs of New England are low, heavy rain is reported from the Libyan desert. When the Atlantic seaboard is parched, the prairie states are fighting floods. The total volume of water throughout the world is constant, never less, nor more. It is present in three forms: water in seas, lakes, streams; water in vapor form in the air and clouds; water in the earth and inside of trees and leaves. Between these three forms water revolves restlessly. Although evaporation from seas, lakes and streams is a tremendous agency for getting water into the air, the world's greatest waterworks (the trees as well as all vegetation) taps the vast invisible reservoirs in the ground and keeps the water moving up and out. Locally this may have an even greater effect than evaporation from exposed water surfaces in determining rainfall.

Obviously with all this lifting, an enormous force is somehow exerted. Yet a tree is not equipped with a pump. It is essentially solid and stationary in all its parts.

One might suppose the tree could pull up water like a suction pump. If you create a vacuum in a vertical tube that has its lower end in water, the water will rise in the tube. It is drawn up by the suction. This sounds plausible for a tree. If water evaporates at the top, a vacuum could be formed somewhere lower down inside the porous tube system of the trunk. But this won't work, for two reasons. First, suction is due to air pressure and some free surface of water must be exposed for gravity to push down on it. But the roots of a tree are in the soil and not in a well of water, so that there is no water for gravity to push on. Another objection is even more final. The weight of a column of water balances air pressure at 33 feet. If a man wants to raise water with a suction pump, he can lift it 33 feet at sea level, even less on the mountains, and not an inch higher. That height would serve for small trees but not for tall trees. Water goes up to the top of trees a hundred feet or more without the slightest difficulty, even up to 300 feet in the sequoias of California. A redwood called "Founder's Tree," considered the tallest tree in the United States, lifts water 364 feet with the same efficiency as a strawberry plant a couple of inches tall.

Another theory is that roots exert pressure. Root pressure is the accumulated force of absorption. Liquids will travel up fine tubes. They call it capillary attraction. It's the principle of oil running up the wick in an old-fashioned oil lamp. The same force makes blotting paper work. The inside of a tree with its innumerable little empty spaces arranged into series of tubes is ideal for capillary attraction to go into action.

However, this theory only explains how water gets into the bole of the tree in the first place. The minute threads and tubes of the roots absorb the water and push it along into other minute tubes in the lower part of the tree trunk. This is an explanation of why sap flows in a tree trunk in late winter. When the snow is still on the ground and the buds have not yet loosened their scales, the Vermont farmer can tap his trees for maple syrup. The clear sap, ninety-five per cent or more water, drips into his bucket possibly as fast as 100 drops per minute. This means that root pressure is working down where the water is loosening up in the frozen ground! If he tapped his trees higher up, he wouldn't get more sap, he would get none at all.

Atmospheric pressure is fifteen pounds to the square inch at sea level. The maximum force of root pressure measured is two atmospheres. This gives 30 pounds to the square inch. But it would take 300 pounds to the square inch to lift sap to the top of the tallest trees.

The most plausible explanation of the mighty lifting force possessed by trees is something entirely different.

It appears that the world's greatest waterworks relies on cohesion in a column of water. From roots to tiptops runs an unbroken "rope" of water, woven out of countless threads. Pull on the top of this by evaporating water out of the leaves and you simply pull up more water by its own rope. This implies that throughout the tree, every single twig and bud and leaf is connected by unbroken threads of water with the roots. Not every tube may be full of water but enough are full to keep the lines unbroken. By the process of growth from the first shoot out of the seed, the inside of the tree is endowed with water. And it stays endowed, as it grows larger. When the leaves fall off in winter and the pull at the top on the rope stops, the fineness of the tubes tends to hold the water in the standpipe by capillary attraction. It doesn't fall back into the ground. Indeed, the loss of water by evaporation is halted when the leaves fall off and so the total volume of water inside a tree gradually *increases* in winter as it creeps up the tubes.

What is the tensile strength of sap—that is, how hard can you pull on it lengthwise without having it break? Will it hold together as a continuous stream, say 300 feet, against the pull of gravity? Sap has been found to have the amazing tensile strength of 2,250 pounds to the square inch, equal to 150 atmospheres. This is 150 times greater than suction, 75 times greater than root pressure. This strength could lift sap to the top of a tree 4,950 feet tall, almost a mile high.

To what end do trees lift so much water? It is certainly not for our delight since these mighty fountains are invisible. Water lifting by plants is not an indispensable link in the restless transfer of water from earth to clouds, as evaporation from open water in seas, lakes and streams is far more important. It is not to deliver water to the top of a tree for its own use, although a small percentage serves as a carrier for tree food. Water simply comes in at the bottom and goes out at the top. Botanists have not found any final explanation as to why so much water is lifted. Philosophically, the world's greatest waterworks are all the greater because they are not subordinate to anything else. Only a utilitarian mind asks why they lift so much water. They do because that is their nature. Like Keats's Grecian urn a tree is the "foster child of silence and slow time." A hundred years of patience and sunlight lifts an inestimable amount of water and builds a great waterworks system.

More remarkable than the quantity of water lifted by a tree is the intricate beauty and perfection of roots, trunk and leaves. These represent three departments of the waterworks system. Each department is different from the other two, not only in appearance but also in the way it works. Let us examine them.

ADDENDUM to CHAPTER TWO

Three topics of fundamental importance have been touched upon in this chapter, and each deserves further discussion since they have been the subjects of much research since 1942. These are the molecular basis of inheritance, the nature of development to attain the pattern of form that is characteristic of each species, and the water relations of plants. Each topic has been the subject matter of many books.

Since 1944, the nucleic acids, very large molecules or polymers in the nuclei and chromosomes of all organisms, have been recognized as the molecular basis of inheritance. These are the molecules containing the information that, when translated into structure and behavior, makes you what you are, why I am what I am, and what spells the differences between orchids, oaks and oats. The structure and behavior of these nucleic acids—known universally known as DNA, or deoxyribonucleic acid—was revealed in 1953, and since that time the world of biological research and study, and our understanding of the nature of individual differences, has undergone a complete revolution. Without question, this discovery ranks as the most important piece of biological knowledge gained in the twentieth century. This judgment is borne out by the fact that a dozen or more Nobel prizes have been awarded to researchers in the field of inheritance.

The information bound up in DNA in the form of genes—segments of nucleic acids of varying length—is the blueprint of an individual. But like any blueprint, this information must be expressed as shape and substance if it is to be recognized as something beyond its molecular nature. It must be used to govern the growth processes of development of an individual as it progresses from the embryo in a seed to the adult plant, and it must be released and transmitted if it is to be passed on to future offspring, and so participate in the perpetuation of the species. A mother cell divides to produce two daughter cells. The latter—barring accidents or mutations (changes in the molecular structure of DNA)—are exactly like each other and like the mother cell from which they arose, in that they have the same number of chromosomes, the same amount of DNA, and hence the same quality and quantity of hereditary information. This came about because DNA, making up the bulk of the substance of chromosomes, can *replicate* itself with great exactitude, and the chromosomes, splitting lengthwise and passing the separate halves to daughter cells during cell division, insure that all cells in a given individual are basically similar. This process, however, is the conservative side of evolution; it preserves and transmits information, but does not make use of it.

In addition to being replicated and transmitted, the information of an individual organism contained in its DNA is used for two basic purposes: for organizing and controlling the machinery of the cell in its day-to-day existence, and for directing the processes of development as the organism passes through its life cycle from conception to death. The means for performing these actions are complex, but in its simplest sense, the information in DNA is extracted by a process called *transcription*, during which DNA makes RNA, a complementary molecule called ribonucleic acid. RNA contains a readable message which, by a process of *translation*, is realized in the form of proteins. Like DNA and RNA, these too are macromolecules, or polymers consisting of sequences of smaller molecules. If we can think of DNA as the library of information of a cell, and RNA as the means by which that information can be released for use by the cell, then the proteins are working and structural molecules of the cell: working in the sense that all enzymes are proteins, and these catalyze and govern all reactions taking place in the cell; structural in the sense that the proteins are crucial elements in the formation of membranes which shape the cell, compartmentalize its interior to serve various functions, and act as an exterior sensor capable of appraising the external environment.

The attainment through development of a pattern that places each individual in a given species is, of course, a whole sequence of events that occurs at the right time, in the right place, and to the appropriate degree of activity. Much of what takes place in development is known, but the heart of the mystery is yet to be fully explained: it is that coordinated activity of hundreds of genes acting in concordance and in sequence that enables oak DNA to produce oak trees, never maples or pines or peach trees.

The third topic, that of water transport, is more a physical than a biological one. When a tree is in full leaf, it is in the green leaves, and during the daylight hours, that most of the activity is taking place. It is here that the leaves are making food through the process of photosynthesis, and to do this requires a constant supply of radiant energy from the sun, of carbon dioxide from the atmosphere, and of mineral nutrients and water from the soil. Since there is insufficient root pressure, as a result of water absorption, to push the water to the top of a tree, it must in some way be pulled up. This is done by the cohesion (capillary action) of water in the long conduction cells of the wood, by the tensile strength of water which is surprisingly great, and by the constant loss of water through the leaves (transpiration). This "transpiration stream" is a continuous and uninterruped flow, and if broken it cannot be reestablished. So while the leaves persist, the flow of water persists, taken in at the roots and passed off at the leaves.

Nothing moves in this world without the expenditure of energy, so the movement of water is expensive, paid for by the energy bound up in sugar molecules. Water supply and food production, as a consequence, are tied together in an inseparable way, and the green plant has never invented a better way of satisfying both needs in a less expensive manner.

The movement of sap in a maple tree in the spring comes about in a somewhat different way. Among the long and dead conducting cells of wood are sheets of living cells, oriented perpendicular to the vertical axis of the tree. These ray cells, as they are called, are full of starch, stored there in the previous year. With the advent of warm days and cool nights of spring, the starch, which is insoluble, is converted into soluble sugar, thus increasing the concentration of soluble materials in the sap: water moves in through the roots by osmosis to dilute the sap and to equalize the concentration of soluble substances, thus creating a pressure that forces the sap upwards, and causing it to drop-by-drop fill the maple sugar buckets.

—C.P.S.

CHAPTER THREE

Hundred-Mile Roots

A fine summer shower splashing down on the lindens, maples and birches around my house seems to bring the trees an abundant water supply. It soaks trunks and leaves and drips off every twig. If the interior tissues of the tree, especially those of the green leaves, are thirsty they ought to profit by this drenching. But this is not the case. A tree's internal waterworks system does not gain a single drop, until the rain has filtered into the earth where it can be picked up by the roots.

On the face of it this sounds simple. It suggests to our minds a picture of water-soaked earth or underground streams tapped by big roots resembling rubber hose that somehow suck up the water. But most of the water in the ground in which roots grow is not "wet" water. Where you turn up earth in a normal condition it is dark and damp. You can't squeeze a drop out of soil like that. The water is locked to each particle of soil in the form of a microscopic film. The proposition of collecting water through a root system under these circumstances and sending it upward in a stream of sap is unique and would baffle the ingenuity of man.

We think of roots as being thick, muscular, brown. We know them as the main canals which, as branch lines join and flow together, build up ever greater carrying capacity into the trunk. Big roots are merely underground wood. When an old stump is blasted out of the ground you can make furniture out of its woody anchor. But the most wonderful and active part of a root system, the true water collecting mechanism, consists of fine white hairs, smooth as pearl, polished with moisture, delicate and sensitive. These one almost never sees; they vary in length from $\frac{1}{250}$ to $\frac{1}{3}$ of an inch. They are attached just back of the tips of roots, where the root itself is scarcely bigger than the strand of a white cotton thread. They are produced by the presence of moisture which causes the outside cell of the rootlet suddenly to go into action and poke out sideways, making a hair of its own cell body. You can actually see these root hairs grow if you catch them in a microscope. Their number is in proportion to the amount of moisture in the adjacent soil. They are like little fingers that reach out only when there is water to grab. Given plenty of water, many, if not all, of the cells just back of the root tip will elongate into hairs so that the root-tip looks like a bit of felt. Each of these will wriggle and turn to reach and lay hold of particles of soil. It spreads and wraps itself around each particle as snugly as a catcher's glove is wrapped around a baseball. It then unlocks the film of water from the soil particle and absorbs it, doing this all along the length of the hair, wherever it touches moisture. While this is going on the thread of the rootlet is pushing forward to reach fresh supplies. New hairs are springing out while the older hairs farther back, having done their work, are shrivelling up. This little clump of "felt," which is perhaps the liveliest part of the whole tree, is never longer than a small fraction of an inch near the tips of rootlets.

Yet so deliberately, so intensively does this gossamer explore the soil, that it turns microscopic films of moisture into gallons of water! The thoroughness of this process is suggested by the density of hairs that may permeate a single cubic inch of soil. The best official records of the numbers of lengths of root hairs that a plant has packed into a cubic inch deal with little plants like beans and grasses. They can be grown in specially prepared light soil, easily washed off. Possibly these conditions and lack of competition stimulate root hair growth, but let's look at the record. A certain species of grass grew four thousand feet of root hairs—that's about ⅘ of a mile—*inside one cubic inch* of soil. The mileage varies enormously. A soy bean had only forty-seven feet of root hairs in a cubic inch. A scientific estimate made for a single plant of winter rye shows that it produced a total of fourteen billion hairs with a total length of 6,600 miles! I hasten to credit these incredible figures to Dr. H. J. Dittmer of Chicago Teachers College who has made studies in connection with finding the best plants for soil conservation.

The root systems of grass plants are constructed on a different plan from those of trees. Grasses have what is known as a "fibrous system" where countless little roots shower out from the base of the grass stem. Trees use the "tap root system." The infinite branching, ever smaller until the ultimate branches are as slender as needles, all communicate with the great central tap root. A tap root system extends not inches, but yards beneath the plant. No patient wizard will ever be able to unearth and measure the total mileage of the roots and root hairs of a mature tree. If you want to claim that a big oak tree on your place has built a system that if laid end to end would reach around the world at the equator, no authority can contradict you.

The swiftly growing root hairs conjured up by the presence of moisture constitute the water collecting apparatus of all root systems, large and small. Their enormous mileage is one of the little-realized wonders of the trees around us.

Another arresting fact about roots is the way a tree builds its vast and intricate system of tough and twisting branches, the "hinterland" of the growing tips, inside of solid ground. This is accomplished without so much as a quiver on the surface, in contrast to the labor and confusion when a man heaves up the earth to get the roots of a sizable tree into the ground!

In the late fall I found an acorn lying on the floor of the woods, split open, with two little white shoots emerging from each side. One made a sharp right angle and pointed upward. That was the beginning of the trunk and leaves. The other shoot also made a sharp right angle but pointed straight downward into the ground. That was the beginning of the roots. I reversed the acorn. Twenty-four hours later each shoot had turned around and started to grow in the opposite direction. Regardless of what position the acorn was turned the shoots always responded as fast as they could so that the future trunk always pointed toward the sky, and the future roots always pointed into the ground. How could such a tender little root, first out of the acorn, get *into* the ground? Even though a seed may be lightly buried, thanks to a squirrel or the action of wind, water or falling leaves, it is obvious that the problem presented to the downgoing roots to penetrate and burrow into solid earth is a tough one.

The end of the first radicle out of the seed, like the growing ends of all future root branches, is equipped with a hard tip. This can take punishment when it is shoved against an unyielding substance. Back of this hard tip is exerted the power of growing pressure which is the combined push of the dividing cells. This is about three pounds in a downward turning rootlet first trying to get into the soil. However, the most important secret of soil penetration is not so much the few pounds' pressure behind a tough point, but the fact that a root *gropes* and *wriggles* into the earth. The cells in the growing end of a root are sensitive to hard things. Where resistance is encountered the root actually bends away and proceeds in the direction where the resistance is less. This enables roots to shy away from stones and to get around and between impenetrable barriers. Coupled with this is a marvelous spiral motion, called *circumnutation*. Instead of pushing straight ahead, the growing point rotates slightly. This becomes an eccentric motion as it is modified by the bending away from stones and other resistances encountered and by the varying amounts of moisture on each side—moisture has an attraction for growing roots. This spiralling tendency, a great contribution to the problems of soil penetration, was invented by plants long before corkscrews.

Roots exert another and still greater force. This is the force of expansion. Pioneers once used the swelling of wood instead of dynamite for splitting rocks. A tiny cell turgid with sap will swell out with tiny force. But a billion cells doing this all at the same time will multiply the pressure by a billion. Because of a broader surface with which to push out, the horizontal growing pressure of a root is greater than the longitudinal. Thus, the action of roots penetrating through the ground is not so much that of a nail driven straight ahead as of a wedge that expands as it pushes forward—a wedge that is able to split the toughest wood or rocks.

By this process of thrust and twist, of expansion and growth, the underground root department is built. The maze of branches, with their twistings and turnings, shows how a tree goes after water with monstrous tenacity. Where soft earth is lacking it will burrow through clay and gravel and into the cracks of solid rock. In the upper twigs of a tree there is nothing to compare with the extent and speed of growth in roots. As for their speed we must refer again to the roots of a grass plant because they have been officially measured. The roots, not counting the hairs, of a plant of wild oats grew 54 miles in 80 days. The roots of a crested wheat plant grew 315 miles in three years. That averages 100 M.P.Y. (miles-per-year)!

CHAPTER FOUR

Inside Information on Tree Trunks

A hundred yards in front of my house at the foot of the hill the torso of a linden lies on the ground beside the brook. At first glance it looks as though some workmen had forgotten a section of a big cast iron pipe. Instead of cleaning it up as untidy I have left it untouched. Nature, having cushioned it in grass, wild strawberries and cinquefoil, is transforming it into a busy world with colonies of ants and thousand-legged crawlers, and magma of fungi. Both patiently built insect communities and fungi are doomed because a wrecking crew of invisible bacteria are tearing apart fibers and tubes and crumbling the corky bark that took a generation to build. These wreckers will unlock the salts and minerals bound in the wood, so that the rain can carry them back into leaf mold and loam. Eventually these elements may be supped up by another root system and built into another tree, perhaps a maple or a birch or a cherry. This is the never ending cycle of organic chemicals, whose molecules are used over and over again, first in one kind of organism, then in another. These salts and mineral elements are never reduced in quantity, never impaired. Even after being locked in wood for hundreds of years, when released and returned to the soil, they are fresh and ready for building another plant. As long as a tree trunk is connected with living roots below and transpiring leaves above, it offers a lease for those elements in its wood that are actively connected with its system. Healthy wood in the service of a tree never decays. The activity of sap and food moving through its perforations has an antiseptic effect.

Outside my window a sixty-foot linden leans across the brook. Farther along an eighty-foot white pine, with its billowing horizontal branches, looks like a square-rigged ship in full sail. Facing these on the west boundary my largest sugar maple raises a tall symmetrical oval. These trees appear to be as fixed as the unchanging mountains. In fact, trees are legally considered to be fixed points on the landscape, as many a survey is paced from an old cedar or oak and so entered in the deed. Incidentally, this has put lawyers to the test, where a boundary is in dispute after several generations, and the landmark having ceased to operate as a waterworks, has returned its elements to the soil and vanished.

It may seem unduly imaginative to say that there is constant activity inside a tree trunk. The trunks of this linden, pine, and maple, that look so solid and changeless, actually expand every year with the addition of a fresh cone-shaped layer of new wood. Of this action the bark offers vivid evidence. Rough outer bark is formed when a smooth, tight-fitting covering of young bark is unable to expand or stretch, and therefore bursts apart when succeeding layers of new wood are added beneath it. Strange to say, each species has its own way of breaking its bark and this forms the characteristic patterns by which many trees can be identified.

Only a few trees are able to stretch and extend their bark as each year's annual ring pushes it farther and farther out. In most cases the bark splits and breaks—but always in a certain way. The chestnut oak, sassafras and black locust develop the most deeply sculptured bark. The elm has shallow ridges running longitudinally with the trunk. The ash forms crisscross ridges that give it diamond shaped markings. The hop hornbeam and red cedar acquire a shredded appearance. Famous is the outer covering of the shagbark hickory that breaks off like the loose shingles of an old house. That of the sycamore has so little stretch or give that it promptly breaks off and exposes the characteristic white patches of the inner and more elastic bark. The beech generally manages to keep from cracking and develops a beautiful smooth silver-gray surface. The sweet birch is a deep red brown, very glossy and smooth. This strongly resembles the young bark of cherry, but the cherry doesn't keep its rich smooth bark long, as the swelling of the trunk soon breaks it.

The cones of wood added annually to the trunk are continuing the same activity that built the tree inside the seed. We noted how, when an acorn cracked open, the tiny root persistently pointed toward the ground, while the tiny shoot, forebear of the future trunk, persistently pointed toward the sky. At that stage, although the tree is only an inch high, it is completely organized with root, trunk, and leaves. In fact, it was completely organized while still enclosed in the seed. Every acorn, every apple seed, every bulge on the wing of a maple, linden or ash, contains the three departments of the tree, although it takes a microscope to see them. When still contained within the seed, the embryo of a tree is equipped with root, trunk and two leaves.*

Just as the young root is confronted with the tough problem of getting itself into the ground, the young shoot may be confronted with a similar problem of getting up through a load of dirt or stones or leaves that cover the seed. To this end it doubles the force of its upward push by emerging in the form of an arch. The shoot starts going up while its tip is still embedded in the seed. This gives it two legs to push with. This method of doubling

*Sometimes one leaf. See page 194.

its power when the shoot is doing its heaviest work is, of course, not confined to trees. A familiar example is the arch of the garden bean when it first breaks ground. Ferns and the narrow-leafed sundew have an even more efficient method—using a coil. With a coil the pushing force is the sum of the expansion of each coil, and tests show that sidewise expansion of a stem may be three times as great as the force of elongation. Not so long ago I was walking along the coast of Maine at Kennebunkport. The macadam sidewalk was heaving up in spots and here and there tender-looking little shoots of wild rose and staghorn sumac were breaking through. I could hardly believe my eyes. For a seedling to raise itself through a solid sidewalk like that takes the dynamite of moisture. Kennebunkport had been enjoying weeks of rain and fog.

When this rising arch is well up in the air the tip of the shoot lets go from the seed. The whole shoot gracefully rises, straightens, and from that time on, will stab the air as a tree should.

This up-going tree now proceeds in a curious combination of motions. It does not, as you might expect, have streamlined action, pouring up on a vertical line behind its growing tip. As the tip lengthens, it oscillates incessantly. As it oscillates, the tip of the shoot swings round and round, growing upward in a spiralling motion. If it traced a visible path in the air this would form an eccentric corkscrew. The rate and amount of this bending toward various points of the compass constantly vary. It describes ellipses, ovals, triangles, small loops, zig-zag lines as the sensitive growing cells are played upon by various intensities and directions of light.

You might say that it is following the sun in its course, but this spiralling is not as simple as that. Passing clouds and shadows, reflected highlights from a leaf or stone or water cause eccentric variations. Moreover, this bending is inherent in growth itself. It goes on day and night, regardless of light. A young oak seedling, placed in a box cut off from light, traced its spirals on smoked glass by means of a little hair attached to the growing tip. Sometimes these spirals reverse and make figure eights. By itself, without light, these loops are from a fraction of an inch, up to half an inch. But the weakest light will excite this tip. A small taper flame held to one side for a few minutes causes it to bend in that direction with a zig-zag motion far beyond its previous orbit. It may keep on going in the direction of that light for an hour after the taper is extinguished. The spirals of growth are not visible but they may be detected as you would detect motion in the hour hand of a clock. For example, if a piece of glass on which grid lines are marked is fixed horizontally above the tip of a seedling and the positions of that tip are pricked out every half hour on the graph, it traces complete ovals at the rate of about four in twenty-four hours.

These gyrations are not limited to the central stem or trunk. The same behavior is translated to the growing tips of the branches. They, too, revolve with big and little loops, spiralling out horizontally or at their chosen angles. In this respect, a branch is essentially like the central trunk. The only difference is that it is attached to the trunk instead of directly to the root system, and it has an occult endowment for growing sideways or out at angles instead of vertically. Thus the world's greatest waterworks takes form like a creature alive with mysterious motions of its own.

When built, a tree has a beautiful bole, covered, as we have seen, with sculptured or smooth bark. As a cylinder, every tree trunk is graceful by nature, whether it is long and slender, or short and wide. The suitability of this form for its function of holding leaves high up in the sunlight is obvious. But how can that cylinder which looks so solid act as a conduit for a vertical stream of water? What force can inert wood exert to lift the weight of water against gravity? This lifting of water is a remarkable activity of a tree, distinct from growth. It puts to work certain well-known laws of physics and mechanics and raises water to the leaves because of the precise details of its structure.

Although a tree trunk is not hollow like an up-ended water main, it is largely composed of a compact mass of tiny tubes, as we saw in Chapter 2. These tubes, running longitudinally with the trunk, are the grain of the wood. Because of them wood splits lengthwise, with the grain. As they are bound together they add great strength and flexibility like the strands of a hawser or cable, enabling the tree to take a terrific beating in a windstorm. These tubes are all the stronger because they do not have smooth bores. Some are rifled on the inside with spiral ridges; others are reinforced with rings like barrel hoops. A common design consists of extra thick walls checkered with pits on the inside that make the walls much stronger mechanically than if they were smooth with uniform thickness.

When living cells build these tubes, they divide in the direction of the growing trunk, so that one cell is above another, and then the cell walls where the ends touch are dissolved away. When lined up and in position to form tubes, they surrender their protoplasm. Great numbers of these long hollow tubes serve as pipe lines. Other cells, hollow at first, thicken and become solid. These solid cells are also welded end to end. They are called fibers and their function is to add strength to the wood. Similar fibers from the hemp plant are used for making rope.

Most of the hardwoods have conspicuous tubes, buried among tough fibers. You can see these tubes with the naked eye in a cross section of oak. The softwoods (pine) have a uniform texture of big hollow wood cells that are square in cross section. They do not develop spirals and barrel hoop reinforcing but they are always pitted. Instead of long continuous tubes with end walls dissolved away, these pine cells taper at each end so that they overlap snugly. The end walls are so thin that the water which rises through them can readily seep through. These hollow square vessels are so strong that they do not have the extra reinforcing of fibers. Therefore, lacking any tough solid-cell fibers, and consisting entirely of square tubes, the pine is called a "softwood." Such characteristics make some kinds of wood stronger than others, determine whether it will split, saw and nail easily, and give the wood grain and finish.

Another conspicuous feature of hardwood grain, lacking

in pine, is ribbons that radiate from the center. In these ribbons the length of the cells is at right angles to the tubes and fibers, that is to say, the cells are laid horizontally. They are the communicating lines that pass plant food back and forth between the center and the outer regions. You may have seen them as silver streaks in wood grain; they are especially beautiful and conspicuous in oak and maple where they have different lengths. But here we are talking not so much about water lifting, which is mostly longitudinal, as food supply which runs in every direction, moving mostly down through an entirely different plumbing system, to be looked into presently, and then transversely through the "silver grain."

You might say that a common hardwood tree is built with a woof, that is the radiating ribbons of cells just described, between which is woven the warp, that is the bulk of the wood consisting of tubes and fibers. You will agree that the trunk of a tree is neatly put together.

In a very young tree, almost all the interior of the trunk is conducting water. The tubes and their counterpart, the oblong tapering cells of pine, are in good shape for the up-going streams of sap. The standpipe of the bole is a vast interlocking system of tubes and vessels. In order that the waterworks may get into operation in the spring, this system must always maintain an unbroken column of water from top to bottom. In such an intricate system with billions of tubes, this unbroken column of water is possible even though not every tube is filled with water. Many may contain air.

The volume of water in the trunk varies with weather conditions and with the year round rhythm of the tree. If the weather is dry and little moisture is in the ground, when the leaves are out in a warm dry sun evaporation reduces the water supplies in the trunk. Then the outer and younger rings of tubes draw on deep-lying, interior water reserves.

During the winter, when leaves are not out and evaporation is at a minimum, the proportion of water inside the trunk steadily increases. Just before the buds open in early spring, when the leaves have not yet spread their acres of evaporating surface, the volume of water in the trunk is at a maximum. It is pushing up from the roots that are finding the earth full of free water, and is gathering as in a reservoir behind a dam. When leaves are out, evaporation is in full swing, and as the earth loses moisture with the coming of drier weather, the volume of water in the trunk falls as its reserves escape through the leaves.

A large proportion of a young trunk is filled with tubes. In a one-year trunk a big juicy circle of these tubes surrounds a core (pith) that is a mushy heart of food filled cells. In this first year all the tips of fresh branches are growing and there are no obsolete branches or places where leaves had been attached. The tubes of the first year's trunk are bundled into cables leading to these growing tips and leaves. In the sapling's trunk all the tubes are needed and in operation.

But see what happens as the tree grows. Next spring a new circle of tubes, like a long thin cylinder, is laid around the outside of last year's tree. And this *new* sheath of tubes is connected with the *new* year's shoots and their buds and leaves. After some years the first branches have died or ceased to grow. Their buds and leaves have vanished. When you look at a big oak or maple, it is apparent how the first young foliage and its branches have passed into oblivion many years ago. What has happened to the tubes leading to the bygone leaves of those early years?

In the first place, they have not disappeared like their leaves to which they brought water. You can see the old tubes in a cross section of a stump. They constitute the annual rings. The reason you see these rings so easily is that each spring, with the rush of water and dynamic life, large light-colored cells (later to become the tubes) are built. As the summer wears on with less water and lowering vitality, darker and smaller cells are built. During the winter, no cells are built. Then with the next year's spring, suddenly big cells are made again, sharply contrasting with the little cells that tapered off last season. The lines of demarcation between the littlest and the biggest cells make the clearcut outlines of annual rings. Cells turned into wooden tubes are so durable and so well protected inside the tree that they never disappear. These older interior tubes, now having no shoots and leaves of their own to supply with water, are the reserve reservoirs. They hold water which the outer younger tubes that are connected with buds and leaves may draw on in time of drought.

The flexibility of such a system is no little part of its wonder. It explains why, after a severe drought, with little rain for many weeks during the past season, I do not have to worry about the survival of my mature trees. Each has made provision in its own trunk in the same way that the city makes provision by building reservoirs. That is in addition to the deep roots which tap the lowered water table in the earth.

As time passes and the tree grows old, something else happens to the tubes near the center of the tree. The cubic capacity of a tree bole with a diameter measured in feet is enormously greater than that of a slender trunk only an inch or so in diameter. The capacity of the outer rings of the big trunk that are actively lifting water is enormous, and so is the storage capacity of the interior tubes. Under such circumstances, the oldest and deepest tubes are superfluous as part of the waterworks system. They fill up with gum and resin that toughens and hardens them. Just when the bulk and weight of the tree need strengthening, it gets this mighty reinforcing of heartwood. In red cedar this heartwood is purplish red and exudes an aromatic fragrance which discourages moths. The heartwood of black walnut is dark brown. Ebony is nearly black. In pines, poplars and tulip trees the heartwood scarcely changes color.

After some years have been spent laying one thin cone of tubes snugly around the preceding year's until the mighty bole is built, and never stops building while the tree lives, a strange and wonderful secret of its life may be revealed. The cylinders of tubes, the reinforcing fibers that interlace them, and the central core of the heartwood are all alike inert and dead. Water flows up through a multitude of fixed channels from which the living protoplasm has vanished. Since this is true and ninety-nine per cent of the bulk of a living tree is dead non-growing material, how can it go on increasing its diameter from top to bottom? The answer is found in a thin sheath of living cells, only one cell deep, that completely encloses the structure. So thin is this sheath that it can be seen only through a microscope. It is a membrane of life not thicker than the breadth of a thread in a spider's web. Yet this coat of almost invisible texture, called cambium, envelopes without a single gap the entire trunk and all the limbs and branches.

This diaphanous veil of life has the form of a long tapering cylinder, necessarily like that of the tree trunk. Its living cells are slender and placed in a longitudinal position. However, annual rings must be formed, not longitudinally, but one outside another . . . that is in a horizontal direction. A cross-cut log has radial symmetry as seen in these concentric rings, with the rays of the wood cutting across them like spokes of a wheel. To form a ring, a cambium cell may split down its length, leaving one cell *beside* the other. Or if the cell is Split crosswise, one half will *glide up alongside the other!* This, by the way, is one of the most remarkable events in tree building. Eventually the cell on the inside may turn into a wood element while the other retains its living protoplasm as a cambium cell ready to do the trick again the next year.

If you drive a nail into a tree four feet above the ground, the nail stays there. It isn't lifted with the growth of the tree. Here is the explanation of why, as a tree grows in circumference and height, its wood does not pour up or stretch up. The bole is built horizontally. Once a cell is in position in the trunk it never shifts that position. Cells are never transported like bricks and placed one on top of another. They are created where needed—and stay put.

Now anybody, even without an engineering mind, can readily see that in building the world's greatest waterworks up to this point, something important is missing. To build root systems, rings of wood around the trunk, as well as increases in length in the growing tips of trunk and branches, much food must be provided. So far we have a structure to convey water from the soil *up*, but what about conveying food *down?* Since food is manufactured almost entirely in the leaves above, some system must be provided to carry it down to the bole, even to the depth of many feet below the ground, where it is needed for root development. There is no food in the soil ready to use. Chemicals dissolved in water must first be carried up and transformed into food in a leaf, and then carried down again to the deepest growing root.

To accomplish this purpose an entirely separate conveyor system is installed. This is as wonderful and efficient as the water lifting system but much less conspicuous. The food conveyor belt is only a few cells wide and is found as a very thin sheath *outside* the living cambium. It is squeezed in between the cambium and the bark.

This system for promoting a downward flow of food also consists of great numbers of tubes. But instead of the end walls of cells dissolving away completely so as to make pipelines as in the sap conducting system, the end walls are perforated. They look like sieves under a microscope. In fact, they're called *sieve tubes*. The food flows bodily through these sieves. It flows slowly through the perforations and thus plenty of food is available for building wherever needed in the tree. The texture of the food is, of course, not like breakfast cereal or baked beans, but neither is it liquid. It's a jelly fluid (colloidal), highly concentrated but still in good shape to flow to all parts of the plant.

The same cambium cells that build the tubes and fibers of the annual rings also build the sieve tubes around their outside margin. After a cambium cell has turned into two cells, side-by-side, the inside one may turn into a wood element (part of the water lifting system) in which case the outside one remains cambium. Or the reverse may happen. The outside cell may turn into a sieve (part of the food system) and the inside one remain cambium. It's about a fifty-fifty chance which way the cat will jump.

Why, then, are there not annual rings of sieve tubes? Theoretically there are. But one can't see them, since these food conveying cells never become woody, tough and long enduring as do the interior wood elements. They are always more or less soft and squashy and, as a result, they are squeezed into oblivion as a fresh new ring is built each year.

You can easily detect the presence of this marvelous food carrying system. In the early spring, when the waterworks are in full swing and the newly built sieve tubes are bulging with supplies of jelly food, the bark slips. If you rub your finger along a fresh young twig the tender bark pushes off easily, as though it were loose. Actually it is not loose, but just beneath the bark the new tubes are loaded with damp and glistening food which makes them easily squashed and loosened.

Before we leave the bole to look at the third department of a plant's waterworks, it is interesting to note something that lurks in the annual rings, which has nothing to do with their mechanics. In recent years science has awakened to the remarkable records of weather written across these rings. These records antedate the U.S. Meteorological Bureau by thousands of years. As the width of a ring varies in proportion to the amount of water, or rainfall, a graphic record of rainfall is written across the succession of wide, medium or narrow rings. All the trees in a locality will vary in the same way. Thus a new science is discovered—a branch of meteorology, pointing both backward and forward. Backward because the inside rings of a hundred-year-old tree living today overlap the outside rings of a tree felled a hundred years ago. And so a weather chart has been made for some localities, reaching back to prehistoric times. When such a chart is compared with the Weather Bureau's records of sun spot cycles which have been kept for only a hundred years, it corresponds exactly. Sun spot cycles averaged $11\frac{1}{3}$ years during the last century. Tree rings tell us that previous to that time the sun spot cycles varied considerably. Sun spots bring meterological disturbances, storms and rain. Thus tree ring cycles tie up with sun spots, and we have in the tree ring chart a record for sun spots for thousands of years back. Does this suggest a possibility for long distance weather prediction for the future?

The archeologists are interested, too. The tree ring chart is like a yardstick with exact years marked on it. Professor A. E. Douglass of the University of Arizona took a beam out of an adobe Indian hut, slid its sequence of big rings along his master chart until they fitted exactly, and asserted that the beam was cut in 1410 A.D.!

CHAPTER FIVE

Green Leaves as Food Factories

With their spectacular leaves, the trees about my hill put on a striking pageant from May to November. For leaves have everything it takes to arrest attention: color, action, mass and sound effects.

They raise flexing towers of clear green against smooth sky blue. Ever changing, they turn into jet black silhouettes against flaming orange, jade, lemon yellow, or the pearl gray of fluid skies. After a shower my leaves are glittering with diamonds. When the leaves of the sugar maple or poplar are agitated by a sudden updraft they appear to make invisible wind visible by the flush of silver that rushes up the tree.

When trees bow before a sudden squall they move with the uniformity of violin bows in an orchestra. Each species imparts its own individual motions to its leaves. This is the net result of their size, their length of stems, the manner in which they are attached, and the flexibility of limbs and twigs. Most conspicuous are the motions of the leaves of the trembling aspen. Thousands of tiny wings flutter all over the tree. If you concentrate on an individual leaf you will see that it executes a whimsical, eccentric dance. The cause of these gyrations of trembling aspen leaves even in the merest whisper of a breeze is easily discovered. The leaf stem is flat and flabby like a ribbon, so that it catches the wind and gives the leaf a comic wiggle.

Willows sweep back and forth because their twigs are as flexible as pendant strings. Oak leaves rise up and down on branches that behave as though hinged to give vertical motion. The leaves of an elm, hanging from slender drooping twigs, move like pendulums.

In October the colors of a prairie fire sweep through the leaves, and then they let fly singly or in flocks, each leaf for an instant making an independent escape, before settling in its place, to be woven into a gold and brown ground cover.

Leaves are the most articulate part of a tree. They never sound discords, just as they never have color disharmonies. Their range of tones is symphonic. They produce high clear notes, and deep thunderous roars. They effect a few seconds of suspense in utter silence broken by an intimate whisper. They hum in a steady breeze, or swish like waves on a beach. Many times in the winter woods I have paused before an oak almost as well clothed with leaves as in summer and listened to the crisp high notes of the leaves as they rattle in the wind like distant sleigh bells. Forests of pine and spruce have a characteristic sound, hard to describe in words, like steam escaping from a whistle that doesn't work. These evergreens are pitched higher and softer than the broad leaf trees.

Not only are leaves arresting *en masse* in their color, motion, and sound, but also the designs of single leaves are so magnificent that, of all objects in the world, they have been a source of inspiration for art, second only to the human figure! Everybody recognizes the rugged outline of an oak leaf and the trident of a maple. They bear a subtle resemblance to the form

Maple Leaf as Art. Note how it makes a perfect pentagon around a point where the diagonals intersect.

of the trees on which they grow. The oak leaf has a firm straight axis with its lobes stabbing out at right angles. The maple comes to a broad peak with its lobes pointed upward. These are also the habits of their trees. Even more striking is the resemblance between a maple leaf and the form of the buds found on the tip end of maple twigs in winter. These buds grow in threes, with the longest bud in the center and two smaller buds pointing out on each side so that all three form a trident like the three lobes of the leaf.

The elm leaf has a graceful, smooth contour and its heart-shaped base has the same curves as the fountain-like branches. The poplar leaf is a narrow tapering ellipse like the silhouette of its tree. The jagged outline of a hawthorn leaf reflects the sharp angles and irregularities of its tree. The redbud is a squat round tree that bears squat round leaves. The hackberry is long and tapering and slightly lopsided in a graceful way, and that also describes its leaves. Although there are exceptions and many species have leaves whose outlines are not easily recognized in the habit of the whole tree, it seems logical that the inherent characteristic of growth should be expressed both in a tree's architecture and also in the formation of its leaves.

But merely to distinguish an oak leaf from a maple leaf is to miss most of their meaning. There are many forms of oak leaf, and they are not capricious forms. The angles, size and shape of every detail of the leaf, including the pattern of the veins, is remarkably constant in each species. Between species, the differences may be great or small but they reveal a continuity of form, a sort of leaf personality that dominates the genus.

For example, the oaks fall into two general series: the Black Oaks and the White Oaks. You can easily tell to which group an oak belongs by looking at the tip of a leaf lobe. If it is one of the Black Oaks this tip has a sharp point or a bristle; if it is one of the White Oaks the tip of the lobe is rounded and smooth.

In the Black Oak group the black, red, scarlet and pin oaks (*Quercus velutina, borealis, coccinea,* and *palustris*) are all typical and similar in aspect but the depth of the sinus (that is, the cut-in space between the lobes) varies progressively. That of the Black Oak (*Quercus velutina*)—there is a specific Black Oak tree as well as a group—is the shallowest, with broad lobes. In the red, scarlet and pin oaks the sinuses get progressively deeper and the lobes progressively narrower. In fact, pin oak leaves are incised almost to the middle, offering a vivid example of the evolution of leaf forms which, going to extremes, makes compound leaves on hickories and other trees. When you compare these four oak leaves you can see the evolution of leaf forms and how each is related to another.

Members of the White Oak group appear to be more distinctive as to leaf forms but they flow one into another, nevertheless. The specific White Oak (*Quercus alba*) is deeply cut, with smooth lobes that curve in and out with beautiful sinuosities. The post oak leaf (*Quercus stellata*) has the same form modified to wide lobes that are squared off. The leaf of the chestnut oak (*Quercus montana*) has wavy edges. The interesting point here is to see how another of this group, the burr oak (*Quercus macrocarpa*), abundant in the Middle West, combines the features of the leaves of the chestnut oak and the post oak. It is half-way between those two. But it is impossible to say which

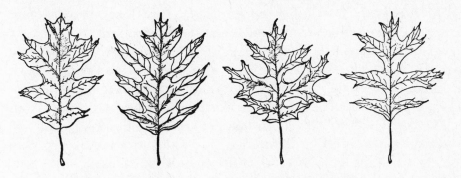

COMPARE depth of sinus in these black oak leaves.
Left to right: black, red, scarlet, pin.

type comes first—probably leaf forms are evolving back and forth in several directions at once.

An individualist of this White Oak group is the live oak (*Quercus virginiana*). This leaf forms a simple oval without a trace of lobe or sinus. The edges are usually inrolled. It is the king of the oak trees in the Southern states. One live oak at Middleton Gardens, Charleston, S. C., has a spread of 144 feet. I have always felt that the name live oak is unfortunate. It refers to the evergreen nature of the tree. Evergreen in the sense that

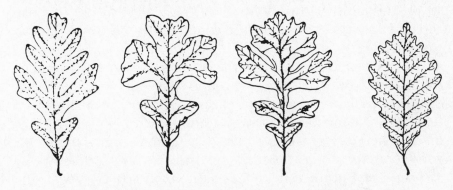

COMPARE the way these white oak leaves have combined
slender lobes, squarish lobes, and wavy edges.
Left to right: white, post, burr, chestnut.

4 5

this oak is always clothed with leaves ... old leaves fall off and new leaves unfold from their buds the year round.

Compared to the oaks, there are but a few species of maple trees and maple leaves; all bear the family resemblance. The typical leaf is the sugar maple (*Acer saccharum*), emblem of Canada. Another common American maple is the red maple (*Acer rubrum*). Superficially, their leaves are alike. But look closely—there's an interesting difference. The sinus of the sugar maple is rounded at its inner end, while that of the red maple comes to a sharp angle. You can also note a difference in the lobes. Those of the sugar maple are broader and pointed outward at a wider angle, while those of the red maple tend to point forward. To put into words such comparisons as these is like describing a person's expression by referring to his turned-up nose or dimpled chin. The actual difference between a sugar maple and a red maple leaf is something instinctively known after seeing them a few times, just as you know the face of a friend.

The box-elder (*Acer negundo*) is a member of the Maple Family which, at first glance, appears to have produced a leaf unlike other maple leaves. It is compound, usually composed of three little leaflets. If you live in the Middle West where this clean cut little maple abounds, note how the three leaflets are always held in a position that forms the trident maple leaf pattern. It's as though the three lobes of a big typical maple leaf had separated completely, and then continued to grow together as three leaflets.

Of all leaf forms, those of the birches are the most constant. All birches have oval leaves with fine sharp teeth on the edges. As a group they are soft and delicate in texture compared with leathery or shiny leaves of some other trees. Also birch leaves are attached to very slender twigs. The common gray birch (*Betula populifolia*) has a wide base and narrows suddenly to a sharp point. But the others, for example, the paper, sweet, and yellow birches are difficult to distinguish by their leaves alone. Their close similarity of leaves is interesting in view of the vivid differences birches exhibit in their barks.

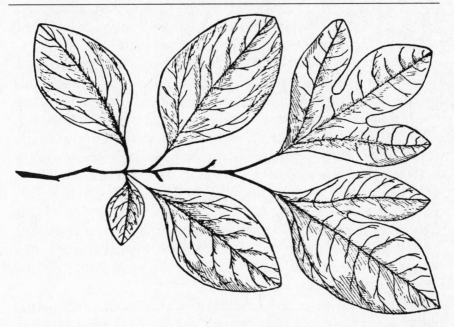

A VIVID EXCEPTION to constancy of leaf design is seen in the sassafras.

On the other hand, the instability of the leaf forms of sassafras and mulberry trees is an arresting characteristic of those trees. If you see a tree with bright green twigs and three forms of leaf: an oval with a smooth edge; or an oval with one lobe projecting on one side like a mitten; or two lobes projecting on opposite sides . . . you can be sure it's sassafras. The leaves of mulberry trees are even more capricious with fancy teeth on their edges and with lobes and sinuses appearing unexpectedly through the leaves of a single tree.

These many instances give us a suggestion of how leaf outlines, with all their marvelous variety, are systematic and offer the quickest, easiest introduction to trees. By far the best way to realize the schemes and patterns that link various series of leaves together is not to look at pictures or read about them in a book, but to find them on the trees. In an hour's walk in the countryside you can collect a good percentage of all the common tree species in your part of the country. Why don't more people enjoy com-

paring leaves? It's surprising how accurately and with what exquisite variety leaves are planned and formed.

However, a leaf was never created just to be admired. That
is an aspect added to it in our minds . . . it helps us to know that
life can be lovely and interesting and orderly. In reality, a leaf
is a hundred per cent functional. Let us examine it from this
point of view. The texture of a typical leaf appears to be continuous and without openings. Yet, as a terminal of a twig, we know
that it acts like a nozzle spraying water vapor into the air. Water,
collected by the root department, is carried up through the trunk
department—because *the leaf pulls it up*, as we shall see. It's the
dynamo of the waterworks. At the same time the leaf is making
food. Both these operations are carried on in a mechanism that
is packed between the upper and lower surfaces, although the
leaf may seem as thin as paper.

If any man invented a machine which would run by the
power of sunlight and make good food out of water and air he
would be considered a genius. In a sense, he would also be
wasting his time. Green leaves have been on the market a long
while, making food out of water and air most efficiently. The
patent is held by chlorophyll.

Chlorophyll is almost the same as human blood. They have
a similar chemical nature. The chief difference is that in blood
the chemicals are arranged around a nucleus of iron, while in
chlorophyll they are arranged around a nucleus of magnesium.
Blood, by carrying oxygen, can aid in purifying foods and res-
toring them for use, while chlorophyll can make foods originally.
How it does this is a secret formula. All we know is that elements
of water and air are combined and then transformed into a
substance that resembles neither water nor air and that contains
sun energy, as a storage battery contains electric energy. This
substance has an excellent name, *carbohydrate*. Carbon is the
element used from the air, and hydrogen is the element used
from water. Other names for this substance are sugar, glucose,
and starch; they are all variations of the same thing.

This synthetic food made by chlorophyll is the only food

POINTS TO LOOK FOR IN LEAVES

The curves and proportions of leaves are related to their tree spirals as described in Chapter Six. Each leaf also has interesting little earmarks that help in its identification.

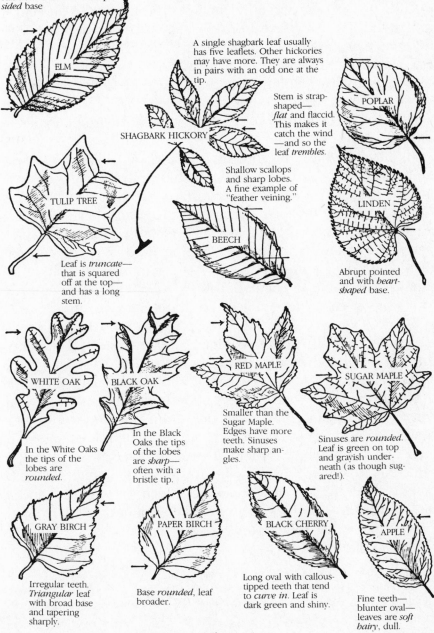

Has *double* teeth and a *lop-sided* base

ELM

A single shagbark leaf usually has five leaflets. Other hickories may have more. They are always in pairs with an odd one at the tip.

SHAGBARK HICKORY

Stem is strap-shaped—*flat* and flaccid. This makes it catch the wind —and so the leaf *trembles*.

POPLAR

TULIP TREE

Leaf is *truncate*—that is squared off at the top—and has a long stem.

Shallow scallops and sharp lobes. A fine example of "feather veining."

BEECH

LINDEN

Abrupt pointed and with *heart-shaped* base.

WHITE OAK

BLACK OAK

RED MAPLE

SUGAR MAPLE

In the White Oaks the tips of the lobes are *rounded*.

In the Black Oaks the tips of the lobes are *sharp*— often with a bristle tip.

Smaller than the Sugar Maple. Edges have more teeth. Sinuses make sharp angles.

Sinuses are *rounded*. Leaf is green on top and grayish under-neath (as though sug-ared!).

GRAY BIRCH

PAPER BIRCH

BLACK CHERRY

APPLE

Irregular teeth. *Triangular* leaf with broad base and tapering sharply.

Base *rounded*, leaf broader.

Long oval with callous-tipped teeth that tend to *curve in*. Leaf is dark green and shiny.

Fine teeth— blunter oval— leaves are *soft hairy*, dull.

there is for men and animals, as well as for plants.* Bakeries, cereal and candy factories, and the like are simply converting and packing this food after it has come off the end of the production line created and operated by chlorophyll. Milk and eggs, meats and fish, all derive from the same plant-made food. The difference lies in whether you eat carbohydrate first, second, or third hand. Cattle get it by grazing; poultry by snapping up grain or insects; fish by gulping water bugs which in turn derived their substance from algae or other plants. Even oysters grow squashy and fat on one-celled water plants (diatoms) that are biologically like microscopic leaves.

Chlorophyll was invented before any animal life could exist in the world. Then green leaves put chlorophyll to work so well that they made a big surplus of food, far more than plants needed for their own sustenance. Because of this available surplus, animal life could be sustained. Animals, including ourselves, have never found any other way of getting food. We are entirely dependent on green leaves! Every last man of us is upheld by them as surely as the Statue of Liberty is upheld by its pedestal.

How does the green leaf go about making this miracle substance? First, the plan of a leaf presents a broad surface to the sunlight so as to catch as much radiant energy as possible. The several hundred thousand leaves of a good-sized maple spread about half an acre (over two thousand square yards) of green to the sun. When in full operation a square yard of leaf surface will manufacture about one gram of carbohydrate per hour. A gram is so little you can't feel its weight if balanced in your hand. It is approximately the weight of a common straight pin. Yet that square yard of leaf surface, working eight hours a day during June, July and August, can turn out a pound and a half of carbohydrate. That's around 3,630 pounds of pure food concentrate made in a season by one maple tree with its half

*An exception might be made for protein, a nitrogen compound synthesized in living plant cells without the aid of chlorophyll. However, it is a question whether protein could be created without carbohydrates being available for its composition.

acres of leaves. To do this, a leaf must be equipped with a two-way system that will supply water to every chlorophyll speck and carry away the food made by that speck—plus a means of inoculating the chlorophyll with air.

We noted that wooden pipelines in the trunk of a tree become bunched together into cables which run out through branches and twigs, and terminate in their allotted leaves. As these water bringing tubes reach the base of the leaf stem they are joined by the food conveyors (sieve tubes) which have followed an entirely separate course in the trunk. You will recall that the sieve tubes formed a cylinder around the outside of the trunk just under the bark, while the water pipes ran up and down inside the trunk. As they reach the stem of the leaf these two conveyor systems—one bringing water into the leaf, the other taking food away—are combined. You can easily see their cables as they emerge from the stem into the leaf and spread out as a network of veins. The big veins bulge out, especially from the lower surface of a leaf. But all these visible veins constitute only a small part of this marvelous two-way conveyor system in a leaf. They keep branching smaller and smaller until they end as single microscopic veins only one little cell in thickness. So finely is this network divided to supply every leaf cell with water and take away its food that no cell throughout the entire leaf is more than $\frac{1}{125}$ of an inch, an invisible distance, away from a pipeline.

Because the vein system spreads out in the pattern of a broad thin leaf we can hardly realize how it branches in depth as well as width. The organization of a leaf in depth illustrates one reason for its marvelous efficiency.

As viewed in cross-section through a microscope, the roof of this factory (the top of the leaf) is airproofed and waterproofed with cells tightly welded, forming a surface covered with wax. This roof is one cell thick, clear and transparent, like a modern glass-roofed factory. As sunlight pours through this roof, it drenches myriads of vertical cells hanging like clusters of sausages from the ceiling. Because of their vertical position, these cells are

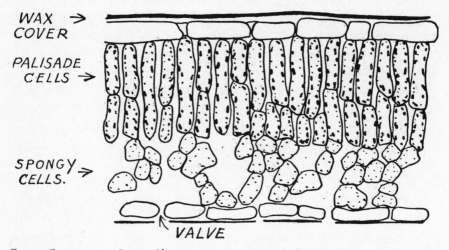

WAX COVER →

PALISADE CELLS →

SPONGY CELLS. →

← VALVE

CROSS SECTION OF LEAF. Shows arrangement of palisade cells for absorbing maximum sunlight; and that of the spongy cells for exchanging air and water.

called *palisade* cells. They have a perpendicular fluted aspect like the Palisades of the Hudson. They are placed to get the full power of the sunlight coming through the transparent roof and to trap the maximum amount of light throughout their length. They are swollen with streaming protoplasm shot through with countless specks called chloroplasts, filled with green chlorophyll. Most of these chloroplasts cluster around the outer fringes of the stream, just inside the cell wall. However, they are detached and may be carried around freely in the river of protoplasm. An individual chloroplast is microscopic. But they are concentrated in the palisade cells of leaves in such enormous numbers that they alone give foliage its green color.

Pause and consider what this means. These palisade cells just beneath the top surface of a leaf are the receiving antennae, not only of the tree but also of the whole world of organic life. They first receive the radiant energy of the sun. Their chlorophyll traps that energy, transforms it, passes it along. This is the vital link between our world of plant and animal life and the radiant energy shot out from the sun through limitless spaces of ether.

The palisades fill only about half the depth of the leaf; below them are other interesting parts in the well-balanced mechanism. This lower half contains cells of miscellaneous shapes and sizes, jumbled together loosely, so as to leave ample air spaces between them. These are juicy living cells with a few specks of chlorophyll in their protoplasm that catch and use the remainders of light rays that may not be trapped by the palisades. These remarkable loose clusters are called spongy cells. They are perfectly designed to promote the exchange of air and water, as they are bathed in air from the spaces between.

Underneath these spongy cells is laid the floor of the leaf factory. This lower surface is transparent, waterproofed and usually airproofed with wax, like the roof of the leaf—but with one remarkable difference. This floor is perforated with tiny air valves that open and close automatically to control the flow of air and water vapor in and out of the leaf. These valves are so small you can't see them without a microscope, but their size is compensated for by their numbers. When the valves are open they make the underside of the leaf practically porous so that air and water vapor can pass in and out. The actual number of valves depends on the kind of tree. An oak leaf has about thirty-five thousand to the square inch; an apple about twenty-four thousand; a maple only ten thousand! The top of the leaf often has a few of these valves, but the great majority of them are in the lower surface. Interesting exceptions are leaves that float on the surface of water, for example, a pond lily. In that case the air valves are necessarily all in the upper surface.

These valves are shaped like mouths. In fact, their official name is *stomata*, Greek for mouths. The opening is a slit between two slightly curved, somewhat swollen cells, resembling kidney beans. This slit opens and closes as the two cells swell up or deflate. The action is amazingly simple. Imagine two rubber balloons shaped like these "kidney bean" cells, laid side by side, with a slit between, while the upper and lower ends meet. Suppose that the rubber on the outside of each balloon (that is, on the side opposite the slit between them) is thinner and more elastic than the heavier rubber on the side toward the slit. As such balloons are inflated, the outside with its thin rubber will bulge out much farther than the inner side with its heavier rubber. In fact, the bulging side will actually pull the opposite side with it in the same direction. Thus, when distended, each balloon will form an arc that widens the slit between them. When less turgid they will tend to straighten out which causes them to come together and close the slit.

The cells forming a leaf valve have a thin outside or far side wall and a thick wall adjacent to the slit. This opens the slit as the outer wall is distended with water. When there is a good supply of moisture, the tree can grow faster, needs more food; the cells are turgid and the slits open wider. In a drought, the cells give up water and this reduces their volume so that they deflate. Deflating closes the leaf openings, thus checking evaporation of water out of the leaf. Too much loss of water through leaves in dry weather might be fatal by the draining of reserve sap inside the trunk. For this reason, the leaves automatically close and cut down the loss of water from the wood during a dry spell.

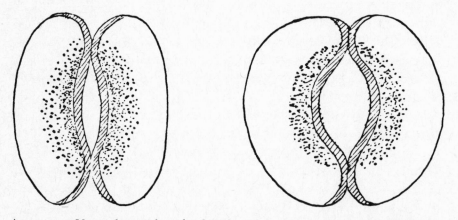

Automatic Valve (stoma) in leaf. Left: valve almost closed by deflation of cells. Right: as cells inflate with water, thin outer walls bulge out, pulling apart thicker inner walls to open the space between.

Another marvelous thing about these valves is that they open and close in response to light. The food factory operates only in daylight when it can get sun energy. Full sunlight is not required. An overcast day will do, but the brighter the day the faster the factory works and the wider open must be the factory ventilators.

To open the valves with light involves an ingenious chemical stunt. One of the characteristics of the two kidney-shaped stomata cells is that they contain green chlorophyll, while the adjacent cells in the leaf surface have no chlorophyll. Therefore, these valve-control cells can make sugar in light. A sugar solution inside a cell pulls in water through the cell walls (osmosis). This addition of water makes the cell swell up. As we have just seen, when these valve cells swell up they open the valve! To summarize this marvelously simple operation: the more light there is, the more sugar they make, the more water that enters the cells, the more they swell up, therefore the wider the slit becomes. In the dark the reverse happens because the sugar turns to starch. Starch does not dissolve in water and so as the sugar solution is reduced, the water is lost from the cell by osmosis. All this causes the cells to deflate in proportion to the reduction of light, so that the valves of leaves become much smaller at night—in fact these automatic controls may close them entirely. This action is not as swift as the arrow on my Weston light meter, but it's surprising how sensitive these devices are. Experiments show that when a bright light is turned off the stomata will close in half an hour.

CHAPTER SIX

The Dynamic Spirals of Plants

Stand off and look at the crown of a tree. Although the leaves are beautifully massed, they may at first appear to be placed haphazardly. Look again. Stand under the arching limb of a beech or elm, or the flat angular branch of a dogwood. What do you see? A mosaic—one of the wonders of the plant kingdom. Note how this mosaic is pieced together, detail by detail, throughout the entire pattern of the tree.

Think of branches as projecting from a circle made by the cross-section of the trunk. If the distance between two successive branches is one third of the way around this circle their angle is 120°. As the branches mount the tree they go round and round with equal spacing. One kind of tree may put forth its branches at an angle of 90°, or 144°, or 180°—whatever the angle of the species *it is constant throughout that tree*. These angles made by the branches always divide the circle equally. In mature trees, of course, all limbs will not be in place but that is only because as twigs they were damaged or failed to develop. Their traces would be there; not one is missed at its true angle.

This same angular succession is true of twigs that grow out of a limb. Look still closer and you'll see that a leaf emerges from its twig at the same angle from its neighbor as the limbs make with the trunk. In place of twigs and leaves you may see unopened buds, and these too project from the bark in the same succession of angles. Limbs, twigs, leaves, all originate in buds, and these four structures are homologous. Throughout the tree, from trunk to the tip of every twig, both the leaves themselves and the skeleton on which they are hung are dispersed at equal angles in every direction. At least that is their basic plan although their equal angles may become distorted by later conditions of wind or light. The leaf mosaic is further perfected by the variation of the lengths of branches and the lengths of the stems of individual leaves, so that each leaf may be held away from its neighbor. Often the twigs and the stems of leaves are bent around or twisted to achieve a position more in the clear.

The net result is that thousands of leaves can grow together, above and below and around their tree, without overlapping or getting in each other's light. This is functional beauty in one of its purest forms.

Nature has two ways of dividing the circle around the trunk in order to give leaves the maximum dispersion. One of these is an *opposite* arrangement of leaves (or branches, twigs and buds). That is, two leaves grow out from the same height on the twig and they are located exactly opposite each other. You can see this arrangement in the dogwoods, maples, ashes and horse-chestnuts. Now look along the twig to the next pair of leaves. They are exactly at right angles to the first pair. The third pair will be exactly over the first. If you look at the twig end-on you will see the leaves project from the bark in four ranks of 90° angles. If, instead of a pair of leaves, the tree produces three or more at the same height of the stem (the catalpa, for example, produces leaves in whorls of three) then the next whorl is turned exactly the right amount to bring its leaves directly above the intervals. Each leaf has emerged with perfect accuracy at the best angle to give it the greatest clearance.

The second method by which nature divides the circle *is* based on *spiral* arrangement. This is far commoner. The chances are you will find it on almost every tree commonly seen with the four exceptions just mentioned of dogwood, maple, ash and horse-chestnut—and, of course, the catalpa with its whorls. The spiral arrangement is indicated when a single leaf or bud emerges from a given height on the twig and with no bud or leaf opposite.

Follow with your eyes the points where leaves or buds emerge along the twig of an elm. As you travel along the twig the point of attachment of each leaf is discovered to be exactly 180° around the stem from the preceding leaf. Every second leaf, therefore, is in a straight line. If you look at the twig end-on, you will see two ranks of leaves, alternating first on one side, then on the other. The linden has the same arrangement.

If I take a piece of string and attach it to the bases of the leaf stems or buds along an elm or linden twig, it makes a steep spiral as it goes round and round the twig. To reach the next leaf directly above the starting leaf the string makes one complete turn of 360° and touches two leaves, not counting the first leaf. You can write this as a fraction by calling one complete turn the numerator "1" and the two leaves needed to complete that turn the denominator "2." This makes ½. In other words, each leaf is exactly one half of the way round the circumference of the stem. This is another way of saying that elm and linden branches and leaves are spaced at 180°.

The distance between leaves along the twig may vary considerably, according to the caprice of growing conditions. In wet spring weather the twig may grow vigorously and elongate far, or in dry weather it may push out slowly. *But the angle between two adjacent leaves never varies.*

Next I attach my string to the leaves of a beech. This time, instead of traveling half way round the stem to touch the next leaf, I go only 120° or one third of the way. To reach a leaf directly above the starting point my string makes one complete circle, but this time it touches *three* leaves. This gives me the fraction ⅓. In other words, if I look at the twig end-on I will see three ranks of leaves, diverging at 120° regardless of how much the distance between them along the twig may vary.

Now see what happens to a string diagram of the spirals along the twig of an oak, cherry, apple or poplar. This time to reach a leaf placed directly above my starting point, the string makes two complete circuits and it touches five leaves, not counting the first. This gives me a ⅖ spiral. The angle of each successive leaf is 144°. This is the commonest spiral of all.

In doing all this we are on the trail of one of nature's most fascinating mysteries. To discover it and build up a series of fractions, attach our string to one more tree. This time try a holly tree. Here it takes three complete circuits around the twig to reach a leaf in a straight line with the starting point. In so doing the string touches eight leaves, not counting the first. Here we have a ⅜ spiral. Three eighths of a circle are 135° and that is the angle of divergence in a holly tree and some others.

Have you detected a remarkable sequence in these spirals? Put them down in order: ½, ⅓, ⅖, ⅜. When you add the numerators and denominators of any two consecutive fractions you get the next one! This series can be continued thus—5⁄13, 8⁄21, 13⁄34 and so on ad infinitum. And that is exactly what nature does! Lurking in these numbers is the abstract quality of perfect dispersion. Here are beauty and function expressed as a mathematical formula.

Typical leaves on trees use spirals described in the small numbers of the first four fractions. The higher fractions are found, however, in hundreds of places where leaves grow more compactly than on trees, such as in mosses or in plants that make rosettes like cabbages and artichokes. Also, higher fractions of this series are found in plant parts that are leaf-like, such as bracts on daisies or the scales of pine cones. Our fifth fraction, namely 5⁄13, belongs to the white pine cone. In this cone the 14th scale (or leaf) is located exactly above the first and to reach it the spiral goes round the axis of the cone five times!

The centers of flowers (like that of a daisy or sunflower) are arranged in spirals whose proportions are identical with those of pine cones, although the fractions are different. Consider the beautiful spirals of the florets in the center of a daisy. At first glance these do not appear to resemble the spirals of branches and leaves on a tree. The latter are on an elongated axis like a corkscrew, while the center of a daisy is a more or less flat surface. But imagine looking at the spirals of the tree end-on and then imagine them collapsed into a plane instead of elongated and you have the same basic scheme. The spiral fractions of a daisy center are $^{13}\!/_{34}$, $^{21}\!/_{55}$ and in an extra large daisy $^{34}\!/_{89}$. Oxford University has a record of a sunflower head (the same family as the daisy) 22 inches in diameter of which the spiral fraction, officially counted, came out $^{144}\!/_{377}$. You will arrive at that if you add three more fractions to those just assigned to the daisy center.

With this spiral curve nature divides the circle equally, so that the leaves on a tree stand as far apart as their number permits. One of the properties of this curve is space. The other is time. Wherever this curve is found in nature its parts differ in age; they are produced serially.

This curve is identical throughout nature. Just as the circumference of a circle always has the same ratio to its diameter (3.1416 as we learned in school), the spirals in nature all have a uniform ratio.

Refer to the series of fractions—if you multiply any numerator by 2.618 you get its denominator, whether it's the leaves of an artichoke, or the scales of a spruce cone, or the intersecting curves in the center of a daisy. Thus, in the leafy crown of a tree we have discovered a fundamental principle of art, *dynamic symmetry*.

Behold then the world's greatest waterworks complete with its three departments:

The root system with its hundreds, perhaps thousands, of

miles of minute channels and apparatus for collecting the tiniest molecules of moisture and merging these into a river of sap. This astonishing system is so endowed with power and pliancy that it can permeate solid ground which man needs dynamite to burst open.

The bole, or trunk, with its millions of tubes to carry sap upward, compactly organized between the core and the bark, its film of food channels running down the outer part of the cylinder where the tissue is young, all so deftly put together that every single twig, bud or leaf is connected with its own lines of communication.

The leaves placed by nature's universal spiral so precisely that each is given its chance for a maximum amount of light; each leaf with a dynamo powered by light, making, out of water and air, food by which alone all plants and animals are sustained.

This tree is fluid and beautiful. Non-essentials are eliminated. It is an honest expression of a purely utilitarian mechanism, well planned, with its parts grouped and all in proportion.

So considered, the tree is a marvelous invention and all the more so because it operates silently, efficiently, and continuously.

What Happens to Make Autumn Colors

At the foot of my pasture stands the graceful long oval of a sugar maple. It is set in a stone wall with the parabolic curve of its roots like great muscles seizing the ground beneath rocky projections—beautifully characteristic of this famous New England tree. The oval of this maple throughout the summer is clear leaf green. It is not dark blue-green like the elms, nor yellow-green like the poplars, nor gray-green like the willows. It sets a standard for leaf color. Yet about the tenth of October this dependable green will vanish. In its place, the same oval, composed of the same leaves, will appear flaming orange and yellow. In moister ground beyond this sugar maple a grove of red maples will all at once turn to bright crimson. Back of my house a line of birches will become as yellow as butter; while a fine ash on the north side will turn as purple as prunes. The effect is that of a swift change in scenic colors as complete as anything on the stage of Radio City Music Hall. It all happens soundlessly, smoothly and on schedule.

The key to this miracle is a tiny band of cells at the base of the stem of each leaf, where that stem is attached to the twig. As summer draws to a close these special cells—and no others in the leaf stem—begin to loosen and dry out. Eventually they will become so brittle that the leaf will break off and fall to the ground. Before that happens the tree prepares to heal the scar where this break will occur by converting other cells just below these brittle cells into tough corky tissue. The toughening of these cells interferes with the plumbing system in the leaf stem by stopping up the pipelines that bring the sap into the leaf. The result of this series of events is to shut off the free flow of sap a couple of weeks before the leaf is ready to fall. These are the two weeks of the fall foliage. This is the time when the pipelines in the leaf stems are plugged up by cork. The procession of color begins with the little things like the strawberries and blackberries and various herbs. Little plants have autumn colors like the big ones. Then in the vanguard of the trees come the red maples, and after them the sugar maples, elms, ashes and last of all, the hickories and birches.

As soon as a leaf has its supply of fresh sap cut off by this plugging of its pipelines, photosynthesis stops. Chlorophyll is an unstable chemical that must be constantly renewed to exist. Therefore, the green chlorophyll, isolated in the leaf by the cutting off of sap, is destroyed by the sun's rays and disappears. In this way green color which is the dominant pigment in the leaf is removed. What is left becomes a vivid demonstration of chemistry.

One pigment that comes into its own when the chlorophyll disappears is carotin. Carotin was in the leaf all the time, floating around in the cell sap in little specks called plastids. But despite the fact that these carotin plastids are bright yellow or orange they are masked by the powerful green of chlorophyll. Carrots are colored by carotin and give their name to this remarkable pigment. It makes butter yellow after the chlorophyll in the grass has disappeared in the cow's milk factory. Carotin is also the pigment of egg yolks. The fact that it survives in the evolution of cream and eggs is proof of its stability. When a leaf is cut off from its sap, carotin is not destroyed as quickly as chlorophyll; it shows up when the green chlorophyll is gone. Sugar maple leaves are rich in the orange and chrome hues of carotin. Birches have pure yellow carotin.

What about the autumn crimson of the red maples and Virginia creeper, the scarlet of oaks, the dark red of sassafras leaves, the plum coloring of the ashes? These red and bluish tones are caused by a sugar chemical in the cell sap called anthocyanin. Anthocyanin is not a pigment whose specks float around in the sap as chlorophyll and carotin do; it is a sugar in solution. It colors sap just as a drop of iodine or ink, dissolved in water, colors that water. Anthocyanin is a chameleon-like chemical. It behaves like the litmus paper that home gardeners sometimes use to test garden soil. If soil is acid when the litmus paper is pressed into it, the litmus turns red; if the soil is alkaline, the litmus keeps its bluish color. So with anthocyanin. If the sap in which this sugar is dissolved is acid, it turns red. If the sap is relatively alkaline, it turns blue or purple. Whether sap is acid or alkaline depends on the chemical make-up of the species. The red maples are acid, so they turn red; ash trees are relatively alkaline, so they turn plum color.

These pigments and sugars do not account for brown which is so prevalent in the fall foliage. Brown does not appear in the spectrum. As we shall see in Chapter 10, it is a degenerate orange. That is, our mind's eye sees brown when orange wave lengths of light are low in intensity. After the yellow or orange of the leaves is exposed for some days it loses its intensity and is keyed down—turns brown. Another cause of brown is a substance found in the wood cells, a powerful astringent called *tannin*. This acid stiffens proteins in animal hides so that they become insoluble and incidentally turn to a rich *tan* color. This is the process of tanning hides. The same thing may happen in leaves. One of the most beautiful and distinctive effects in the fall is contributed by the American beech leaves. They turn to a duo-tone, tan streaked with yellow along the veins, from tannin in the cells of the leaf and carotin in the veins. Because every tree has its own individual chemical make-up of sap each species turns its own distinctive color (with some variations due to soil conditions). You can often identify trees by their hues in the fall.

Some trees do not contribute vividly to fall foliage and the reason is interesting to note. For example, black walnut and butternut trees drop their leaves so swiftly when the brittle cells are formed that their branches are bare when other trees are flashing with colors. The locusts retain chlorophyll green until the leaves drop off. This implies that the corky cells which heal the scar may not cut off the supply of sap to the leaves. To verify this, examine the leaf scar of a locust in winter, or any time after the leaf has fallen. You will find, instead of a clean unbroken scar as on other trees, an irregular and broken callus with a little hole into the bark where the buds are buried.

Autumn colors and dropping leaves are part of the same phenomenon. To strip a tree completely of its leaves is a device of nature to preserve the life of that tree. Those handsome broad leaves are pouring out water in the form of invisible vapor into the air. This water is lifted out of the ground. But the supply of available water in the earth is curtailed when the ground freezes in winter. Therefore, the leaves must be "shut off" before winter or they will dissipate vital sap when it cannot be replaced from the roots. The most efficient way to shut off the leaves is to knock them off. Nature does this by forming those brittle cells which with their adjacent corky cells plug up the sap system and cause the spectacle of the fall foliage.

The brilliance of the fall foliage may be enhanced by the weather conditions. The intensity of light has much to do with the intensity of the red and purple of the sugar chemical. For this reason, the brightest colors are formed when the fall season is bright and clear. If there's an excess of overcast weather, the yellow and orange of carotin are not affected. They glow on moist and misty days with exquisite rich pastel hues. On the other hand, the reds and purples of the anthocyanin are dulled by cloudy weather.

Autumn colors do not depend on the frost. Probably they did in some prehistoric age when the ingrained habits of the broad-leaved trees were being formed. But in our day this behavior is automatic. The hardening of that tiny band of cells at the base of the leaf stem occurs early in October, signalling the end of the life cycle of their leaves. Its perfect timing is another of those engaging mysteries of plant life.

CHAPTER EIGHT

Winter Buds and How They Work

When, in the growing season, you see twigs elongating, vast areas of leaves unfolding, clusters of flowers spraying out, this growth is not suddenly formed out of air and wood. It was manufactured a year ago. All through the previous spring the twigs, leaves and flowers of the year to come were being formed and cells for them earmarked. Then this foliage of a year later was folded and packed and tucked away in such a manner that, after many months, it could be unfolded and expanded without a crease or imperfection.

Thus, a tree puts in motion a dual program of manufacturing in the spring. It conjures up from elementary cells tiny forms of foliage and flowers with their twigs and stems packed together into buds; and at the same time it cracks open the buds made last year and unfolds their contents. These two operations are related and balanced by the directing of available food supplies. Food is always most fiercely expended in making something bigger. Therefore, when spring arrives the current season's growth gets the lion's share of food. At the same time the little units for next year are being processed but at first they do not grow much larger than the head of a pin and their food requirements are slight. In early summer, around the last week in June, twigs are apt to be as long as they will grow that season; leaves are full-sized; flowers have set their fruit and dropped off; down in the trunk the new rings are well along to completion. At this stage, food expenditure (growing force) shifts its balance to the little parts for next year which have been barely started. During the two midsummer months, with the food factory in full swing, the tree concentrates on building, folding and storing the miniatures of these next year's shoots. This is the principal construction job of a tree through most of the summer.

By the innate adroitness of organic matter, the leaves and other parts of next year's shoots remain miniature. They grow to a predetermined fraction of an inch and stop. They are folded, bent, overlapped, twisted, crumpled, in order and precision, then wadded tightly together and packaged inside a variety of tough and waterproof wrapping materials. In this condition we call the shoot a winter tree bud. It is completed around the end of August and lives without stirring for seven months.

When future tree life is thus packed into a tiny unit protected from drying and freezing, the contrivance bears some comparison to a seed. Both seeds and buds offer a way by which plant life can live without the usual requirements of water, air and warmth for months or even years, and then go right on where they left off when conditions permit. To put much into little space and keep it alive on a standstill basis is the chief purpose of these unique devices. Literally, the contents of a bud or a seed do not live without oxygen and water. The amounts of these are relatively small, for just to keep alive without growing bigger takes an infinitesimal amount of air and water—in fact, it takes no more than can be imprisoned with them, while the antiseptic quality of their protoplasm keeps the leaves and flowers sweet and pure.

Why has more news of winter buds not leaked out? Chiefly because they are so little in comparison to the grand scale of the tree. You have to peer closely to see them. But seeing them does not strain the eyes. The smallness of winter buds is greatly exaggerated. Most tree buds and big shrub buds are larger than precious stones. They come in a fascinating variety of forms and colors and markings. They seem to be every shape except square. Nature has few sharp straight lines and right angles. She builds in spirals and curves and radii that make circles. This is the property of fluids, possessed also in turn by growing cells constituted of fluids.

On an overcast day in midwinter a tulip tree (*Liriodendron tulipifera*) that stands alone in the upland pasture back of my house appears to shrink in proportion to its surroundings. It is like a small etching done in India ink in the center of a large sheet of drawing paper. The line where the pasture meets the sky at the crest of the hill is almost invisible, and earth and sky are a continuous expanse of gray. Thus the tree has no evidence of life. The business of leaves and flowers, the colors of fall foliage, and even the earth that supports the tree have vanished. Little wonder that the branches of trees in winter are considered to be stark and bare.

Yet if I come within touching distance of the twigs of that tulip tree I can see that they are studded with life. The tip of each twig is equipped with a spoon-shaped bud about half an inch long, that stands up at a slight angle. This smooth and graceful object is broader at the top than at the base, and somewhat flattened, much like a duck's bill. The sides meet at the edges and are glued together. Because of their form these sides of the tulip tree bud are called valves, a word used to describe clamshells. Near the base they are tinged with lavender, shading to golden brown. Every twig, and there are thousands throughout the vast tracery of the tree, holds out this lovely bud so distinctive in color and shape. No other tree bears anything like it.

Along the twig I find smaller replicas of the end bud. These are not scattered around haphazardly. Since they contain the future foliage they are fitted into the spiral system of the tree and are located with precision. Wherever the leaves of last summer were attached and their stems made an angle with the twig, a bud was born. So, in winter, these buds along the twig always appear just above the scar where a leaf fell off in the fall. It's the same on all trees. You can't miss finding them if you focus your eyes as you do to read the words on this page.

In looking along my tulip tree twigs to find buds and enjoy the geometrical order in the way they are placed, I promptly find a twig which seems peculiar and distorted. Instead of a smooth flow of young twig bark with leaf scars and their adjacent buds spiralling at their fixed angles, the twig is short, heavy and roughened by circular ridges of bark. The tip is crowned with a beautiful duck's bill, but no little ones are found below it. These unlovely twigs are called spurs, and far from being abnormalities they reveal an interesting resourcefulness in tree building. We have seen that three kinds of things may be packed into a bud: leaves, flowers and twig elongations to thrust them forward. Since a twig can exist only in length, its form inside a bud is necessarily primordial—that is, certain cells are earmarked and in position all ready to become a twig. But if all the lower twigs, which generally point out laterally, were to thrust out their full length, the tree would tend to grow as wide as it is tall, or twigs would collide and get tangled up, choking the tree with too much foliage. A spur is a twig that has not extended itself. It opens its end bud and puts out leaves or flowers but the embryonic twig does not elongate. The spur forms another end bud in practically the same position, leaving a rough ring only a fraction of an inch wide where the bark is disturbed by the end bud. The number of these bark rings in a spur shows its age. Such a twig may be only an inch long with eight rings, showing that it took eight years to grow that inch. Some trees let their lower branches languish and die, while others, like the tulip tree, and especially the apple, cherry, and birches go in for the spur method as one way to hold back underbranches and keep the tree's symmetry. A vivid example is the larch (*Larix sp.*), where a large majority of the twigs are spurs and lend a distinctive appearance to the tracery of the twigs. Quite often, after several years, the shaping of the tree calls for some of the spur twigs to resume elongating in a normal manner. So that is what occurs. You can often see twigs with a zone of rough ridges well back from the tip, indicating that they "spurred" for a few years and then changed their minds and shot out again with normal twig growth. This sort of behavior suggests that a tree has an instinct for growing in an intelligent way. Spurring may be a response to reduced light as it occurs so often on lower branches. But that raises the question as to why, under reduced illumination, twigs would not elongate more than the average to reach the light. Moreover, many twigs cease elongating when they are fully exposed to light, and their spurs simply promote compactness and symmetry. After all, the reason why trees make spurs instead of long twigs at just the right times and places to build the most advantageous structure remains a good mystery.

The opening of buds is also selective. Once I tried to estimate the number of buds on the tulip tree by counting buds in a portion that seemed to be about a tenth of the volume of the branches. This was a naïve experiment. It would be much easier to estimate the number of beans in a glass bowl. The labyrinth of branches and twigs quickly baffles the eye and hand. A friend at the Brooklyn Botanic Garden quoted an unnamed authority as saying that a full-grown elm will have seven million buds. Whatever the figure, it's enormous. If they all opened at once the tree would be choked. So, by some inherent logic, only a percentage of the leaf buds open in the spring, perhaps half of them. The others just sit tight. They may never open, and as the tree outgrows them they will shrivel and fall off. But for a year or two they are perfectly capable of opening. It is a marvelous fact that if anything happens to a bud that has elected to open so that the tree is deprived of a leaf at that place, the nearest bud to it, which has not stirred, will then spring into action. I have watched without misgivings a squirrel feasting himself in the branches of a beech tree in late April, when the young leaves are like tender morsels of lettuce for him, knowing that plenty of reserve buds will be called into life and make up the deficiency of leaves. This practice does not suggest "thinking" by the tree if you regard it as the result of competition for food. Opening buds are gluttons and the food supply from stores within the wood are probably not enough to put more than half of the buds into operation. If one is broken or eaten by a squirrel, a nearby bud then gets enough food to open. This does not explain why all the suppressed buds do not open after the new leaves are out and making a surplus of food. Posing questions like this is part of the pleasure of reflecting on the superb practicality of a tree's behavior! Instead of opening all its created leaves and then stifling half of them for lack of light, it opens just the right number to form its leaf mosaic.

The biggest buds are usually the end-of-the-twig buds. That is because they contain more parts and therefore come in a bigger package. End buds may have both leaves and flowers. Even if, as sometimes happens, the end bud contains only flowers, it still has to be larger than a leaf bud. Look at the dozens of flowers in a cluster of lilac, and consider how these were all completely formed and tucked away in the bud at the end of the twig. The enormous magnolia flower is housed in the biggest bud commonly seen. It crowns a magnolia branch like a fat pear an inch in length. Perhaps that is the only bud that many people have ever seen in winter. An end bud may be bigger even though it contains only leaves and stem and no flowers. In that case it must have more of these parts than the buds lower down on the twig. For the end bud is building the main line. The end of a branch thrusts farther and stronger, for which it needs more twig primordia and more leaves to fill its spiral.

Some of our most familiar trees are equipped with two kinds of buds, entirely different in appearance. The flowering dogwood (*Cornus florida*) is an excellent example. In winter you'll find flower buds (always on the ends of the twigs) that resemble fat silver-gray shoebuttons. They're wider than they are long—about a quarter of an inch in diameter. They consist of four segments, glued together at the edges, and curving to an abrupt little peak, like the bulbous top of a Russian church spire. The opening mechanism of these dogwood flower buds is unique. Instead of rupturing the outer cover as do so many buds with inelastic and non-growing covers, the glue at the edges of the segments softens with the running sap. Thereupon, they separate neatly, and then grow from their bases like finger nails. The enlarging bases become creamy white, bigger and bigger they grow, opening out like enormous white petals, and become the conspicuous part of the flower which makes the flowering dogwood famous. The quarter-of-an-inch, silver gray segments of the winter bud do not change color and they can still be seen as tiny "discolorations" at the notch in tips of the so-called petals. The true flowers are the little inconspicuous yellow-green clusters in the center. On the other hand, the dogwood twigs which are tipped with the little silver shoebuttons will have entirely different sorts of buds along the twig, arranged in their proper spirals, for holding the leaves. Dogwood leaf buds are extremely slender and sharp. They are composed of two valves that meet at the edges without overlapping, like tiny, sharp stork's bills. When these leaf buds open, the action resembles the stork opening his bill, and the leaves which have been rolled up lengthwise come straight out like a tongue.

The American elm (*Ulmus americana*) is another tree that has two styles of bud, one for flowers and another for leaves. Elm flower buds are not always easy to see because they grow mostly on the upper branches, and the elm is tall. But a steep hillside or a drooping branch enables one to reach twigs bearing marvelous big flower buds (one half inch long). Each is like a well-browned hot tamale, its ends pinched together and the whole golden-brown bud twisted a little, as though the spiralling tendencies of the tree had given a final fillip as it ran off into the buds. When this bud opens it simply untwists and out pours a shower of exquisite flowers. Each flower consists of a little cup, colored with iridescent orange and red. From the center of this rises a big, forked stigma, as white and feathery as eider down, surrounded by deep purple anthers. These details can only be seen with a hand lens but the flowers pouring out of a single bud are so profuse, and elm flower buds are manufactured by so many tens of thousands, that the flowers tint the whole crown of the elm tree with a purple gauze in April. On the other hand, elm leaf buds are little tan pyramids with their tan scales perfectly spaced in rows, like the scales of a fish. They are always off-center and tipped to one side.

The other native American elm, slippery elm (*Ulmus fulva*), is hard to tell from the American elm in summer. It takes some intimacy with the tree to say "That is a slippery elm." You have to know the feel of the leaves—they're rougher on the slippery elm. And the under bark of the twigs is glutionous and slippery, providing an ingredient for cough lozenges. But in winter anyone can easily detect a slippery elm by its red-headed buds. The flower buds are curious and beautiful globes, topped with a thick crop of metallic red hairs. The anthers are a deeper purple than the American elm and when they emerge among the red hairs it is a sight to behold. The slippery elm, like the American elm, has triangular, tipsy leaf buds, but only on the slippery elm do these have red hairs. The twig is ashy gray.

Generally speaking, however, trees do not produce two styles of bud, although many have two sizes of the same general design, as we saw on the tulip tree that had big and little duck's bills. Horse-chestnut is a classic example of a big end bud. This is not a native tree although its cousin, the buckeye, is so native in the Middle West that it owns the State of Ohio. The end bud of a horse-chestnut can easily be opened with a pin and the contents examined without the use of a lens to see a perfect example of bud packing. After the tough outside covering scales are opened and pulled down you find overlapping groups of leaves. These are folded up with accordion pleats and then curved and pressed together so as to enclose, in the very center, a miniature flower cluster that looks like a tiny white cauliflower.

These various contents are packed with a prodigious amount of "cotton batting," masses of moist hairs that keep the inside of the bud from drying out through the winter months. When nature opens this bud the resin which glued together the outside scales melts, the scales separate and fold back. Then the stem primordia are the first to grow so that the leaves and flowers are lifted straight up out of the bud an inch or so before they expand.

Every tree creates its own winter bud architecture. Most of them make the tough protective coverings, or bud scales, out of leaflike parts. These are arranged in accordance with the spiral formula of the tree, even though they may be twisted around so as to obscure their spiral origin. Bud scales don't resemble ordinary leaves; to the contrary, they are miniature, non-green, and grow close together without any stem elongation between them. Furthermore, to increase their efficiency as guardians of moisture they may be covered with hairs, like the woolly buds of the apple tree. Or they may be coated with sticky resin, like the horse-chestnut, the trembling aspen and that classical example of stickiness—Balm-of-Gilead (*Populus candicans*)—whose buds drip amber viscosity as though just lifted out of a glue pot.

The difference in styling between one tree and another lies in the number of "leaves" or scales used on the bud covering, in their vivid colors, and in the way they fit together. We have seen that the tulip tree and dogwood leaf buds use only two scales that meet at the edges. The linden uses only two, but they sweep around the bud like overlapping clamps, and one is always bigger and bulges out like a "corporation," giving the linden bud a lopsided appearance. The elm places six or eight scales in two vertical rows which criss-cross straight up the bud. The oaks, birches, alders and cherries are examples of scales that overlap but spiral as they mount the bud.

If the plan of the tree makes its leaves in opposite pairs, with each succeeding pair turned at right angles to the preceding, that is the way the bud scales are also arranged. The red maple (*Acer rubrum*) offers a brilliant example. A scale is mathematically centered at the bottom of the bud (its opposite is hidden behind the bud), then above this a pair facing on the right and left sides, and above that a top scale directly over the bottom one. Only four show but they duplicate the maple leaf system with its true right angles.

It is my experience that after I have read in a book about some fact or point of view and then have gone out to see it *in situ*, the first specimen I examine has no resemblance to the fact with which I am primed. If you, who have just read that bud scales are produced in series like leaves and are fitted together in interesting ways with edges either meeting or overlapping— if you now go out and examine a willow bud you will be puzzled by what you see. A work of art, about half an inch long, tapers gradually to a rounded top. It is flattened, making an oval in cross-section, and snuggles closely against the bark of the twig. This well-proportioned object appears to be moulded out of dark red plastic material as seamless as sealing wax. The willow is no exception to the general rule in using its leaf-making machinery to make bud scales. Only it is thrifty and makes one scale do the job. This envelops the bud completely and it is treated with waterproofing and richly colored. If you are looking at the black willow (*Salix nigra*), which is our commonest native tree willow, you'll find that these single-scaled buds are dark, glossy red. If it's a swamp willow, the color is orange, shading to magenta; if a pussy willow, it's blue-black, often mottled with red near the top. But all willows have the same peculiar sealing wax look.

You may wonder how a bud without joints or hinges can open. It opens, just as you would suspect, by simply fracturing the case as though it were made of glass. The explosive force, that of growth expansion which, we have seen in other circumstances, can break through a hard sidewalk, is readily released in willow buds. They are the first to break out in the spring. The willows in a wet place will be in full flower and exposing little green leaves to the sun when the snow is still deep in the woods.

Another one-scaler—and they all have a peculiar charm for their neatness and simplicity—is the bud of the sycamore. The "book" says that buds are fully formed by the end of August, and that they grow at the base of every leaf in the angle made by the leaf stalk with the twig. But if you try to find a sycamore bud before the leaves have fallen, not a trace of a bud is visible. The clue to this mystery is found in the way the leaf stalk abruptly widens at its base. Pluck the leaf off and you will find that its stem completely hides the bud as the snuffer of an old-fashioned candlestick hides a candle wick. After the leaf falls, sycamore buds are clearly visible all winter. They are brown conical hats, stocky, and with a suggestion of a fold at the top, like the turned-over peak of a nightcap. To open, the sycamore bud literally doffs its hat. Its scale tears away around the base and it is lifted straight up, resting on top of the outcropping leaves until it blows away. Cast off bud scales are part of that vast organic slough, including bits of bark, parts of flowers, surplus pollen and seeds, that living plants are constantly throwing off to vanish into the earth, their indestructible elements reappearing in fresh cycles of plants of future years.

You will also look in vain for the buds of locust trees. Take the black locust (*Robinia Pseudo-Acacia*) which grows on high, dry, unfertile hills where man has removed the topsoil, near the suburbs of cities, or where nature has left slate and slag. If any tree can be said to have an unlovely winter silhouette, it is this one. It has no symmetry, no pattern, but stands like a dead, ragged, crooked vestige of a tree. But this ragged pole can produce clusters of fragrant sweet peas and duotone spring foliage of unrivaled richness. Where do these leaves and flowers come from in the spring? Their buds are all built and ready, but with its peculiar gift of unloveliness the tree sinks them into the bark of the twig and covers them over with little scabs.

What are the most beautiful winter buds? Since beauty is not a quantity but a quality, this is like asking what are the most beautiful pictures in the Metropolitan Museum of Art. Answering for myself—you will find your own favorites—I would give the following winter buds the highest rating for sheer eye appeal of color and design. Out in front comes the bud of the shadblow (*Amelanchier canadensis*), also called shadbush. As this species often grows as a tree, as well as a bush, isn't shadblow a better name? The scales of shadblow buds are a rich brown-red, edged with a fringe of silver hairs. The bud is large (a half inch and more), a beautiful tapering oval. The scales are curved and they mount the bud with a flourish, giving it a slight twist and zip. This makes it fluid like a candle flame.

Following the marvelous shadblow bud, it is hard to list the winners in order because they are all so different that they have no common denominator for comparison. The sweet gum bud (*Liquidambar Styraciflua*) has formality, style and finish. Broad at the base and tapering steeply, it is like a little heart pointed up from the end of the twig. In color it is rich mahogany and highly polished. The beech has the longest, narrowest and sharpest winter bud. People who see it for the first time are surprised that they haven't noticed this amazing streamlined javelin before. This beech bud may measure three quarters of an inch and longer. The overlapping scales are bright tan and mount the spear-point in a steep spiral. The wild azalea (*Rhododendron nudiflorum*) has a handsome oval bud with overlapping bronze scales, often mottled with purple and pink, and each scale is vividly outlined by a silver edge. When this bud opens, the scales act as though they are hinged at their bases; they revolve all at once like slats of a Venetian blind.

Flower buds of the highbush blueberry (*Vaccinium corymbosum*) are globes of the richest red and the scales are accented with bright orange edges. The blueberry has an entirely different style of leaf bud. Small, hard to see without a lens, they have two narrow, sharp outer scales, partly open like the blades of small scissors. Red maple leaf buds, mentioned above, are easy to find and very striking in the richness of their vermilion. Maples produce their buds in threes at the end of each twig, with a tall one in the center, flanked by two shorter buds. This crimson trident of the red maple is one of the brightest of tree gems. The sweet birch (*Betula lenta*), with buds smaller than the shadblow, has some of the latter's gorgeous flare and twist, combined with red and yellow colors. The yellow is due to the partial emergence of the inner scales, as the sweet birch bud can hardly contain itself but seems to push out and loosen up a bit, even in midwinter. Chokeberry (*Aronia sp.*) has remarkable buds at the end of its twigs. Once seen, they are never forgotten because of the long, oval, curved scales, like spoons painted crimson. Finally, for style but not for color, I never tire of looking at the end buds of the white ash (*Fraxinus americana*). The contour of this bud defies description. It is built out of an arrangement of three buds, each with a pair of rounded scales, as curved as an S and meeting at the top in a peak. Their charm lies in the way the curves of the three buds flow into each other, suggesting ornate terraces. These buds are black suède with sparkling flecks of amber, where resin droplets are squeezed out. This blackness is due to little clumps of flattened hairs that cover the scales. When ash buds open, the outer scales do not dry up and fall off as with so many trees, but they are alive and grow for a while, never achieving, however, the fine proportions of the growing scales of dogwood.

Somebody has said that the difference between people and animals is a sense of humor. Probably a squirrel, nosing around tree buds, never gets a laugh out of the droll faces sketched by the thousands just below the buds. Nature put them there a geologic age before the time of Walt Disney and his whimsical comics. You can know trees by their faces.

Tree faces are found just below the winter bud within the scar left by last year's leaf. This scar is a cross-section of the leaf stem. But stems are hardly ever round in cross-section. Their shapes vary according to the species, just as all other details vary. Thus, the scars left by these stems make ovals, shields, triangles, hearts, and circles in many varieties and sizes. Inside these scars there are small dots where the pipelines, leading from the twig into the leaf, were broken off. Botanists call these "bundle scars," as they are left by the bundles or cables of the sap and food communicating lines. These bundles form the faces; they are so arranged that they suggest eyes, nose and mouth. Hickories bear some of the most vivid and ludicrous faces. Take the mockernut

(*Carya alba*) which has large scars that you can see easily with the naked eye. The head is wide at the top and curves to an elongated chin. Often this is pushed to one side and the features show an agonizing expression like a cartoon of a prize fighter who has just received a terrible wallop. The bitternut hickory (*Carya cordiformis*) has a long oval face with little beady eyes and a nose-wide mustache. The effect of a little sulphur-colored bud is like an undersized hat sitting on top of this face, and this makes it all the more whimsical. You will see camels and monkeys when you look at the walnuts. The butternut (*Juglans cinerea*) is a remarkable animal with a long chin and a pad like a forelock across the top of its forehead. Poplars have pompous and scholarly visages. Their leaf scars form wide solemn faces, surmounted by tall hats, exactly like brownies who have grown very serious and intellectual. In contrast, the elm has a frivolous and dissipated expression. It has a wide oval face as though it were squashed and sometimes one eye is smaller than the other, making it wink. The final touch of this dissolute fellow is that he always wears a conical hat tipped to one side like a New Year's Eve reveler's. The most human expression I have ever seen is in the alder (*Alnus rugosa*). "He" has a little round face with big wide-open eyes and a tiny nose, and looks at you with startled surprise.

Buds and faces are clearer and more accurate identification marks than leaves and summertime characteristics. People who think that twigs are bare and without interest will consider you a wizard when you name a species from a few inches of twig.

But the whole story is not told alone in the buds and faces. Many twigs have vivid colors or taste. The twigs of the sassafras (*Sassafras variifolium*) are bright, clear green and have an unforgettable spicy flavor. A group of dogwoods (not the flowering dogwood) among our commonest native shrubs are famous for the colors of their twigs. For example, the kinnikinnik (*Cornus Amomum*) has deep, red-purple twigs. The red-osier dogwood (*Cornus stolonifera*) has red twigs, sometimes as bright as firecrackers. Against the snow these twigs make a flash of color, well known to garden lovers who often plant them around their homes. Curving, heavy-armed branches of the brambles are sky-blue. The young twigs of willows are lemon yellow. The striped maple (*Acer pennsylvanicum*) has green-brown twigs with long white marks as though somebody had taken a piece of chalk to decorate them. The twigs of the spice bush (*Benzoin aestivale*) have a vivid unforgettable flavor that gives an instant clue to their identity in winter. The spice bush shows its individualism in another way. Whereas most trees and shrubs form single buds, the spice bush builds them in twos and fours and locates them along the twig, sometimes half an inch above the leaf scar. This does not alter the spiral formula, as they are always exactly above last year's leaf, even though a little removed from it.

If you want to delve a little deeper into the marvels of winter twigs, take a sharp knife and split one lengthwise so as to expose the pith, that is, the soft center of young wood where food is stored and kept fresh and moist. There you will find arresting features. Pith varies in color according to its kind. It is not always white but sometimes bright orange, dark brown, yellow or tan. Some trees acquire pith with transverse partitions like the ties of a railroad track. The compartments between these partitions may be stuffed with colorful and juicy pith material or they may be hollow. The butternut (*Juglans cinerea*) offers a vivid example of a unique pith. It is dark brown, with strong cross partitions and hollow chambers between.

On a Sunday in early April the snow is still deep in the woods one hundred miles north of New York. But this snow is glistening wet. Its surface is sinking rapidly, while water is pouring off below across the soggy ground, swelling brooks and darkening the swamps where the snow has disappeared. Mirrored pools are mottled with green grass and skunk cabbages that look like brownies up to their necks in mud. While this is going on the earliest buds have already loosened their scales and poured forth the tassels of the willows suspending a golden gauze above the dark wet places. When I look closely at the twigs of these swamp willows I can see the mechanics of opening buds in all stages on the same twig. Some buds have their little orange scales clamped shut as though still on the defensive against freezing nights. Others are sending out spikes of green leaves and fluffs of pistillate flowers. From winter bud to leaf and flower makes a beautiful diagram of the succession of events— all on one twig for a brief time.

Where the snow still lies deep in the woods the hazels are in full bloom. This is the American hazelnut (*Corylus americana*), not to be confused with the witch-hazel which blooms in the fall. Few people may have seen these flowers. They are an example of minimum bud opening. The little egg-shaped flower bud, only a sixteenth of an inch long, loosens its scales at the tip and pokes out a cluster of wriggly branches that appear to be made of crimson paraffin. It has the charm of a small jewel wrought with the utmost simplicity. You can see it with the naked eye if you focus closely.

At the same time on the open hillsides, where the light is brighter and the sun is warmer in early spring, the high crowns of the maples and elms are in full bloom. The tall columns of the poplars are studded with what you might take to be huge buds. It is impossible to appreciate what is happening on the poplars when you see these swellings silhouetted black against the sky. But if you reach for a twig and pull it down where you can read its details, you will see that the poplar flower buds are pushing out an object about the size of your little finger, colored with bright yellow and red plaid. This effect is produced by the expanding and elongating contents, as they expose catkins bearing hundreds of closely packed wine-red pollen sacs. Between each two sacs the tree has inserted a yellow scale as packing material. These inner scales separating the delicate clusters have the same function as pieces of corrugated paper or excelsior used to separate fragile glassware in a packing case. The pollen sacs gather strength and size so fast you can almost see them grow. In a day or so they throw away their inner scales, leaving a glistening red tassel that soon turns to orange.

So for these few swift days in the spring the mechanics of

the winter buds are in full action. The contents which have been so tightly packed, so carefully guarded through the winter, pour out, expanding, elongating, twisting, turning as they adjust themselves to their positions in the sun and wind. The unrolling leaves set themselves at right angles to the sun's rays. The flowers are held aloft, waving sticky feathers and arms to catch the air-borne pollen. The catkin tassels droop and dangle so that they can be whipped in the breeze and pour out their pollen. For this climax, as we have seen, each bud operates in its own peculiar way. On some the scales merely loosen and fall off; some scales separate and then revolve on their bases as though on a hinge, opening like a Venetian blind; a few instil growing life into their bud scales, as in the dogwood's beautiful white structures; and then there are others, like the hazelnut, which simply opens a tiny pore at the top to let the contents spray out.

This activity is the triumph of winter buds—and with it they vanish.

CHAPTER NINE

The Spectrum Marches Across the Pasture

So far we have explored chiefly among trees. Many tree characteristics—such as the sap-conducting tubes, the spiral plan, sun-powered factories in leaves, dynamic root behavior, and the chemical wonder of fall colors—are also those of the herbs and wild flowers. In the chapters that follow we shall turn our attention primarily to these companions and relatives of trees. It is the flowers of fields and woods that afford us the most intimate experiences with color, and whose mechanical behavior and equipment we can see if we peer closely.

On or about June twenty-first, the year's Long Day, a spectacular event occurs in the pastures and roadsides. Hordes of compact little flower buds, whose presence has gone unnoticed because their green coverings have made them invisible in the surf of grass and leaves, are suddenly cracked open. Bits of the spectrum are scattered around like confetti, speckling the landscape with red, orange, yellow, blue, white, pink, purple, violet and magenta.*

*On June 21, 1942, I counted 47 species from 20 families in bloom within a half mile of fields, woods and swamps in northwest Connecticut. The following is the list:

Black-eyed Susan	Enchanter's nightshade
Daisy	Rue anemone
Daisy fleabane	Partridge berry
Robin's plantain	Meadow rue
Heal-all	Blue-weed
Yellow hawkweed	Alfalfa
Devil's paintbrush	Wild bean
Bluets	White sweet clover
White lychnis	Yellow sweet clover
Deptford pink	Rudbeckia hirta
Slender lobelia	Chrysanthemum Leucanthemum
Yarrow	Erigeron ramosus
Red clover	Erigeron pulchellus
White clover	Prunella vulgaris
Hop clover	Hieracium pratense
St. John's-wort	Hieracium aurantiacum
Wild basil	Houstonia caerulea
Wild rose	Lychnis alba
Wild parsnip	Dianthus Armeria
Common milkweed	Lobelia spicata
Swamp milkweed	Achillea Millefolium
Wild radish	Trifolium pratense
Tall buttercup	Trifolium repens
Columbine	Trifolium agrarium
Forget-me-not	Hypericum perforatum
Chickweed	Satureja vulgaris
Tall anemone	Rosa sp.
Blue-eyed grass	Pastinaca sativa
Herb Robert	Asclepias syriaca
Beard-tongue	Asclepias incarnata
Iris	Raphanus Raphanistrum
Panicled dogwood	Ranunculus acris
Blackberry	Aquilegia canadensis
Water hemlock	Myosotis scorpioides
Yellow cinquefoil	Stellaria media
White cinquefoil	Anemone canadensis
Ox-eye	Sisyrinchium angustifolium
Elderberry	Geranium Robertianum

This is the Festival of the Summer Solstice, celebrated annually in the open country. It occurs as surely as the sun spends close to fifteen hours above the horizon on a single day, as we shall soon see in this chapter. It is the outstanding color miracle of the seasons. Autumn foliage, which is on a different scale and more massive than the scattered brilliance in the Festival of the Summer Solstice, cannot hold a candle to the variety of hues.

Ever since the flowering season began early in May the fields have exhibited bright colors. But, until this third week in June the effect is that of one dominant color followed by another, rather than a medley.

My house is built in a pasture, formerly grazed but which has been unmolested for several years, an ideal condition for producing field flowers. It is astonishing to watch them come and go, completely changing the color of the field from week to week through the spring months. The ground color, of course, is always green from spring to fall. But even the hues of green vary with the seasons. They begin with the fresh, brilliant green of new spring grass when it overtops the winter straw. This grass soon is mottled with the blue greens of clover leaves, and the various tones of strawberry, cinquefoil, sorrel and countless little herbs that spread their leaves among the grass. Against this back-

Pentstemon hirsutus	Circaea lutetiana
Iris versicolor	Anemonella thalictroides
Cornus paniculata	Mitchella repens
Rubus sp.	Thalictrum polygamum
Cicuta maculata	Echium vulgare
Potentilla recta	Medicago sativa
Potentilla arguta	Apios tuberosa
Heliopsis helianthoides	Melilotus alba
Sambucus canadensis	Melilotus officinalis

The rue anemone is a hold-over from late spring. The ox-eye rushed its season. The bulk of this list, however, is opened by the long day during the greatest flower opening week of the year. And as this list was the result of a rapid survey it is far from complete.

ground the dominant flower colors are both peppered through the pasture and massed together in patches.

The first of these keynote colors comes early in May when the winter cress mustard (*Barbarea vulgaris*) blooms. The keynote is bright yellow, softened with white. These white tints in winter cress are much more pronounced than in the later yellow flowers. After a week or so, the yellow of the mustard vanishes into green pods. Then, as if by magic, the keynote color changes to blue with the coming of the bluets or Quaker ladies (*Houstonia caerulea*) while a carpet of light blue field violets appears on the north slope (*Viola fimbriatula*). The specific name of bluets, *caerulea*, literally means sky-blue. This exquisite flower with its salver-form corolla of four tiny petals, each about ⅛ of an inch long, shows every shade of the sky from white to deep blue! At the base of each petal glows a spot of bright yellow, and these four spots make a tiny yellow circle that acts as a bull's-eye for nectar hunters.* For all their small size these little flowers show great perseverance; they do not vanish in a week or two like many other spring flowers, but may be found here and there in the grass from midspring until midsummer. Late in May, the delicate colors of the little bluets are overwhelmed by the golden ragwort (*Senecio aureus*). The ragworts are a middle yellow, halfway between the white-yellow of the mustard and the deep yellow of the buttercups. At this season ragworts suddenly shoot up in numerous scattered clusters taller than the grass. It is their turn to give color to the field.

At the same time, the lower end of the pasture, in moist and partially shaded spots, is putting on one of the most beautiful side shows of any season: the brilliant pink, red, and yellow columbines, the rosy pink-lavender geraniums, the purple-striped Jack-in-the-pulpits. Go and find them when the ragworts unfurl their pennants around the first of June. This is the most thrilling week for spring flowers. Now's the time to see wake Robins and

*Bluets have such a unique mechanism for insuring cross-pollination that we shall return to them later.

baneberries, miterworts and lady's-slippers. These are the more hidden and scattered flowers of out-of-the-way places.

In another week the keynote color of the field changes to pale lavender when the Robin's plantain (*Erigeron pulchellus*) takes the spotlight. Pulchellus is Latin for "beautiful," but the Robin's plantain is sometimes too pale to be beautiful. Only about one plant in ten is pastel purple, with golden or reddish center. Yet it is the most arresting of the fleabanes. Folklore gives the name to the group by claiming that they repel fleas. This plant is often mistaken for an aster out of season, but the asters bloom in late summer and fall. The rays of the Robin's plantain are long and slender and very numerous; the center is bright yellow turning to deep reddish purple as the flower heads ripen. Robin's plantain is larger in diameter than the average aster. Unlike many other field flowers that seem to vanish suddenly when they turn into pods or seeds, the Robin's plantain gradually fades. They stand around pale and wan for several weeks until the hawkweeds start invading the field.

This is a real invasion. The hawkweeds send three regiments across the pasture. The tallest, known simply as yellow hawkweed (*Hieracium pratense*) stands eighteen to twenty-four inches high and bears six or eight deep yellow flowering heads on a single stalk. The shortest, the mouse-ear hawkweed (*Hieracium Pilosella*) has flower heads in wide flat hemispheres that squash down on top of the green grass making solid patches of rich yellow. The mouse-ear hawkweed derives its name from its gray furry leaves that lie flat on the ground in dainty rosettes. This hawkweed is usually mistaken for the dandelion. But the true spring dandelions have turned into domes of tiny gray parachute seeds and blown away a week or two before the hawkweeds arrived. Moreover, dandelions have long hollow stems like smooth translucent tubes, while the mouse-ear hawkweeds have ordinary solid, very short, stems. The third regiment of hawkweeds is the fiery devil's paintbrush (*Hieracium aurantiacum*). And the very devil they are for the farmer when they possess his grazing places. The magnificent crimson and orange of these hawkweeds rivals in brilliance anything in the seed catalogues. This is an example of a gorgeous flower that rates as a weed because of over-aggressiveness and bad manners.

During the second week of hawkweed dominance (around the tenth of June), spots of white appear here and there through the field. The daisies are coming and will take a week to gather their forces. Daisies exert a power all their own. They are the best known and loved of wildflowers, a symbol of cheerfulness and summer days ahead. Their popularity is deserved, for daisies are healthy, unblemished, generous and dependable. You can pick them without qualms and enjoy them indoors and out. Their stems are strong and just the right length for your vases.

Through this succession of hues flooding the fields one after another during the spring, flower colors work up to their climax the third week in June. These dominant colors do not take into account the many little flowers that are born to blush more or less unseen in the "grassroot jungles." Such are the speedwell, one of the prettiest flowers that blooms; the blue-eyed grass; chickweed; wild strawberry; rock-cress; and ground ivy. That is another phase, an intimate, varied and elusive phase, in the colorful history of the unmolested pasture. It will pay one to look a little closer. At each narrowing of the focus he will see new and unsuspected groups of flowers.

The clovers are distinctly creatures of the pasture. They are fragrant, abundant and beautiful. Moreover, they are the farmers' friends because through curious little knobs on their roots they put nitrogen into the soil instead of taking it out as so many forage crops do. There are five common kinds of clover, each different in color and form. The little white clovers that come in bluegrass lawn seed are well known. But the red clovers are the "big shots" of pasture and roadside. Of course, they are not red at all as ripe strawberries are red, but domes of deep magenta. The hop clover, sometimes called yellow clover, looks as though its heads were screwed on upside down. It is clear yellow but with a play of iridescent red and brown in the older blossoms. The two sweet clovers, white and yellow, are usually not recognized as clover at all. Their scientific name, *Melilotus*, means sweet lotus. You often see borders of these tall, graceful flowers along country roads. Although the sweet lotus is a pasture flower, it seems to thrive close to the stony, tarry shoulder of a highway, where the long slender wands spray out over the white fences and hot pavement.

Along with the clovers in this June twenty-first outburst of flowers come daisies, black-eyed Susans, buttercups, sorrel, heal-all, blue weeds and daisy fleabane. These are the true celebrants of the Festival of the Summer Solstice. They are the long day flowers. The sky-blue slender lobelia has just appeared. So have the magenta, white-dotted Deptford pinks.

Two of the most exquisite tints in all nature are also to be seen at this time. The cream of the meadow rue is like butter floating in milk. The beard-tongue, a relative of the garden snap-dragon and digitalis, is usually dismissed as a common tall white weed. Look for its magic tint. The interior of the chalice of the beard-tongue when the sun is full on the flower is filled with spectral blue. The petals are thin and translucent and filter out evanescent blue from the sun's rays.

What is the secret of color in the ever changing landscape? Superficially, on a still bright day in June, the whole scene might be compared to a painting. The plants appear stationary. The hills are solid. A vast universal light drenches the scene and deliquesces silently into the earth. No hint reaches the senses that the color fixed in this scene is the swiftest, most dynamic quality in all nature. Those purples, violets, yellows, greens with the turquoise of the distant hills have just completed the fastest trip recorded in science. They left the sun eight minutes ago as waves of radiant energy. These waves travelled the intervening space of 93 million miles at a speed of 186,000 miles per second until they struck the objects of the landscape which are the first things to intercept them. At the instant a sunbeam is intercepted, a bit of ultra-natural magic occurs. The intercepted sunbeam, collectively called sunlight, is split into a million parts. Some of these are absorbed by the flower or leaf and their energy enters into and creates the life of the plant. Thus, plants are actually compounded out of light. But other parts of this sunlight bounce off. They ricochet, not as ripples on the flat surface of a pond when a stone is dropped into the water, but as ethereal bubbles expanding in every direction. These are the authors of color.

Color is not an inert pigment. It is the culmination of a series of events. This placid colorful landscape is a world teeming with activity. It is teeming not only with animals and insects, not only with sap streaming up through trunks and stems, but with the supreme activity of all: the bombardment of white light, the shattering of the spectrum by leaf, twig and flower, as they consume the wave lengths of light energy exactly suited to their natures and fling off the others. It is these by-products that we see and convert into color in our minds. Light and color are analogous. Light is the raw material; color the converted product.

This conversion, a purely mental process, bears a direct relationship to the mathematical lengths of light waves. The visible spectrum is only a small part of the total spectrum of the sun. The latter consists of rays shorter than we can see, called ultra-violet, and rays longer than we can see called infra-red. Since the nerves of our eyes are not stimulated by ultra-violet rays and shorter, or by infra-red rays and longer, we say they are invisible. Out still further on each side of the sun's spectrum extends the great electro-magnetic spectrum with long radio broadcasting rays at one end and the short gamma rays produced by radium at the other end. Our visible spectrum is a small fraction of this cosmic scale.

The wonder of seeing color is enhanced when you realize what great variety of color the eye can see from inconceivably small variations in wave lengths of light vibrations. To measure them a new unit of measurement has to be imagined. This is called a millimicron. This unit is one millionth of a millimeter. A millimeter, which is about 1/25 of an inch, can barely be seen by the naked eye. When it comes to one millionth of that you just have to imagine it, but happily we can see many things in the mind's eye that we can't see in the physical world. All the visible wave lengths in the spectrum range from 400 millimicrons to 700 millimicrons. Or, putting it another way, the wave length of light is around ⅟₅₀,₀₀₀ of an inch. Yet so sensitive are the nerves of the eye that they convert these infinitely small differences into radically different mental effects which we call blue, green, red and so on. In this respect our eyes have super-microscopic power. The scientist in his laboratory who explores the inner secrets of plant life with magnifications of a thousand diameters has a crude and inefficient microscope compared to the human eye when observing the fine gradations of color in nature.

This infinitely tiny scale of color, ranging through 300 millimicrons, can be divided into three equal parts. The shortest third, namely, wave lengths from 400 to 500, is the blue sector. At 400, where visibility begins, we see deep violet. As these wave lengths increase, we see various tones of blue. From 500 to 600 comes the green sector, ranging from blue-greens at the shortest end to yellow greens. From 600 to 700 we see red, beginning with bright orange-red and deepening to dark red as the waves lengthen until the visible limit is reached at 700. These are the primary colors of light: blue-violet, green, and orange-red. In brief, a primary color is one that can be extracted as a single band from the spectrum. All other colors are blends from different parts of the spectrum. Out of combinations of these three primary colors we can see every hue in the woods, fields and sky.

Where is yellow in this scale? Yellow, one of the most brilliant and recurrent colors in nature, is a paradox. It is not a primary color in light, although for physical reasons it is a primary color in the pigments of a paint box. Yellow is a combination color created by the intermingling of the frequencies of green and red. There is a yellow band in the spectrum around 600 millimicrons where the green and red sectors impinge. But as this band is very narrow and actually a combination of two primary colors it does not rate as a primary color of light. Yellow also results when blue is subtracted from white. In other words, when blue is missing from a sunbeam the green and red left in the spectrum are in just the right proportion to produce yellow. Yellow flowers have an affinity for blue. They absorb blue and the rest of the spectrum bounces off to our eyes, minus the blue, and that makes the flowers look yellow. On the other hand, lobelias and irises are blue because they absorb green and red rays while rejecting rays somewhere between 400 and 500 millimicrons—that is the blue end of the spectrum. We say those flowers are blue because that is the color produced by the length of light rays thrown off. Leaves are green because the pigment called chlorophyll absorbs blue and red rays and rejects the middle lengths which produce green in our minds. The color we *see* is the color from that part of the spectrum which the flower rejects.

This explanation appears to pigeonhole the chemical natures of plants (pigments) according to their affinity for one or more of the three primary colors. That oversimplifies the proposition. In reality, their chemistry is highly complex. They absorb and reject light waves in varying amounts from every part of the spectrum. What counts in producing color is the *majority* of the wave lengths that bounce off and reach our eyes. If the waves of a certain primary color *predominate* we see that color, even if other parts of the spectrum are mingled with it. When that color is exceptionally pure and clear, as the red of the cardinal flower, then the rejected rays from other parts of the spectrum are in a small minority and do not count. But more often the play of color in flowers, the delicate variation of hues, denotes a more balanced intermingling of wave lengths. The purple of violets, the magentas of the wild geraniums are mixtures of blues and reds in their own critical proportions. The turquoise of distant hills is the compound of blues and greens. The pink of the wild rose indicates that flower is throwing off some rays between 600 and 700 millimicrons (red) mingled with a considerable amount of light from all three primary parts of the spectrum which simply means white light.

The vast symphony of tints and tones created out of but three primary colors belongs to the psychological nature of color rather than to its physical nature. The eye sees far more than the spectrum. Red-orange, green, blue-violet, these are the colors of the rainbow, a spectrum thrown into the sky through the prisms of raindrops. There is no black and no white in the rainbow. Yet our minds see black and white with their gradations in the rays. The colors of the landscape are seen in relation to their environment. In that environment white appears on every hand: white flowers, stones, barks, and the reflections of polished surfaces called highlights. On the other hand, plenty of black lurks in shadows, in barks, and in the earth itself. The mind blends these blacks and whites with the spectrum colors. When you combine a pure color with white you get a *tint*. For example, red plus white produces pink. When you combine a pure color with black, you get a *tone*. For example, red plus black produces maroon. The mind is an instrument for producing hues as well as for enjoying them. The mind has a far greater range than the spectrum. Moreover, it borrows long and short rays and mixes them to get purples and magentas. It mixes green and red in definite and precise proportions with the most astonishing result of all, yellow, resembling neither green nor red. It adds "no light," black, unknown in the spectrum, and creates tones. It takes "all waves," white, and combines with other colors to get wonderful tints.

The mind's eye is the converter. There is no blue, green or red, or any tint or hue as we think of them ... until we think of them. These colors are merely radiant energy until they enter our minds. It follows that with a little conscious attention we can see and enjoy much more color in the world around us. Everybody is attracted by the brightest colors in a brilliant sunset and the autumn foliage. But people who require that much agitation of their optic nerves to attract their attention to the colors around them are color "deaf." They are aware only of crescendoes in the colors about them.

ADDENDUM to CHAPTER NINE

In this and the following chapter the reader may well become confused by the discussions dealing with flower color. In physical terms, light coming from a direct source can be classified into primary, secondary and intermediate hues. By passing such light through a spectroscope, each can be identified by a particular band of color along the spectrum ranging from dark red to deep violet. The primary colors are red, yellow and blue, and their respective complementary colors are green, violet and orange. Intermediate hues and their complementaries would fall between these, for example, red-orange would have blue-green as its complementary color.

In his discussion of color, the author has made use of a color theory based not on color as received from a direct source, but rather color as reflected from objects in the environment. The human eye is extraordinary in its sensitivity to color; it can distinguish many different shades and intensities of color without difficulty. In a physical sense, reflected color strikes the retina of the eye, after which it is transmitted via the optic nerve to the brain where it is expressed as the sensation we call color. The primary colors of reflected light, according to this theory, are red-orange, green and blue-violet; these are very close to the complementary colors of the direct light theory. There is a sound biological reason for making this distinction: we see the world around us largely by reflected light, and it is to this kind of light that our visual sense has become adapted. Thus, the cone cells of the retina detect color because of a light-absorbing pigment contained within them; absorption triggers the optic nerve to register a sensation in the brain. There are three kinds of cone cells, red-absorbing, green-absorbing and blue-absorbing, and their absorptive capacities differ because the light-sensitive pigment varies slightly from one kind of cell to the other. Each of the cone cells can respond to a broad spectrum of light, but each responds maximally to colors that are, respectively, red-orange, green or blue-violet. Hence the classification of colors in biological rather than in physical terms.

We are all aware that some people—mostly males—are colorblind. There are several kinds of colorblindness, all of them inherited, but individuals expressing these traits see an environment that is defined in shades of gray, that is, in intensities, but not in color. Presumably the pigment in the cone cells is deficient in its absorption capacity, or the cells in the optic lobe of the brain fail to register sensation properly, but whatever the basis the world to these individuals is far different from that which normal individuals see.

—C.P.S.

Seeing Color the Year Round

Color is always to be seen in the countryside whenever there is light. That includes the dullest day of winter, and overcast and stormy days of every season. The brightest primary colors are always present as well as the most delicate hues. You might suppose that bright red is not a year round color. Let us see. In the June meadow burns the flame red of the devil's paintbrush and the scarlet of wild strawberries. The next month, on the edge of the woods, a wood lily will fling out its red vibrations. In August, at the foot of the hill, along the brook flare glossy rubies of honeysuckle and bittersweet nightshade berries. Later in August the cardinal flower throws out a sharp band from the long end of the spectrum. In September, the Jack-in-the-pulpit fruits and Russula mushrooms are among the countless objects that flash the long red waves of light. In October, the leaves of the red maples, sassafras and sumac will surrender their chlorophyll and throw off scarlet vibrations instead of green. In early winter the climbing bittersweet and the fruit of the cranberry tree will flare from the hedge rows. All through the winter there is no brighter scarlet than the tips of Cladonia lichens called "British soldiers," or the twigs of the red osier dogwood, or the winter buds of willows, red maples and blueberries.

You can see through the seasons a similar succession of yellow, purple, blue, green or any other color or hue you may look for. Color is no seasonal phenomenon; there is always more of it than most of us ever see.

Exploring for bright color the year round brings un-dreamed-of surprises. When you accustom your mind's eye to detect hues, the beauty of the world we live in becomes a revelation. I used to consider that green leaves are all about the same green tone. That is so far from the fact that it is often possible to tell the species of a tree from its distinctive shade of green. Birches are yellow green; poplars, gray green. Sugar maple leaves are a bright rich green above and silvery green beneath. When the wind blows the whole tree gleams with silver. The elm leaves are a polished dark bluish green; the cherry is similar but even glossier. The locust presents a beautiful duotone effect, with lighter and darker green leaves on the same twig. The ash is a dark blue green. The American beech has foliage of clear bright green. Poison ivy starts as bronze red and turns to polished green as sparkling, if it is growing in full sunlight, as though covered with cellophane.

Each conifer, too, has its distinctive shade of green. The white pine is well named not only for its white wood but also for the accents of white light which play through its needles. This effect is due in part to a light blue tint, almost white, in the lines of the breathing pores on the underside of each needle and in part to highlights from the polished surface of the needles. Other species of pine are on the dark side. The three common species of pine native in the eastern United States are named after the tones of their green needles: red, white and black. The famous cultivated variety of spruce, known as blue spruce, has beautiful blue green needles. The hemlock is a dark yellow green and very lustrous.

Among herbaceous plants one of the loveliest shades of green is found in the leaves of clover. The surface is dull, with a bluish tone mottled with light blue angular check marks. In contrast, the mullein is as gray as a woolly blanket, but when you hold it up to the sun the transmitted light is clear yellow green. Of all the bright greens in the world there is none brighter than the pleated leaves of lady's-slipper and Clintonia. They have a high polish in contrast with the blue green of honeysuckle leaves which have a beautiful rich suède finish. Blood-root leaves, when they first appear in early spring, are unique not only for their fantastic design but also because they are a lovely blue green. And the exquisite flowers shoot up on dynamic straight stems through the heart-shaped base.

A vast array of unseen color will suddenly flare when you look for the hues in bark. I used to think that all bark, with the exception of white birch, was a nondescript grayish or brownish tone. That was before I really *looked* at bark and discovered not only a variety of hues of one color but also many different colors. That of the yellow birch is glistening yellow. Sweet birch bark and the younger bark of cherry are maroon. The younger bark in the upper branches of Scotch pine is such a bright orange that the species can be identified by this feature. The white in white oak bark gives the bole its distinctive gray tint by which it can be identified from all other species of oaks. The barks of the American beech and of the red maple are smooth battleship gray. The deeply sculptured bark of the black locust has bright yellow streaks in its fissures. The Osage orange bark is orange, although the name is a coincidence, as the tree is named after its fruit and not its bark. There is a distinct difference in the whites of the two white birch trees: the gray birch is a cold silvery white; the paper birch is a warmer buff white, due to the orange inner bark just below the surface.

So mobile is color outdoors that it changes with every intensity of light. Perhaps this is one reason why certain seasons of the year are considered to be rather drab or colorless. November is the darkest month of the year. Then the sky is frequently overcast and the noon sun is closer to the horizon. The snow which builds up intensities of light in winter has not yet arrived. In these days of reduced illumination, reds turn purple. This is seen in the colors of lichens, twigs of dogwoods or buds of red maple and willow. Yellow turns olive green. Bright green becomes bluish. Look at the foliage of conifers, clubmosses and evergreen ferns in November. Blue turns deeper blue, witness the bloom on the canes of brambles and the metallic blue of the fluted shafts of the scouring rushes. The orange in the carpet of fallen leaves, in catkins, seeds, grasses, and the November hues of hay-scented ferns turns brownish. Brown is a degraded orange. It is produced when the pigments that give off the light waves of orange act as a sort of brake to reduce their intensity —or the same effect is produced when the original source light is of low intensity.

Conversely, outdoor hues are entirely changed by increased illumination. Red appears as purplish pink; yellow becomes warmer; green grows bluer; blue, purpler; and orange, reddish. Violet remains violet but of a paler tint.

This is one reason why it is difficult to discuss precisely the colors of things. Objects which have not changed their color natures take on different hues when the atmospheric illumination varies. All such changes are optical illusions; they are of the psychological nature of color which is so fluid as it plays on the sensitive nerve ends in our eyes.

This fact makes color in the outdoors one of the least known and least understood of nature's phenomena. The terminology for color is incomplete and inaccurate. We speak in generalities, dividing this vast array of hues, tints and tones under a few key labels like red, yellow, green, blue, orange. Violet, purple and magenta are ambiguous words. Even the botanists with all their striving for precision of expression have never finally agreed on a way of describing colors accurately. In the *Manual of Botany* by the great Asa Gray most of the hues from pink to violet are simply called "purple." But if a quality as elusive as color cannot be accurately described, at least it can be felt and the comparison of tones, tints and hues made and enjoyed on the spot while you look at the objects. In this way one can learn to think in terms of color and feel an artist's thrill over its infinite gradations.

It may seem strange that there are no disharmonies of color in nature. If you put pink, green, magenta, yellow and turquoise in a woman's dress, the colors would fight. But the flowers of the woods and fields, the foliage, bark, rocks and hills and clouds never clash. This means, of course, that these colors never conflict in *our minds*; they form our natural environment to which the human eye has been accustomed since earliest time when our prehistoric ancestors lived in caves or swung by their tails from limb to limb among the green leaves. This is the psychological explanation. There is also a physical reason for the unerring harmony of outdoor colors.

We have noted that the red-green-blue bands of the spectrum are always arranged in the same sequence in accordance with the beat (i.e., length) of the light rays from which each color originates. The spectrum emerges out of darkness with deep red; it unfolds through hues of red and orange to touch yellow; then green, blue green, blue and violet, where it vanishes again into darkness. One simple principle in this order is that adjacent colors must be harmonious. If the adjacent bands of the spectrum clashed we should go mad. Thus, blue and green, yellow and green, yellow and red are all harmonious combinations. Consider how nature loves these combinations. Green leaves against blue sky and water; yellow and green fields; yellow flowers with green leaves; red flowers with yellow centers.

Another principle of color is that complementary colors must harmonize by their very nature. A complementary color is one which added to another color makes white. We call it one color, but physically a complementary color is a blend. Think of the three clearly defined bands of the spectrum, which we call primary colors, as three blocks. They are blue, green and red. All three together make white. Now here is blue all by itself.

To turn that blue to white you have to add green *and* red. Green and red, as we have seen, make yellow. Thus yellow is the complementary of blue.

If a ray of sunlight strikes any object, the combination of light waves absorbed would be the complementary color of that which is deflected, giving the color we see. Blue and yellow harmonize beautifully because they are straightforward complementary colors. If combined in light they make white. See how the landscape is filled with blue and yellow: a field of goldenrod against a blue sky; blue flowers with yellow centers; yellow and orange against blue sky or water in fall foliage.

Take the green block. To "complete" it and get white you must add blue *and* red. Blue and red make magenta, and so magenta is the complementary of green. This, too, is a common combination. See the magenta domes of red clover and bull thistle against their green leaves.

Finally take the red. The complementary has no name of its own such as yellow or magenta, but is simply blue-green. Everywhere you see red, you see blue-green. Behold a sunset and blue sky and green foliage.

Another important reason for the harmony of landscape colors, perhaps the most important of all, is the refractive quality of the atmosphere. Moisture and dust particles tend to scatter the blue rays, giving the air a bluish tinge. This tinge has a softening effect on all the colors of the landscape. Distant hills covered with foliage send out green rays that are filtered through the blue gauze of the intervening atmosphere so that we see the most delicate turquoise. Dust and moisture particles even on the clearest day tend to soften the sharp edges of the spectral bands from every part of the landscape. The atmosphere in this way blends colors and ties them together.

This phenomenon of refraction by dust and moisture particles makes the sky blue. In the case of the clear sky where we are looking through great distances the molecules of the air itself scatter the blue and violet waves to make the sky look blue. When the sun is near the horizon in the morning or at sunset, its rays have to pass through a much deeper layer of atmosphere, which may scatter the blue so completely that instead of reaching our eyes from many points, they don't reach our eyes at all. The green rays are scattered in the same way permitting only the long wave lengths of the yellows and reds to reach our eyes. This is the secret of the red and orange colors of sunrises and sunsets.

Distance, which has such a magical effect on the colors of the landscape, is also the dominant keynote in its composition. To say that the landscape on a bright June morning is so still and colorful that it looks as though it were painted on canvas is a compliment in reverse. Depth on the canvas is pure illusion. It must be captured out of the limitations of a flat surface. The eye scans a painting right and left, up and down—that is, at right angles to the glance. But when you look at a natural landscape on a sunny day the whole force of its composition is in the third dimension. Every horizontal angle is multiplied many times by depth. Details are arranged one behind another. Even when a tree is *beside* a pond, the blue water extends *beyond* the tree. The scene literally goes places. This dynamic fact combined with the relation of adjacent colors from the spectrum is the secret of the universal harmony in nature. And every hue is delicately scaled according to its distance from your eye.

The curving pasture in which my house is built is like a brilliant proscenium. Just beyond at the foot of this pasture a curtain of green follows the brook. This curtain is composed of the deep-toned leaves of elms, the yellow-green tints of birches, the clear leaf-green of the lindens and maples, and the blue-green of the ashes. The most conspicuous tree in this group is a veteran white pine whose needles shimmer with highlights. Although this mottled greenery is only a few hundred yards away, a certain amount of blue from the atmosphere is already added. However, the mind's eye is quick to "correct" the hues and sees only the greenest of leaves. To detect the effect of this short distance you must compare the hues of these trees with green leaves a few feet away.

Beyond this line of trees several miles of valley have taken the colors of field and foliage and softly blended them. This is the melting pot of distance. The brightest greens, the reds, oranges, blues, and high-keyed yellows of the hawkweeds are all in there, but they have vanished. Out of the valley three miles away emerges the turquoise of the skyline range of the Taconics. These hills, clothed with fresh spring greens, have merged with the sky. Here are the same materials that comprise the green curtain at the foot of the pasture, but the proportions of hues are reversed. Instead of green with a touch of blue, we see in the distance blue with a touch of green. And finally, beyond and above the hills, the blue sky is tinted with white mist.

A clear summer day usually begins with mist, dense in the depressions and valleys when there is no breeze and the moisture condensed by the cool night air is lifted by sunlit warmth. As this mist rises and spreads, it fills the air with gossamer through which filter yellow hues. As the sun climbs, the mists evaporate into invisible vapor, the yellow light melts into the white sunlight of midday. For this reason a fair day is indicated when the morning begins with mists and yellowish light.

Daylight is white sunlight plus reflected greens and blues. This is true whether the day is clear or overcast. We do not see white light directly. We can see it reflected in the highlights. Even at second hand it is too intense for comfort and many people rush to wear dark glasses. What we see are the blue rays refracted from the sky, or the greatly reduced intensities from white flowers and clouds, or the parts of the spectrum rejected by the flowers and foliage that show their colors. It is then that flowers and trees and rocks may be said to appear in their truest hues. They have the maximum allotment of the spectrum to work with.

After four o'clock in the afternoon, the reds and oranges grow stronger. Shadows enlarge. The light softens until eventually the long rays predominate at sunset. The extent to which this visibly alters the landscape colors depends on the position and kind of clouds in the sky. Often this red is projected from the west to every quarter. Clouds in the north, south and eastern parts of the sky may glow with it. Stones and ponds turn red. A pink glow permeates the evening landscape.

In this symphony of outdoor colors, processes are repeated but effects are never repeated. The ever changing angle of the sun from minute to minute and season to season; the ever changing tones and tints of foliage and field; the ever changing content of moisture and dust in the air and the shifting shapes and textures of clouds—these volatile conditions insure that no two minutes in all time have ever produced exactly the same combination of colors in the landscape.

We have seen how the light deflected by a flower gives that flower its color. But a vast amount of light is absorbed. This puts kinetic energy into the plant. The swallowed light makes the plant grow and operates its whole system. One of its vital results, photosynthesis, is discussed in Chapter 5. A surprising result is the way absorbed light causes flowers to bloom on a timetable, as we shall see in the next chapter.

CHAPTER ELEVEN

The Day-Length Timetable of Flowers

I used to take it for granted, as most people do, that flowers bloom when they get good and ready. There seemed to be no special reason for skunk cabbages to bloom in March, hepaticas in April, violets in May, daisies in June, and so on, with the New England asters and gentians blooming in the fall, while witch-hazel waits even longer and bursts into bloom with the frost. But in recent years, Dr. W. W. Garner, plant physiologist of the United States Department of Agriculture, has proved that the succession of bloom through the seasons runs on a timetable keyed to the length of the day. Soil, moisture and temperature control the building of the plant. They mature its growth, putting it into shape so that it can bloom. But these factors do not crack open the flower buds. These often wait for just the right number of hours and minutes of sunlight per day.

When you stop to think of it, rainfall and temperature are

highly variable. If the blooming of the wild flowers depended upon these factors there's no predicting when violets would appear, and the dogwood might become mixed up with the fall foliage if the weatherman produced a humid Indian summer after a cold dry spring.

Recently I saw interesting graphic charts showing how many species out of one hundred popular native flowering plants are in bloom each calendar week from March through October at the wild flower reservation of the Missouri Botanical Garden, Gray Summit, Mo. The number of different species in bloom makes a peak around the first of May, then for a week or two drops rapidly, and rises again for another peak in midsummer. These two peaks of blooming are constant year after year. When these charts are compared with charts of the rainfall and temperature of the same periods, it is seen that there is no relation between the two. The blooming is scarcely affected by variations of rainfall and temperature. For instance, one year at the midsummer blooming peak there was a fierce drought, and the rainfall line touched bottom. But the flowers all bloomed on their fixed schedules.

Flower buds must be exposed to light for a certain number of hours and minutes per day, absorbing their chosen energy-giving rays, in order to bloom. This sensitivity to length of day is so critical that changes of only a few minutes will determine whether certain flowers will open or not. The intensity of light doesn't make much difference. Overcast days do not alter the situation. For some plants the length of day may be altered with an electric light having only a fraction of the intensity of sunlight, yet that light is enough to produce the same results as sunlight. It is continuous duration of light that counts. If a plant is keyed to bloom on a day-length of ten hours, alternating with fourteen hours of darkness, it will refuse to bloom if that ten hours is divided into two five-hour periods with an hour of darkness between.

A flower that is tuned to a certain day-length will wait for that day-length regardless of where the flower may be located.

The wild azalea (*Rhododendron nudiflorum*) is about a 15-hour flower of both north and south. I have seen this flower opening its buds in mid-April in Florida and early June in Massachusetts. The blue toadflax (*Linaria canadensis*) is in its prime in South Carolina in late April, and I have found this flower blooming June 10 in Connecticut. They were both on schedule.

A certain duration of daylight per day acts as a curtain raiser. Once the flowers are open, they stay open until the curtain is lowered, not by any change in the length of day, but by completion of the flower's function, the fertilization of its seeds.

In central New England the day is about eleven hours long on February 21. From then on it increases at the rate of a little over two minutes a day, until June 21 when continuous daylight is around fifteen and a half hours. Then the day decreases at an equal rate and around October 21 it is again about eleven hours long. During this period of the flowering season, flowers open in succession. They may be a week or so late in the spring when frost in the soil and cold temperatures may prevent the earliest spring plants from maturing, but after that the flowers stick to their schedules. Thus the early spring flowers are known as *short day* plants; those that bloom around June 21 are *long day* plants; and late summer and fall flowers are again *short day* plants. Plants that bloom more or less continuously through the seasons are *indeterminate*.

A good example of an indeterminate wild flower is heal-all (*Prunella vulgaris*) that blooms continuously through lengthening and shortening days. Because of this characteristic, heal-all is one of the most universally distributed plants. It can travel not only on the latitudes growing wherever the soil is favorable, but also on the meridians of longitude. The distribution of these indeterminate plants is much greater than of the light-critical plants, an important fact if the plant is valuable commercially. Tomatoes, for example, are indeterminate and can therefore be grown from the tropics to the Arctic. Tobacco is somewhat more choosy but fairly indeterminate so that tobacco can be raised in Cuba and in New England.

Growers of chrysanthemums, which are short day plants, force them into bloom, not by increasing the light but by using a black cloth to *darken* the plants when the length of day is longer than their critical flowering period. Varieties of lettuce differ in their criticism of day length for flowering. As lettuce heads best when flowering is prevented, the farmer who is raising long day lettuce will darken his plants below the critical day length of the variety to prevent flowering. On the other hand, if it is a short day variety, it will head better if the day is lengthened by artificial light. This great discovery that flowering plants are day-length sensitive offers alluring possibilities to horticulture.

The question may be asked why, if twelve hours and fifty minutes is just the right day length to make Johnny-jump-up bloom, that Johnny-jump-up does not bloom when the same day length is reached in September? The answer is that it may bloom. I have often found violets and other spring flowers blooming in the fall. On November 11, 1938, at Pocantico Hills, New York, I found violets, dandelions and fleabane, all spring flowers. I have seen shadblow, one of the most conspicuous early spring shrubs, in bloom at Lake Mohonk in November. These plants were perfectly true to their natures as far as the day length was concerned. They bloomed in the fall because their vegetative growth was not built and ready for blooming in the spring. By some outside influence these fall-blooming spring flowers were delayed in maturing until the day became too long for them to bloom, so they waited until the right length day came around again.

A rainy or cold spell may temporarily delay the opening of a flower beyond the time when its sensitive day length arrives. A critical flower cannot open *before* its day, but if when that day comes its vitality is reduced by chill, it may delay for better weather conditions. The sunlight has pulled the trigger but the gun doesn't go off because the ammunition is wet. If the cold snap is prolonged beyond the critical period, the flower may not bloom. I suspect that the spring flowers that I found blooming in November were caught in that way. This theory is supported by the evidence of the weather bureau for the spring season of

1938. When spring flowers should have been blooming they were victimized by extraordinary cold.

The life cycle of each plant usually prevents this off season blooming. Succulent little perennials like Dutchman's breeches, spring beauties and violets have no wood to build and not much in the way of stems and leaves so that they mature early in the spring and are ready to open their short day flowers. Once the flowers are open, the plant must go through its cycle which takes a year, including the production of seeds. Therefore, it does not bloom twice—once in the spring and again in the fall.

The middle-sized annuals and perennials like daisies and black-eyed Susans are characteristic long day plants. They have had more time since growth started in March to build up a fairly good-sized stalk and a respectable number of leaves. They are ready in all their middle-sized maturity to flower with the arrival of the summer solstice. The tallest annuals and perennials, the late goldenrods, asters and thoroughworts, are short day plants. When the short days of late summer come along they have enjoyed many weeks to develop great-sized plants to maturity. However, the relative sizes of the little early short day plants, the middle-sized long day plants, and the very tall late short day plants is only a matter of general interest, and by no means a constant factor. Flowers of different day lengths may be in any size that suits their inner beings. The fringed gentian, one of the last flowers of the parade, keyed to an exceptionally short day, averages only a foot and a half in height.

Woody plants are usually short day types. Their structures are built over a period of years and the preliminary steps to maturity have all been accomplished before the first thaw in March. They don't even have to wait for leaves. Their flower buds were formed eight months before. When these buds are tapped with the right day length of light they bloom promptly. The willows are tuned to the shortest day length of all the shrubs and trees. For this reason the opening flowers of the pussy willows are a symbol of the coming of spring. The flower buds of American hazelnut are short day and therefore may bloom while the snow is still on the ground. The silver and red maples come next, bursting into bloom before their leaves appear. The elms follow. The oaks require a little longer day, flowering when their leaves are half grown. The linden is a long day plant, waiting until June in central New England and opening its flowers after the leaves are fully grown. Among shrubs the elderberry is a perfect example of a long day plant. It blooms when the day is around fifteen hours, that is, in mid-June.

Compared with northern latitudes the flowers of the tropics are *short day*. The day at the Equator is constant around twelve hours. A plant like the poinsettia which is a critical twelve hour plant will not flower outdoors in New England and therefore is not native that far north. Planted in a northern garden it may grow vegetatively for a season but will not bloom unless darkened every day after twelve hours of light.

Thus we see that the succession of flowers in the woods and fields is far from haphazard; each flower is geared more or less critically to the rising and setting of the sun. The colors of the flowers unfurl across the landscape as the sun mounts a little higher and stays a little longer day by day.

Not only flower buds but also the entire mechanism of the plant is operated by the amount of light it absorbs. Early in the spring I left a board on the ground in the pasture. Green blades of grass had just begun to appear and field plants among them were little incipient rosettes. At that juncture I deprived those plants under the board of all light for a month while the rest of the field was boiling over with vitality. After all that has been said about life-giving sunlight we should expect that the plants plunged into darkness under the board would at least be stunted, if not killed. But when I lifted the board, exactly the opposite had occurred. The grass had grown long blades, which far outstripped the grass growing normally in the sunlight. The rosettes had developed long, pallid, yellow stems that sprawled around like ghostly giants in the darkness. These plants, grown in darkness, were unlike their true selves . . . out of balance with too long stems and too small leaves. Lacking chlorophyll, which can be formed only in sunlight, they could not manufacture their own food and were living off the reserves stored up in the roots. But they illustrated a surprising fact. Growth in size of plants occurs chiefly at night in the darkness. They assimilate vitality by day. They grow by night. It's like marching. First one step, then another, alternating accumulation and expenditure. These plants had grown into freakish lengths in their enforced night.

For the same reason plants that grow in feeble light may be taller and have larger leaves than those in full sunlight. They are fundamentally weaker, more succulent and they have smaller roots. You often see herbs or young oaks or maples growing in the shade in a forest with enormous leaves, ten times as large as the normal sized leaves that are hung up in the sunlight. On the other hand, plants growing in great light intensities assimilate more strength in mighty roots, stout stems and thicker leaves. This type of plant is characteristic of the high mountains and the far north and deserts. *They are stunted by light!* But they can stand a lot of punishment as you can imagine if you have noticed the heavily twigged heaths and gnarled pines on a stony mountain top.

The pathetic fallacy endows nature with reason. She is adept, clever, cruel, vain or desirous of being lovely. Of course, the truth of the matter is that nature possesses none of these qualities in a rational sense. She is a force, an all-embracing ceaseless force. Utterly impersonal and indifferent to you and me. She can be endowed with any virtue we wish, however, because the only reality is in our own minds. Leonardo da Vinci pays a man's tribute to nature when he says, "Human ingenuity can never devise anything more simple and more beautiful and more to the purpose than nature does." But if ever plants seemed to have a logical purpose it is in the elongation of stems in low intensities of light. By this adaptation the plants appear to reach for the sunlight. A sunflower will move all day so as to keep its head nodding toward the sun in its course from east to west. The heliotrope is named after a similar characteristic: helios is the Greek word for "sun" and trope means "turning."

If light shines on one side of a plant more than another the branches grow in the direction of the light. See how lopsided become the trees and shrubs on the edge of the woods. A house plant on the window sill will nod toward the sun outdoors in preference to the people in the room. If you turn it around, in twenty-four hours it will be growing toward the light again. What makes it turn? Plants don't have muscles and nervous systems. This turning, called *tropism*, is caused by the greater growth of the cells in the stem on the side away from the window, that is the side with the least illumination. The stem is pushed around or bent over by the force of these enlarging cells. This is part of the same phenomenon as those overgrown, sprawling plants in the darkness under the board, whose stem cells elongated through the stimulus of darkness.

A certain moss grows near the mouth of a cavern where it receives only the faintest glimmer of light. This moss is covered with a plate of clear cells that act as focussing lenses. They gather what light there is and concentrate it in the chlorophyll of that plant.

Plants that reach up for the light; plants that twist and turn to win the light; plants that carry lenses to focus the light ... nature is, indeed, ingenious.

ADDENDUM to CHAPTER ELEVEN

Tulips, snowdrops, myrtle (*Vinca minor*), violets and blood-root bloom in the spring, daisies in the summer, and chrysan-themums and asters in the fall or later. If we subscribed to the doctrine of special creation instead of the theory of evolution we could interpret this distribution of flowering species throughout the season as the Creator's way of providing plants for man's use and delight. Even without any theoretical basis, however, one can, perhaps, understand the blooming of spring bulbs; cut open a tulip bulb, and there will be a flower in miniature, waiting for the first warm days to push itself into open air and display its colors. But is this true for the fibrous-rooted myrtle and violet, or the marsh-marigold? In this age of molecular biology, however, we are far more likely to search for a chemical and hereditary basis of this phenomenon.

We now recognize that there are short-day plants, long-day plants and those that are light-neutral. All exhibit the phenomenon of *photoperiodism*, defined as a response—flowering in this instance, although in some animals it may be the initiation of the breeding season—to a variation in the proportion of light and darkness over a 24-hour daily cycle. Each species, except those that are light-neutral, must be exposed to a critical duration of light if it is to flower. If that duration is too short, long-day species will not bloom; if it is too long, short-day species will put out only vegetative growth. For some species the critical period is quite precise, with a variance in some instances of only 10 to 15 minutes, one way or the other. Since this is a response to radiant energy, an examination of spectral significance reveals that photoperiodism is governed by the red end of the spectrum, and that a chemical called *phytochrome* is involved in the induction or inhibition of flowering. Phytochrome exists in two different forms, and it can switch back and forth between these two states, depending whether it was last exposed to red-orange light around 660 millimicrons, or to far-red light of about 730 millimicrons. The quality of light behaves, therefore, as a switch, shifting the phytochrome from one form to the other. Whether the red-orange is an on-switch, and the far-red an off-switch, or the reverse, depends upon the species in question. Thus, and in terms of flowering, far-red is an inhibiting wavelength for short-day plants, but a flower-inducing one in long-day species. The reverse would be true for red-orange wavelengths. The response of the cocklebur (*Xanthium strumarium*) will serve to illustrate the effect in a short-day species: it will flower only when it has 10 hours or less of light, but its dark period must be uninterrupted by light. A single flash from an ordinary flashlight during its dark period is sufficient to inhibit flowering.

It is possible, then, to manipulate the light regime of a species, and thus induce flowering in any species whenever one wishes. The fact that we can now find chrysanthemums at any time of year in the florist shops is an example of this. Photoperiodism is also under genetic control. Some strains of wheat, for example, are long-day plants, blooming in the long days of summer. By selection, however, appropriate strains were isolated that were light-neutral, and would come into flower and fruit regardless of the length of light or darkness. It is these strains that were developed for the Green Revolution; they are productive wherever grown.

—C. P. S.

CHAPTER TWELVE

Tree and Grass Equipment for Wind Pollination

The true wonder of flowers is not their appearance but their *action*.

To the last detail a flower is designed for one great purpose. Color, fragrance, form, size, the length and shape of each little part—all fit, with the utmost perfection, into the overriding purpose of reproducing its kind.

Plants, like animals, must obey the laws of eugenics. The most inexorable of these laws is that inbreeding weakens a race, whereas cross-breeding strengthens and perpetuates it. This is simply another way of saying that an organism equipped with a variety of characteristics can cope with life better than an organism with a single set of characteristics.

We think of the life cycle of a plant revolving from seed to shoot, stalk, leaves, flowers—and then back to seed. We say that a flower "goes to seed." This implies an uninterrupted cycle smoothly revolving along the course of the species. But this oversimplified life cycle takes no account of a violent interruption which is the most exciting fact in that cycle.

This interruption occurs in the heart of a flower at the moment that flower reaches the climax of its size and beauty. All the characteristics of the plant, to the last detail, are distilled into strange little ribbons of matter, called chromosomes, which can be seen only through a high-powered microscope. Despite their infinitely small size these chromosomes contain the essences that predetermine whether the plant shall be a tiny chickweed or a towering redwood.

During all the growing, up to the time of flowering, the life stream of the plant has been flowing along a single channel by virtue of its inherent vitality. When it flowers this life stream suddenly breaks apart, and the two parts pursue separate and far from parallel courses.

Some sets of chromosomes, complete with all the characteristics of the plant, are locked in little undeveloped seeds called ovules, and these are enclosed in a swelling at the base of the pistil. This swelling is called an ovary. Other complete sets of chromosomes are locked into tiny grains of matter called pollen. The ovules are anchored in the flower. The pollen is turned loose from a little box called the anther. Before the pollen grains are forced to leave the plant, the personality of that plant has been divided into hundreds of thousands of duplicate sets. Each grain contains one complete set of characteristics. They then set out on trips that seem amazingly haphazard and perilous. But, after discounting all the perils, the plan works and that is all that matters in nature.

Ovules and pollen are the end products of the plant. Each contains chromosomes with all the features of the parent but by themselves they have no future. An ovule cannot automatically turn into a seed. The plant's life stream has literally divided! Outside forces are required to reunite this life stream and complete the cycle. Usually these forces are wind or insects. To

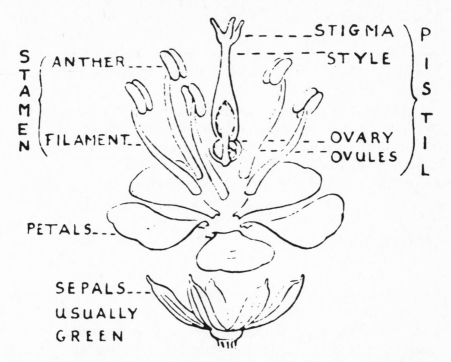

TYPICAL FLOWER. Refer to this diagram for explanation of words used for flower parts. The anther is the pollen box. An ovule is an unfertilized seed, one or more of which may be contained in the ovary or seed box.

harness these forces to their will, flowers have many ways of going into action.

The pollen that has gone travelling must somehow return to a pistil of the same species from which it came. When the pollen grain arrives at the tip end of a pistil ready to receive it, it will adhere because that tip end, called the stigma, is sticky. Now, after a brief lapse of time, that pollen grain begins to grow, like a tiny independent plant suddenly come to life. But instead of forming a normal sort of plant with root, stem and leaves, it simply grows a long tube that penetrates and travels down the inside of the pistil until it reaches an ovule. This rapid growing form of plant life, the pollen tube, resembles in some ways the translucent threads that fungi build so rapidly—bread mold is a familiar example. Then the chromosomes of the pollen grain with the set of characteristics from another plant travel down this pollen tube and fuse with chromosomes in the ovule of the new plant. The result is a seed with the characteristics of two separate plants.

As you look across the landscape when pollination is in full swing, the marvelous sequence of events and the play of countless fantastic mechanical devices are not conspicuous in the stability of the trees and the fields of grass and flowers. Here and there bees buzz or butterflies flap seemingly as aimless as tossed leaves. You catch the glint of an occasional dragon fly or slap at a few flies. It seems incredible that these capricious creatures and the even more fickle winds are the agents of a well ordered routine of scientific precision.

Consider the problem. A target the size of a pinhead must be hit by a microscopic grain of pollen at exactly the right time. The distance to be traversed may be a fraction of an inch or miles. But the grain lacks any motive power within itself and the outdoors is vast. Moreover, the right kind of grain must hit the right kind of target. No other will do. Yet never in all the ages of the flowering plants has this feat failed to clothe the earth.

One of the real wonders is that nature accomplishes this miracle by the help of *incidental* agents. Pollination by insects and wind, vital as it is, is a by-product of actions not directed to its purpose. Nature seems to have found a way of doing what Mark Twain had in mind when he said that some way ought to be found to harness the wagging of dogs' tails to run sewing machines.

Wind pollination calls for a super shotgun. Vast numbers of grains are discharged into the air so that by the law of averages each little pinhead target waiting for a particular type of pollen will be hit.

Whether this method is efficient or inefficient depends on how you look at it. The waste is staggering. Apparently millions of grains are thrown away to one that is used. On the other hand, the pollen producing mechanism must be enormously productive. How efficient this mechanism is, at least in ragweed, can be confirmed by hay fever victims. Ragweed is a wind pollinated plant. When its anther geysers are in action the invisible pollen dust from this plant alone is found in every cubic yard of air over the ragweed belt. Doctors estimate that it takes about twenty-five pollen grains per cubic yard as a minimum to produce hay fever symptoms. The load of pollen in the air is usually much denser than twenty-five grains per cubic yard during the ragweed season.

Because of the curse of hay fever scientists have recently contrived to measure the amount of ragweed pollen in the air in various localities. The plan calls for exposing microscope slides coated with a sticky substance to catch the dust in the air, and then counting the number of ragweed grains through the microscope that are found on a given area of the slide, caught in twenty-four hours. To do this eighty-seven localities were organized with the aid of the U. S. Weather Bureau. The average amount of pollen from ragweed plants alone falling on each square mile in the vicinity of New York City, during the pollinating season, is 101 pounds. Boston has 50 pounds, Indianapolis has the largest with 826 pounds. Buffalo has 568 pounds, St. Louis, 519 pounds. California, relatively ragweedless, measures 6 pounds at Los Angeles and 2 pounds at Sacramento. The only localities in the United States where no ragweed pollen was found by this survey were Seattle, Washington, and Portland, Oregon. Scientists estimate that the total ragweed pollen crop of the country amounts to at least a million tons. And they are talking about grains that are invisible, microscopic, so that it takes billions of them to make an ounce. This is shotgun production with a vengeance.

Although ragweed, the villain of the drama of pollination, has received more attention than other plants to determine the quantity and distribution of its pollen, other kinds of plants may far exceed its per plant record of production.

The oak has developed a curious arrangement of its flowers for quantity production of pollen. It is called a catkin. Each pollen flower is a knob a little larger than the head of a pin. Each knob has up to a dozen stamens with two pollen chambers in each stamen. These knobs are strung along a cord making a flexible thin tassel, several inches long—the catkin. This tassel whips in the breeze so that the pollen may be thrown out and caught by the wind. These tassels grow in clusters, thus multiplying the pollen yield many times. A great oak tree may be covered with these catkin clusters, giving a yellowish or reddish tone to the entire crown of the tree. For a few days in April an oak becomes a veritable fountain of pollen; the number of grains released by countless stamens in countless catkins defies imagination.

Pine trees have an equally efficient mechanism. We call their flowers cones, although structurally they are much like catkins in that many tiny flowers are strung along a central axis. A cone is apt to be rigid while a catkin is flexible. The pollen producing cone of a pine tree is a fat spike an inch long and a quarter of an inch in diameter. Within this cone little delicate scales each about ⅛ inch long are packed tightly together in symmetrical spirals. A single tiny scale bears two little anthers with twin pollen cavities, each manufacturing thousands of grains. These pollen cones grow in clusters of about a dozen near the ends of the topmost branches. One pine tree may bear thousands of clusters. All this adds up to an organization for producing pollen in quantities measured by astronomical figures. In fact, it is a common sight to see yellow "smoke" coming out of a pine tree when a puff of wind strikes the ripe anthers.

Most trees are wind pollinated. The exceptions are those that bear large colorful flowers such as the fruit trees, locusts, horse-chestnuts and magnolias, and a few like the linden that bear honey and fragrance, although lacking colorful flower parts. Each wind pollinated tree has super-shotgun gears for quantity production. The pollen flowers are designed not only to multiply anthers, but also to make it easy for the pollen to be snatched up by the wind. For example, the tassel, or catkin, arrangement of the oaks is ideal for these two functions. Catkins are used also by the beeches, chestnuts, birches, alders, hazelnuts, walnuts, hickories, willows and poplars. The shapes and sizes of catkins in these trees have great variety—but the principle of the breeze-whipped tassel is the same in all.

Pollen flowers of the sycamore, instead of growing in catkins along a slender central axis, are packed in countless numbers into a tight round ball that waves back and forth on a long flexible stem at the end of a branch. This pollen sphere is less than half an inch in diameter and quickly collapses and disappears after discharging its load. The seed-bearing flowers of the sycamore are also arranged in round balls at the end of long stems but these are larger—an inch and a quarter in diameter. These are the balls which you usually see hanging from the sycamore, giving it the name of buttonball tree. The sweet gum also uses the round compact formation of pollen flowers. But sweet gum balls have short stiff stems. To offset this disadvantage in not being able to swing in the breeze so freely, they grow on the tips of the topmost upturned twigs.

The pollen producing mechanism of elms is combined with the seed producing mechanism, making a "perfect" flower. In other words, elm flowers have both stamens and pistils. Elm flowers grow in clusters that spray out at the end of long, flexible stems. To give the pollen even greater access to the breezes the anthers are thrust far out beyond the rest of the flower on stems of their own. These flowers have no colorful petals, but the sepals are fused to form an iridescent bowl of mottled red, yellow and green out of which the stamens are thrust at different angles. Long before garden clubs made flower arranging a fine art, nature made a flawless arrangement of the elm flower in its vase. The elm is brightened by countless masses of these spraying flowers which mature before the leaves come out, making it that much easier for the wind to snatch at the pollen.

The stamens of red and silver maple flowers also project far out. The clusters of these maple flowers grow in whorls and sprays of brilliant firecracker red color. Although they are only about a half inch across, without petals, they are produced in such enormous quantities that the flowering of these maples is one of the color treats of early spring.

The plan of the ash is so well developed to insure a hundred per cent crossing that the pollen flowers grow on different trees from the seed-bearing flowers. This rules out all chance of in-breeding. The pollen chambers have short stems but they make up for this by a lofty position, growing in massive clusters like green furry ringlets a few inches below the tips of the highest twigs. Other common trees that have achieved this method of producing pollen and seed flowers on separate individuals, equivalent to the separation of the sexes in animals, are willow, holly, sassafras, persimmon, Kentucky coffee tree, poplar, mulberry, and osage orange.

Despite their mighty and enduring frames, all wind polli-nated trees seem to be in a great hurry to get the matter over. A tree flower may discharge its pollen and its stamens may wither after a few hours of full bloom. All the trees of a species in a given neighborhood may have their flowers appear and disappear within a week. Each kind of tree has its own time for blooming. In early spring the willows, silver maples, red maples and elms lead the procession in the order mentioned. These trees all flower before their leaves come out. The oaks flower in mid-spring when the leaves are half grown. Then come the hickories. The time of pollination for each species is remarkably constant.

Like the wild flowers, tree flowers are tied up with the sched-ule of the sun as it increases the length of day. A few minutes more of daylight acts like a trigger to open the flowers of another tree as spring marches on. The timetable of field flowers keyed to the length of day is discussed in detail in Chapter 11. The minute inconspicuous tree flowers are even more perfect ex-amples of sensitivity to length of day. Year after year their pol-linating mechanism ripens to the explosion point precisely on the calendar. Having reached that point, the first dry sunny day will set them off. Dr. R. P. Wodehouse, a leading authority on pollen, has made a chart showing what kinds of pollen may be expected in the air during each week of the flowering season at his location a few miles north of New York City.

Another group of plants that dramatizes the efficiency of wind pollination is the grasses. Let your mind wander across landscapes where valleys and hillsides are furred with timothy; or across the ranges of the West where buffalo grass and curly mesquite sweep up the piedmont; even to northern Canada where tufts of green foxtail push up between the cracks of Arctic ice on the shores of Hudson's Bay; again along the prairies where the path of the reapers makes huge parabolic curves over the horizons of wheat and corn which also are grasses. Everywhere you look, grass sways and shimmers in the breezes.

As a seed factory grass is nature's most remarkable exponent of mass production. This is true not only in the number of seeds produced but also in their high percentage of viability. Grass seeds sprout if given the least excuse. A trace of soil in the crevice of a rock and a few drops of rain will do. Grass can fill a square foot of receptive soil with hundreds of individual plants. Yet to produce their myriads of seeds, each stigma, before it can op-

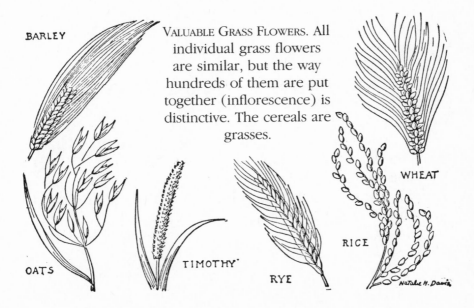

BARLEY

VALUABLE GRASS FLOWERS. All individual grass flowers are similar, but the way hundreds of them are put together (inflorescence) is distinctive. The cereals are grasses.

WHEAT

OATS

TIMOTHY

RYE

RICE

Natalie H. Davis

erate, must be touched with the spark of life in a grain of pollen, as the fuse of a firecracker must be touched with the glowing tip of a small boy's punk.

Like the wind pollinated trees, grass is well equipped for gushing pollen. One investigator with a microscope and a genius for mathematics says that a single stalk of corn will produce fifty million pollen grains. When tassels are ripe and the wind is fresh and puffy you may see pollen rising like wisps of spray above a rustling field of corn, which, as we have said, is grass. Moreover, grass usually grows in dense masses, giving it an added advantage. As compared to trees, what it loses in height grass more than makes up for in numbers. Pollen blowing across a field is intercepted by myriads of hungry stigmas.

Few people other than students of botany have ever seen an individual grass flower or have any conception of what one looks like. This is true despite the fact that these flowers can be found all around us by the millions in their season. Grass flowers are one of nature's most precise, quick-acting little gadgets, beautifully designed for their purpose. Mechanically, all grass flowers are alike. The differences between the individual flowers of various grass species lie in botanical minutiae or minor variations; although the ways in which the flowers are arranged in their aggregations (inflorescences) are conspicuously different. These inflorescences may take the form of dense cylindrical spikes typical of foxtail and timothy, open triangular forms of the well-known Kentucky bluegrass, loose dangling clusters of the wild oats, or the spearheads of broom.

To understand a grass flower it is necessary not only to change your perspective, as most of them are only about ⅛ to ¼ of an inch long, but also to put aside all notions as to what a flower should look like. A grass flower has no petals or sepals. Instead of emphasizing radial symmetry as do other flowers it is designed like a miniature plant or tree which has a central stem and leaves projecting at angles along this axis. This unit is known as a *spikelet*. The "leaves" are broad and curving, contain no chlo-

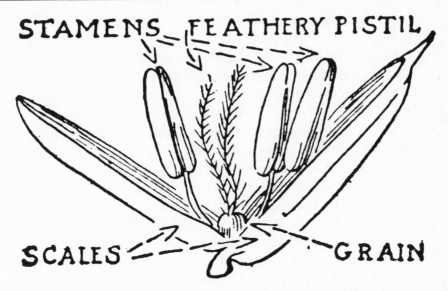

GRASS FLOWER DIAGRAM. About ⅛ of an inch long. Blooms only once for only about an hour. Countless numbers of these little flowers make up the spikes of grasses.

rophyll, but they do have veins. They are closed around the floral parts most of the time and make snug little containers of shiny waterproof texture, sometimes translucent like parchment. The two outside leaves, called *glumes*, are the largest and are attached nearest to the base of the flower's stem. Above these come *flowering glumes* (later these will be the chaff if the flower is wheat). A spikelet may have two or more of these flowering glumes, or perhaps only one, depending on the species. Above each flowering glume a pistil and three stamens are attached to the stem of the spikelet.

There is nothing particularly charming in this design of a grass spikelet, but the remarkable thing about it is the way it works. *A grass flower opens only once in its life and that for only an hour or so!* Most of them open in the morning between 6:00 and 7:00 A.M. Wheat opens at 4:30 P.M. Oats open between 2:00

and 4:00 P.M. Canary grass (from which seed for canary birds is obtained) is another exception to the morning opening: it opens between noon and 4:00 P.M. Each day some flowers of the inflorescence open. Remember that the inflorescence of a single plant contains countless numbers of these little flowers. At precisely the same hour the process is repeated the next day, and this goes on until all the flowers of the plant have opened, shed their pollen, and all are closed up permanently.

A remarkable occurrence makes the closed glumes of these flowers swing open. When the stamens are ripe and ready to discharge their pollen the entire mechanism is poised for action, waiting for a dry sunny day (no use trying to blow pollen around on a rainy day), the right temperature (around 61°), and the right hour of the day. It is easy to speculate on the effect of humidity and temperature, but just what the connection is with the *hour* of the day is not clear. Possibly the angle of the sun's rays exerts an effect. When the right combination of conditions exists, two particles that are otherwise insignificant and unnoticed inside the glumes suddenly expand by taking in water from the plant. From little dry scales they become in a few minutes swollen bladders. This overcomes the elasticity of the closed glumes and pushes them out. The stamens elongate, the anthers are pushed far out. At this moment they revolve, and, turning completely over in one great sweep, they split open and out spouts the pollen. The speed with which this occurs is unbelievable and again refutes the notion that plants are quiet and static objects. A report for oatgrass records that the stalks of the stamens increase their original length three or four times in ten minutes.

To get the advantages of cross-pollination, the pistil of the same flower which has opened in this spectacular fashion frequently holds back. After the pollen of its flower is discharged out comes the pistil and pushes up two long feathery prongs ready to catch the pollen floating around in the air from another plant. Occasionally this order is reversed and the pistil emerges first. After the pistil has caught pollen, the stamens of its own flower follow. It should be added, however, that whereas this mechanism is designed to promote cross-pollination this result is not inevitable and many of the grass flowers are self-pollinated. However, the average of cross-breeding is high enough to maintain hardy colonies of grass everywhere, as the landscape bears witness. If some seeds are inbred they are in the minority and the chances are that the grass resulting from inbreeding will be cross-bred for the next generation. Wind pollination is a great success for trees and grasses.

Cross-pollination is a recent discovery of men of science. The facts were not fully demonstrated until Darwin published them in 1859. Previously to that time seeds were seeds, and men never suspected that those seeds could only form after the little ovule is touched by the spark of life in a pollen grain. The earliest mention of the part which pollen plays was by an English naturalist, Nehemiah Grew, in 1682. The subject was so revolutionary that scientists promptly got up in arms over its absurdity. A half century passed before Linnaeus, in 1735, came out with more proof supporting Grew's theory. Still the crossing of pollen by the aid of insects was not dreamed of. Men observed the bees and other insects visiting flowers to eat their pollen and nectar, but they simply supposed that the flowers were generous and hospitable. As one authority put it, flowers have a "sweet reasonableness."

All this time the fact that many flowers hold their pistils high above their stamens so that a flower's own pollen cannot drop on its own pistil, or the fact that in some flowers the stamens project out at wide angles, well away from their pistils, went unexplained or ignored. It took a German schoolmaster, named Sprengel, in 1787, to point out that bees transport the pollen from the stamen to the pistil. Sprengel was on the right track but he made a great error. His bees, after they sipped the nectar and collected pollen on themselves, climbed up on the pistil of the *same* flower to deposit the pollen. Since he was so close to discovering the truth about flowers, it's surprising that seventy-two years more had to pass before Darwin announced *cross-*

pollination. Wisdom seems to consist of waking up to obvious and long established facts.

The fundamental fact that flowers are mechanisms for cross-breeding was received with incredulous awe. Jean Henri Fabre, the insects' Homer, expressed his feelings about cross-pollination by saying. "Before these mysteries of life reason bows, helpless, and abandons itself to an impulse of adoration of the Author of these ineffable miracles."

ADDENDUM to CHAPTER TWELVE

Cross-pollination, or self-incompatability as it is more generally known today, is a significant feature of sexual reproduction in the flowering world, as indeed it is in the animal world as well. It is a phenomenon which promotes diversity, and diversity is necessary if evolution is to function. There is no preconceived plan in bringing this about; it just happens because the heritable information of species is unstable, and constantly gives rise to variant forms. Just as human beings vary among themselves, so too do plants. It may not be obvious to the casual eye—one plant of Queen Anne's lace looks very much like any other member of the species—but a closer look would reveal minute differences of structure, color or the biochemical reactions that lie beneath our scrutiny. When cross-pollination occurs, therefore, plants of different genetic constitutions mingle their genes to produce the seeds which, in turn, will give rise to the next generation of offspring. Because the offspring will differ in their heritable constitutions, they will be variously adapted to the environment in which they find themselves. Some of the seeds will be eaten by predators, some will not make it to maturity and reproduce because they land in infertile or unsuitable sites —echoes of the Parable of the Sower (Mark: 18)—and others will die because they lack the combination of genes that permits survival. Of those that do survive and reproduce some will simply add to the diversity of the species; others may spin off from the mother species to form new species; or the mother species itself may undergo such change that it will lose its old identity, but in the process gain a new one.

Not all species, of course, reproduce through cross-pollination. Some are self-compatible, and these may be either self- or cross-pollinated; whichever kind of pollen arrives first and lands on the stigma will bring about fertilization. Indian corn or maize (*Zea mays*) is an example of such indiscrimminate pollen receptivity, as are most, if not all, of the wind-pollinated species.

Have you ever seen a huge field of "hybrid" corn in the state of Iowa? If you stop to think about it, it is really a most remarkable sight. Each plant is just like every other plant in the same field: same height, same color, same productivity. There is no variation among them. It is as if they came off the same assembly line, stamped from the same die. In a sense, this is not a far-fetched analogy, for hybrid corn is an engineered plant, engineered by man.

The term "hybrid" needs further explanation. A hybrid is a term applied to organisms resulting from a cross between two unlike individuals of the same species, or two individuals of different species. The mule is an example; it is an *interspecific* hybrid, a cross between a mare (female horse) and a jack (male donkey). The mule also exhibits something that is often characteristic of hybrids; it shows hybrid vigor. Pound for pound it is stronger and more durable than either the horse or the donkey. This is true also for hybrid corn, but it is an *intraspecific* hybrid. It results from a cross between two or more strains of corn, each of which has been closely inbred (that is, self-pollinated) until it is highly uniform is structure and behavior. Inbreeding, as a rule, results in each strain being relatively weak, and possibly exhibiting traits which are agronomically undesirable (the same genetic reasoning underlies the law that prohibits marriage between first cousins). But the inbred strains are different from each other, and none would survive for long without the intervention of man. When crossed, however, the offspring of the next generation frequently show a good deal of hybrid vigor as well as an extreme degree of uniformity; further, they are unlikely to exhibit any of the undesirable traits of their parents since the "good" genes from one strain would very likely cover up, or offset, the effects of the undesirable genes of the other strain.

Since it is an important facet of sexual reproduction, it is not surprising that self- and cross-pollinations are governed by interactions resulting from the combined influence of the genetic constitutions of both pollen and style. The basis of this interaction is determined by sets of sterility genes called S-loci, which exist in many varied forms. They are lacking, of course, in self-compatible species. These genes are usually labelled S_1, S_2, S_3, etc., and the number of different S-loci may be in the hundreds. Each plant, however, has two S-loci, one of which it received from its male parent, the other from the female parent. Each pollen grain can only possess one such locus, or gene, at a time, while the stigma and style possess two.

In self-incompatible species, these two loci cannot be similar to each other. For example, the loci can be S_1S_2, S_2S_3, or S_1S_{10}, but not S_1S_1 or $S_{10}S_{10}$. The reason for this is as follows: if pollen from an S_1S_2 plant lands on the stigma of another S_1S_2 plant (or on its own stigma), a pollen tube will not emerge from the pollen grain and grow down the style. Some inhibitory factor in the style will prevent the growth of either S_1 or S_2 pollen, and fertilization of the egg in the ovule cannot be accomplished. If such pollen should land on an S_3S_4 stigma, either or both of the S_1 and S_2 pollen grains are capable of growth. If the S_1 or S_2 pollen lands on the stigma of an S_1S_3 plant, the S_2 pollen can function but the S_1 pollen cannot. The situation is analogous to the antigen-antibody reactions in man, but in a reverse way; that is, like does not react adversely with like in blood transfusions, but like reacts adversely with like in a self-incompatible circumstance. In addition to the shape, color, nectar and odor that may aid in bringing a pollinating insect to a flower, and thus assisting in cross-pollination, many species have most effective and efficient backup systems to accomplish the same thing.

—C. P. S.

CHAPTER THIRTEEN

Pollen Jewelry and How Flowers Guard It

Yellow dust dulling the surface of a little pool, yellow dust on spotless flower petals, yellow dust dropped from a bouquet of catkins onto the polished surface of the dining room table—it all seems a little distressing. Dust cloths and vacuum cleaners somehow come to mind.

But pollen is no shapeless dust. Pollen is not dull, unattractive, haphazard. It is an individual organism with a behavior and existence all its own, making a fresh and exciting chapter for today's botanists. Each pollen grain is like an exquisite piece of jewelry. Its size, shape and sculpturing are distinctive for the kind of plant which makes it. One might say that the air, woods and fields in the flowering seasons are filled with myriads of microscopic golf balls, footballs, canoes, helmets, water-wings, dumbbells, sunbursts and crystals.

Each pollen grain is a single cell, unlike all other plant units,

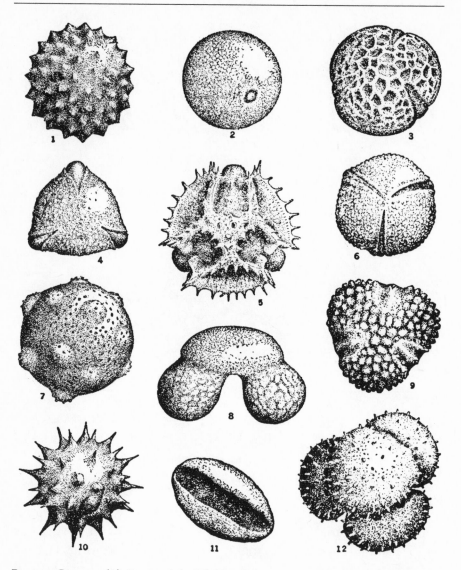

POLLEN GRAINS: (1) Ragweed; (2) Timothy grass; (3) Privet; (4) White Oak; (5) Dandelion; (6) Beech; (7) Sweet gum; (8) Pine; (9) Holly; (10) Sunflower; (11) Ginkgo; (12) Venus flytrap.

which are compounded out of many cells. This pollen cell is enclosed inside two covers, like a football that has a leather case enclosing a rubber case or bladder. The outer cover, the leather case, is made of protein and sugar, impregnated with waterproof wax, and stippled or ridged. Often it is extremely ornate with geometric designs of crests and spines. This outer case is marked by three deep furrows which open and close in a remarkable fashion as we shall see. The inner cover, corresponding to the bladder of a football, is made of cellulose, like ordinary wood cell walls.

The contents of a pollen grain are similar to those of all other cells, with protoplasm in which is a tiny dark speck called the nucleus, consisting of little bars and ribbons called chromosomes. All this can be seen through a microscope. But what cannot be seen is the spark of life into which has somehow been impressed all the forms and peculiarities of the plant that spawned the grain. Into this speck of protoplasm all the essentials for originating a great tree, or a frail little herb, are distilled. This pollen grain is a minute bottleneck in the life cycle of a plant. But every characteristic of its species, as outlined to the last detail in a manual of botany, flows through this speck when it is transmitted by its phenomenal mechanism to an ovule to make a seed.

The sizes of pollen grains are not in proportion to the sizes of their plants. The pollen of a sequoia tree that grows to a height of over 300 feet happens to be the same size as the pollen of a violet. The biggest pollen grains are made by pumpkin vines and measure about $\frac{1}{100}$ of an inch in diameter. If held so as to reflect light this is just barely visible to a person with sharp eyes. Althea and hibiscus and the members of the Four-o'clock Family are also famous for their large pollen grains. The smallest grains are produced by the forget-me-not. They are about one tenthousandth of an inch in diameter. The wind-pollinated plants produce the middle-sized grains. They seem to be just right for floating freely in the air. The big grains are too heavy for blowing around, but bees and wasps can carry them about, sticking to various parts of their bodies, without knowing they're carrying the freight. The smallest grains also use insects, because, due to their minute size, they are affected by molecular attraction and tend to stick together and do not blow out of their pollen boxes (anthers) easily. They need the brusque treatment of an insect to dislodge them.

Even more arresting than the sculptured form of pollen is the way it acts. A pollen grain is not an inert speck or even a dormant cell. Pollen is ready for hair trigger action and, once the anther doors open to set it free, it behaves in its own independent way, however dependent it may be on outside forces for transportation. It collapses by pulling in its joints which consist of the three furrows in the outer cover. A grain that may be spherical when expanded suddenly becomes a cylinder or an ellipse resembling a very small wheat seed when it folds up. When moisture touches the grain it quickly expands again. To perform this swelling and folding action, the furrows in the outer cover behave like pleats. When expanded they suggest an open human eye, with the thickened margins of the furrows resembling lids; the inner membrane, the white of the eye; and a round pore in the center of this membrane, the iris of the eye.

This blowing up and contracting of the grain under moist and dry conditions is characteristic of all kinds of pollen. The pollens of grasses, however, have but a single pore and no furrows. The change in shape and volume in this type is accomplished by the elastic expansion of the outer cover as with the blowing up of a toy balloon.

Pine tree pollen, and that of its relatives the spruces, firs and cedars, offers another striking exception to the three-furrow mechanism. Pine pollen is equipped with bladders so that it looks like the old-fashioned water-wings used to teach children to swim. Between the bladders a single furrow closes and opens as the bladders fold in and out. Each bladder is almost as large as the main part of the grain. The bladders themselves do not expand and contract. They are always expanded and filled with air. To prevent their collapse they are reinforced with a network of structural material laid on in geometrical designs.

More startling than this expanding and contracting which goes on at the least touch of moisture, is the activity that begins after the pollen arrives on the stigma of its species of plant. Suddenly a long pollen tube emerges from the grain and grows through the entire length of the pistil. As the stalk (style) of a pistil may be very long (that of a lily, for example, is several inches) the length of the pollen tube is enormous in relation to the microscopic size of the grain. Corn is an extreme example. Corn stigmas are pink threads perhaps eight or ten inches long, which you have often seen and called corn silk. Each thread leads to an ovary which is a potential grain of corn. A microscopic pollen grain landing near the outer end of this silk will produce a tube that travels the eight or ten inches to reach the ovary and ripen a grain! Many pistils have a number of ovules, although they have a single style. In that case a number of pollen grains must be caught. Each pollen grain produces its own tube that grows down inside the stalk without interfering with other tubes doing the same thing—until it finds an ovule. Garden peas are a good example of a compound pistil. To bring about fertilization takes as many grains of pollen landing on one pistil as there are peas in the pod. If too few pollen grains land on that pistil, some of the peas will fail to ripen.

A grain of pollen may keep its spark of life for only a few hours or for several months, depending on the species. This comparatively short life has nothing to do with its ability to irritate the mucous membrane. If hay fever pollen is kept dry it can cause violent sneezing after twenty years or longer. The same is true of its ability to puff and fold which seems to work mechanically long after the protoplasm has perished.

The outside cover of pollen with its wonderful sculptured armor is practically indestructible. This fact has written a fascinating chapter in the fossil history of the lush plant life of prehistoric times. Pollen is preserved perfectly, as though prepared for a scientist's microscope slide, in the coal measures of the carboniferous age, after 250 million years. These grains show that the plants of that remote time were relatives of the pines, ginkgoes and cycads. A more "recent" story of plant life is written in the peat bogs deposited since the disappearance of the glaciers over a period of thirty thousand years. For instance, a study of a peat deposit thirty feet deep (a foot every thousand years) in Central Ohio shows different kinds of pollen at different levels. Although all other identifiable traces of plant life have been erased, it has been possible from these pollen fossils alone to make a chart showing what kind of plants grew in the vicinity during each ten million year period.

Plant fossils are important and exciting to paleobotanists. Recently they plumbed the oil shales in the Green River region where Colorado, Utah and Wyoming meet. Few traces of fossil leaves or other plant parts had ever been found there, but those oil shales hold enormous quantities of beautifully preserved pollen grains. This now becomes an accurate, authoritative manual of the flora of the region written forty million years ago. Over one hundred species have already been listed and they are still turning up pollen. When you look over the list and see such plants as fig, palmetto and eucalyptus, it might seem that some mistake has been made. These are sub-tropical plants, identified with Mexico, Central America and the northern part of South America. Actually, it shows a drastic change of climate in Colorado, Utah and Wyoming. The mystery forest of the ancient Green River region left only its pollen preserved in the amber matrix of oil to tell the tale long after the grosser structures of those plants had been erased by time.

However, this kind of longevity is interesting only to man and not to nature. The brief life of most kinds of pollen requires that it be launched, transported and go to work on a pistil quickly—usually within an hour or two. All this must be done between showers, too, for pollen is damaged by rain. To keep their powder dry flowers are equipped with special structures as well as the ability to twist and turn to protect their anthers from rain drops.

It is always a wonder to me to look at the Queen Anne's lace in my pasture on a rainy day or when rain is threatened early in August. The round discs of freshly blooming flower heads in which pollen is ripening have tipped 90 degrees so that they stand vertically like those round tables that tip up to get them out of the way against a wall. This is caused by the stem suddenly becoming flabby a couple of inches below the flower head in wet weather. It does not revolve as stems sometimes do but simply flexes just the right amount so that the weight of the flower will let it fall at a 90° angle. But as you look across the pasture on a rainy day not all the Queen Anne's laces are tipped over. The older heads which have shed their pollen remain in the horizontal position. In some mysterious way the presence of ripe pollen to be protected determines whether or not the stem will flex. Wild geranium and buttercups exhibit the same behavior, drooping dejectedly in the rain, *if* the blossoms are young and the anthers ripe. When you consider that this is part of the floral mechanism it's not as gloomy a prospect as it appears to be.

Other field flowers (for example, hawkweeds, dandelions and chicory) close up tight on a dark, overcast day and at night, protecting their pollen in this way from dew as well as when rain is threatened. This is true also of crocuses and pond lilies, and the Star of Bethlehem. Indeed, these flowers appear to vanish on a rainy day by closing up until it stops raining. Many little spring flowers such as the windflower, rue anemone and bloodroot are exceptionally cautious and only open wide on the brightest, driest days. This is equally true of the fall blooming fringed gentian. Clear bright sunlight is needed to separate the marvelous petals. Its near relative, the closed gentian, never does open except for a small hole at the top to let a bee in.

Other flowers are built so that they never have to take action to keep their pollen dry. A beautiful example of well-housed anthers is the Jack-in-the-Pulpit with graceful and sturdy hood.

The flowers of the wild ginger and May apple grow under a broad protecting leaf. The quivering bright orange touch-me-not (*Impatiens*) often has a leaf, like an umbrella, over its blossom.

The structure of the flower itself may help to keep its pollen dry. Some have petals always closed over the stamens. This is vividly true of the clovers and all other members of the Pea Family. Corydalis, butter-and-eggs of the Snapdragon Family are other examples of stamens protected inside their petals. In the iris a great broad stigma makes a roof over the stamens. In the cornflower (bachelor's button) the pollen is contained in a tube where it is protected from rain and dew. The stalk of this tube is irritated at the least touch so that, when an insect strikes it, this stalk suddenly shortens and crumbles, dumping the pollen onto the insect. Perhaps the commonest form of protection is seen in the large number of flowers that open laterally, like mints, bluebells and roses which are tipped enough to prevent their corollas from being filled with water. Many others like the Solomon's seal, bellwort, columbine and milkweed dangle face down.

If flowers are well equipped to keep their pollen dry, their devices for attracting insects surpass in variety and ingenuity the wildest imagining. The subject is as vast as the numbers of species which use insects for cross-pollination. It has stirred writers to eloquence and filled many books. Let us examine in the next chapter a few of the most arresting examples of this interdependence of flowers and insects . . . one of the marvels of the world around us.

CHAPTER FOURTEEN

How Flowers and Insects Fit Each Other

I used to wonder how so many flowers that grow in the great outdoors could depend on being pollinated by insects. Here, in a single acre which is a pinprick in the landscape, half a hundred different kinds of insect-carried pollen will be produced through the summer. This pollen must be both transported and sorted, so that the pistil of each flower can receive its own kind of pollen. The work must be done swiftly. A flower does not wait long to be pollinated, perhaps only a few hours. Moreover, a single daisy contains several hundred flowers, each of which must receive a separate grain of pollen; and a meadow acre may be white with daisies. The same astronomical numbers are seen in the hawk-weeds, black-eyed Susans, goldenrods, and asters. Then, too, the mustards, heal-alls, speedwells, and bluets, to mention only a few, are ripening and calling for pollination that only insects can deliver. To touch each little flower at the right time with the right pollen would seem to be an impossible prospect, even for armies of insects, going about it in a hit or miss fashion.

One warm sunny day in midsummer, I focused my camera on two square inches of a yarrow flower cluster. Here was a tiny sector visibly detached from the other flowers on the same plant, from the other flowers of the field, and from the world at large. Insects of many kinds, most of them very small, landed in that sector at the rate of about one every five seconds. This makes twelve per minute, or at the rate of 5,760 visitors in an eight hour day. They were busy, preoccupied, even avaricious. They scurried around, dipping in here and there with lightning strokes, quivering with excitement. Ants also were numerous, perhaps one every minute, and they can walk fast and work fast, like nothing else in the world. After a few minutes of watching this activity, feeling almost breathless myself, I saw a wasp zoom into focus. He looked like a colossus in contrast with the minute insects. The wasp did not scurry around but simply planted himself in the middle of the feast, poked his proboscis swiftly in and out, jerked his thorax violently up and down, and when an ant stepped on his toes, he kicked like a mule. All this activity in two square inches of flowers in a vast and busy world!

The best time to see insects in action is on a warm, clear morning after the sun has dried the dews of night from the flowers. If the preceding days have been cloudy and cool, or rainy, the numbers of insects are multiplied when the sun shines. The longer they have remained in hiding, getting hungry, the faster they work. This fact apparently makes up lost time in the pollination schedule of the flowers, many of which remain closed during the rainy days. Too much wind drives away the insects, especially the butterflies, which are very choosy about eating their flower food on a warm sunny day. In comparison to moths, bees, and flies, butterflies are grandiose, vain and sluggish over a field of flowers. They would rather catch the glint of sunlight on their wings than eat. They would rather be warm than eat. On a sunny crisp day in September, they often alight on warmth-reflecting stones or shiny leaves in preference to flowers.

But, in general, so intense is the preoccupation of insects after nectar and pollen or luxuriating in the sun-filled bowls of flowers that you can approach very near them. Their rapid movements are directed at their job on the flower and they show little alarm at the human monstrosity who looms up beside them. You can even pick some of them up in your fingers. Not so flies. They are as elusive as ever. Also the sphinx moth is always a timid spark of lightning—the most you can usually "see" of him is a resounding buzz. And the amazing dragon fly, which we used to call the devil's darning needle, always keeps a good two yards between you and him.

For sheer tragi-comedy the spectacle of insects on flowers is the greatest show on earth. The height of the season for spectators is in August. Then big round-topped Queen Anne's lace, great yellow arches of goldenrod, domes of magenta thistles, pink clouds of Joe Pye weed, and sharp purple spires of vervain are flooded with sunshine. These set thousands of stages ready for the performances of countless actors. Focus your eyes, concentrate your attention, and in a few minutes you are lost in the spell of this world of little things.

Players are unbelievably agile, colorful, whimsical. Some, like clowns, appear to be awkward and lumber around bearing great shields (stink bugs), or lug off other insects twice their size. Still others dart past your head with shrill whirring, or buzz with ferocious resonance out of all proportion to their size. The carefree and easy-going butterflies flutter with eccentric motions like wind-tossed leaves above the flowers. A clear-wing sphinx moth charges straight at a flower head like a dive bomber. The bees are purposeful, buzzing deliberately from flower to flower with tireless and never failing precision. Other insects may pause for rest, just sunning themselves on flowers or leaves. This is especially true of butterflies, as we have just said, which often gather in twos and threes on a flower head, raising their spangled wings slowly with the gestures of a beautifully gowned woman before a mirror. Butterflies also love to play, and go whirling off in a gay tussle with a chance comrade. Not so the bees. They always go earnestly about their business of laying up riches. The dragon flies are like streaks of blue light, suddenly stopped in midair. Their sharp streamlined bodies quivering, they appear to be creatures of electricity. Dragon flies travel in pencil-straight lines, while hover flies, that are also electric-swift, describe curves, throwing off sparks of color like glass tinsel. And all the time there is a great coming and going by the hoppers and the crawlers.

Many of the little insects are simply interlopers or hangers on. Many kinds of flies, for instance, don't need pollen; they prefer a bit of carrion or decaying vegetables to flowers. Spiders kill other insects for food. They use flowers only for hitching posts from which to drape their spiral traps, knowing that among the flowers are many prospective victims. Ants certainly don't belong on flowers, but are much more at home in their underground labyrinths or wherever they have their cows to milk. All these insects are attracted to the flowers primarily because of their color or the warmth of the sun or perhaps for the sake of company. They help to carry pollen around in a haphazard way. On the other hand, bees are indigenous to flowers. They can exist because flowers exist, and if it weren't for bees half of our most beautiful species of flowers would disappear. Bees are almost as much a part of some flowers as stamens and pistils.

Of all types of bee, the honey-bee does the most work and covers the greatest territory. She is the chief engineer in activating cross-pollination. Her relative, the bumblebee, is larger, rounder and makes a bigger buzz. But the honey-bee has better pollen baskets on her hind legs, and is more interested in pollen gathering than the bumblebee. These baskets consist of rows of stiff bristles placed at equal distances on the hind legs. By packing the pollen, moistened with honey, in between these hairs, the bee can accumulate a good-sized ball of pollen sometimes a quarter of an inch in diameter, containing over 100 thousand grains of average-sized pollen. When you see a bee carrying two big pollen balls she looks deformed and over-burdened; but she keeps right on with her passionate gathering. I have watched

the honey-bees work, long after the other insects, including the
.bumblebees, have called it a day, up to the very moment when
the ridge of the western hills cuts the sun in half in the evening.
Then finally the honey-bee takes her last pollen ball of that day
back to the hive as food for her larvae.

If you take a pollen ball apart under a microscope it is seen
to contain the grains of only a single species. A bee usually
gathers pollen from only one kind of flower in his day's work, a
remarkable fact which promotes cross-pollination. I have watched
this pollen gathering when there was every opportunity for a
mistake. On the edge of a swamp, vervain and heal-all were
growing together. Both of these flowers are dark purple. Bees
were at work on both of them, so near together that in criss-
crossing from one plant to another they almost collided in mid-
air. A bee visiting vervain would often have his attention caught
by the heal-all. He would hesitate, circle the flower as though
about to alight, go up to within an inch or two, and then pass
it by. On the other hand, a bee visiting the heal-all would act
the same way toward the vervain. They were a little confused
by the similarity of color, but never once, so far as I observed,
made the error of touching the anthers of the wrong flower.

One day I thought this convenient theory was upset when
I saw a bee visiting both poppies and ageratum in the garden.
But close observation revealed that the bee was doing all her
pollen gathering in the poppies, while diving for nectar in the
ageratum. With proboscis folded up she would virtually sit down
among the poppy stamens, work her legs to agitate the anthers,
take pollen into her mouth, moisten it, pack it into her pollen
baskets. In the ageratum the bee kept her pollen baskets up
where they didn't touch the flower, while she drove her proboscis
home for nectar. Since poppies are pollen flowers, and produce
no nectar, it is interesting to speculate that a bee will visit only
one kind of flower on a pollen gathering expedition, but if that
species happens to contain no nectar, she will visit any other
convenient flower to keep her mouth moistened with honey.

Heal-all gives a dotted-line demonstration of the speed with which a bee works. The florets of this plant are arranged on a cylindrical head so that they project at different angles and it is easier for a bee to fly from one to another than to walk. Since a bee buzzes in flight and is silent in a flower, the effect is an intermittent series of buzzes. Each buzz is about a second long spaced by one second of silence. In other words, even with half her time in flight the bee was visiting flowers at the rate of about 30 per minute—a theoretical possibility of 18,000 per day.

A bee on the head of a thistle does not have to fly from one floret to another. She staggers and slips around, bracing her six feet wherever they can get a foothold in the tortuous labyrinth, and thrusts her proboscis every second into one flower after another, pollinating them at the rate of 30 to 40 per minute. Occasionally she rolls over, not playfully for sheer joy, as some sentimentalists believe, but with fervor. She is working hard and when she rolls or stands on her head she kicks her hind legs into the anthers to knock out pollen.

The bumblebee is a more casual pollen gatherer than the honey-bee. Her pollen baskets consist of irregular rows of feathery hairs with which she may carry a pollen ball or dust off the pollen from an anther, while the honey-bee always works hard all day to build up one enormous ball of moist pollen after another to carry back to the hive. The bumblebee appears to be more interested in nectar ... she's a comparatively lazy fat mechanic, possessed of a wondrous long proboscis with which she is able to set off the mechanisms of flowers with deeply concealed nectar that the honey-bee can't reach.

So much has been written about flowers specially adapted for certain insects that an impression is abroad that each kind of flower is visited by its own particular kind of insect. This is true if the phrase is changed to the plural. Each species is visited by its own kinds of insects. For instance, goldenrod is visited by almost every insect a-wing in the field. The little crawling ones like ants will tote pollen from floret to floret in the same flower head, while bees and butterflies and wasps will effect complete crossing between plants by flying from one to another.

It is true, however, that highly specialized flowers do have their gears for cross-pollination adapted to only one kind of insect. The monkshood (*Aconitum sp.*) depends entirely on bumblebees, and it fits a bumblebee as a shoe fits a foot. This well named flower has turned one of its sepals into a big colorful hood, easily mistaken for a petal. Inside this hood two petals have turned into nectaries. These curving organs end in a spur filled with nectar that oozes in droplets from the inner surface of the petals. A bumblebee with a long proboscis, just the right length for these nectar wells, gets inside the flower. If you made a plaster cast of the inside of the hood, it would be the size and shape of a bumblebee's body. Distribution maps of monkshood and bumblebees are identical.

Columbine and delphinium also are built for bumblebees. Their nectar is concealed at the ends of long spurs, exactly the right length and shape to fit the proboscis of the garden bumblebee. One of the commonest and the most beautiful field flowers, the red clover, is another bumblebee flower, but on a somewhat different plan. The big oval head of this clover consists of closely packed little tubular flowers (florets) with nectar deeply concealed at the bottom of each tube. Because of the small size of a floret the bumblebee can get only her head inside, and to do this she must push apart the petals. The bottom petal is shaped like a canoe enclosing the stamens and pistil. As the bee's head pushes on this canoe petal, the stamens and pistil spring up on their stiff stems. The pistil springs up first. Its stigma brushes the bee's face and gets the dose of pollen which had been deposited there from another clover. After that the stamens, which are shorter, pop up and dust the bee's face with pollen for the next flower. The exact size of the bumblebee's head, his weight, and the pressure he exerts pushing down the boat-shaped petal are all nicely balanced by the flower. The mechanism does not operate accurately for any other kind of insect. When red clover was first imported from England into Australia it failed to seed because Australia is not bumblebee territory. When bees were imported to go with the clover, both thrived.

Coordination of flowers and insects is chiefly determined by the location of the flower's nectar versus the length of the proboscis of the insect. This establishes the habits of the insect as to which flowers he will visit and which ignore.

We are apt to think of bees gathering nectar as from a bowl, or perhaps by piercing the flower and sucking its sap. Neither of these ideas is accurate. Nectar is sugar sap, an irresistible attraction for insects, offered in a variety of ways to produce cross-pollination. Sometimes the nectary is a minute depression, just a dot, located on the base of the petals. You'll find this kind of nectary, for example, in the buttercup. Or the nectar may ooze out on lower parts of stamens, as in the wild geranium. Some times a pair of tiny bumps grow beside the base of each stamen and glisten with amber beads of nectar as in the winter cress mustard. Or there may be a raised disc covered with smooth glistening nectar in the center of the flower, as can be easily seen in Queen Anne's lace. In the Composite Family (see Chapter 18) a ridge surrounds the base of the pistil, exuding nectar in such quantity that it rises high in the tube of the flower. In these flowers (goldenrods, asters, daisies, thistles and their relatives) the nectar filling the flowing bowl is literally a cornucopia of honey. Another distinctive type of nectary is seen in the flowers with long spurs, like columbine, touch-me-not, and delphinium, where the nectar oozes out of the inner surfaces of the petals or sepals and runs down into the spurs, partly filling their tip ends.

The vital point is not that each flower has its own peculiar type of nectary; rather it is the *location* of the nectary with respect to the stamens and pistils. The insect is first lured to visit the flower, then, having arrived on the scene, he must act so as to impregnate the stigma with pollen from another plant of the same species and, finally, or at the same time, pick up more pollen. His proboscis must slide in at exactly the right angle. His face must be presented for dusting at the right place. The curves of his belly or back must be just right to pick up or deposit pollen, according to their exact position. Possibly his legs are to be planted so that they will do the trick. All this is controlled with amazing accuracy by the location of the nectary in relation to the length of proboscis of the insect.

A proboscis is one of the mechanical wonders of the world. It is often referred to as the "tongue" of a bee, butterfly, wasp or fly. But a tongue is a muscular organ that cannot usually be extended many times the length of the head. An animal with an ordinary tongue, desiring to reach out some distance, has to have a neck like a giraffe or a trunk like an elephant, or a stepladder like a man. But a bee has an implement more complex than a dentist's gear. It can be extended several times longer than the head and retracted with lightning speed.

The bee has jaws for biting and if she is going to chew some pollen she does so in normal animal fashion with the mouth. But under the lower jaw the bee carries a complicated set of levers, tubes, joints and hairs, all folded up like a pocket knife and tucked neatly into a cavity. When she wants to suck in a bead of nectar that glistens, say three quarters of an inch beyond her head, this proboscis darts out. It's like a split tube made of several long splints that can be narrowed and widened, and through this tube slides a slender hairy pin. This pin touches the nectar and then jerks back a little, drawing the nectar into the proboscis tube. The sweet sap is then passed up toward the bee's mouth by a successive erection of whorls of hairs inside the tube. This is climaxed by a big suck produced by a visible heaving of the bee's abdomen.

When the bee is flying from flower to flower in quest of nectar the proboscis is often carried in the extended position so that it can be shot into a flower before she alights. When collecting pollen for a pollen ball she folds up her proboscis with four swift movements. Then, with proboscis out of sight, she bites off pollen from an anther, coughs up a minute bit of honey to moisten it and deposits it in the pollen baskets on her legs. This pollen is taken back to the hive for the larvae to eat. Cross-pollination results from the pollen grains which happen to cling to the hairs on her legs and body. It takes only one pollen grain to fertilize a seed, and, in order to get just that one, a flower gives away thousands of other grains to raise more bees.

The butterfly and moth proboscis is comparatively simple. It consists of half tubes, like a rubber hose cut in two lengthwise. These two halves are hooked together by sickle shaped devices top and bottom. This makes practically an air-tight tube of great flexibility. The outside of this tube is covered with hinged segments like tiny armor plates. When not in use it is coiled up in a tight spiral under the head. From this position it can be thrown out like a rope to penetrate the deepest flowers. Nectar is simply sucked in through the tube.

Butterflies and moths (*Lepidoptera*) do not gather pollen and they carry no nectar home. They have no responsibility for their young after they have laid their eggs on the food plant of the caterpillar. But butterflies enjoy nectar for their own nourishment, although they never seem to be very hungry. In fact, nectar is their only food. Therefore, they are entirely dependent on flowers and are thoroughly reliable cross-pollinators.

Because butterflies and moths have extra long proboscides the most highly specialized flowers, that is those with the deepest nectaries, are exclusively butterfly and moth flowers. Bees may visit such flowers for pollen but not often, for they can't reach the nectar. One species of sphinx moth that pollinates morning glory and hedge bindweed has a proboscis about three inches long. A tropical species holds the world's record with a proboscis ten inches long and there is a flower to correspond to it.

Wasps also have their own flowers. The social wasps that build paper nests are not in this picture. They are so omnivorous that flower food is unimportant to them, and their casual visits to flowers are only to sit in the sun or attack other insects. But the solitary wasps, those that make cells of mud or sand and dig in the ground, live entirely on nectar as adults. They are equipped with the jack-knife type of proboscis like bees, but these are much shorter than the average bee proboscis. Certain flowers with easily reached nectar have a mechanism for cross-pollination that is exactly suited to these wasps, as we shall presently see.

Flies are playboys. They knock around everywhere. They like to walk or sit on white, yellow and green things. And there is no question but what they effectively transfer a good deal of pollen through the law of averages. One family of flies, the Syrphids, lives on plants almost exclusively. The Syrphids (an exotic name for certain common and colorful outdoor flies) eat pollen and wash it down with nectar, and to that end they are equipped with remarkable proboscides that vary in length from $\frac{1}{12}$ to $\frac{1}{2}$ inch. This proboscis is built in three segments that operate with a sort of piston and hinge action. The outer end is a swollen duplex affair that resembles two clenched fists tied together at the wrists. Ridges, like folded fingers, can open to grab pollen and then grind it and work it back toward the mouth in the channels between the ridges. For sucking nectar, part of this proboscis is turned into a tube. The flies that possess this characteristic are sometimes called hover flies because of the unique maneuver with which they approach their special flowers. A Syrphid, or hover fly, fixes itself at a point in the air above the flower and holds that position for some seconds. Then he darts forward, touches the flower, retreats and holds a fixed position again, three or four inches away. After repeating this performance several times, he lights on a petal, seizes the stamen with forelegs and proceeds to eat pollen. Sometimes during these dartings and stoppings he approaches the flower backward. The Syrphid fly is a great actor, and gorgeously dressed in sparkling bright colors.

Thus, all bees, butterflies and moths, and some wasps and flies are equipped with specialized instruments, more precise than the finest works of a watch, for gathering or eating nectar or pollen. To fit their requirements, flowers are usually equipped on their part with various kinds of nectaries and with the arrangements of flower parts to fit heads, feet, bodies and legs of their particular visitors.

The following summary will illustrate the remarkable relationship between length of proboscis and position of nectary. Bear in mind, however, that any insect may visit any flower by chance. Such chance visitors may or may not promote cross-pollination.

1. POLLEN FLOWERS. These flowers have no nectaries. This lack puts them lowest on the scale of equipment for insect attraction, but paradoxically, having no nectaries, they are more selective than some flowers so equipped. Pollen flowers are avoided by butterflies, moths and wasps which go after nectar. They are usually avoided by bumble-bees that are chiefly interested in nectar and in pollen only as a sideline. Honey-bees are the chief visitors of pollen flowers. They are just as eager to fill their pollen baskets as to collect honey. Beetles also enjoy pollen.

To compensate for the lack of nectar, pollen flowers produce extra amounts of pollen. The wild rose is a conspicuous example. The anthers bulge with great masses of sticky yellow pollen. Other well known flowers in this class are hepatica, bloodroot, star flower, Canada mayflower, baneberry, clematis, meadow rue, poppy, rock rose, cactus, St. John's-wort, elderberry, shinleaf, whorled loosestrife, pimpernel, shooting star, heliotrope, bittersweet nightshade, mullein, and spiderwort.

2. EXPOSED NECTAR FLOWERS. Small hardy white and yellow flowers, always with wide open petals. The nectar is a flat layer at the base of the pistil and sparkles conspicuously in the sun. The fact that the nectar is a thin layer causes the big long-proboscis insects like bees, butterflies and moths to pass them by, although I have seen butterflies resting on them. Since the honey-bee is such a faithful visitor to all other classes of flowers, these exposed nectar flowers can be said to have a claim to distinction in getting along without honey-bees. Their chief visitors are the short-proboscis flies, wasps, and beetles, in addition to miscellaneous crawling bugs and ants.

Queen Anne's lace is an excellent example of an exposed

nectar flower. So are other members of the Carrot Family such as wild parsnip, water hemlock and golden Alexander. Sumac, New Jersey tea, wild grape, false hellebore, bedstraw, the viburnums, boxwood, spurge and some species of saxifrage are all exposed nectar flowers. The flowering dogwood is in this class, the inconspicuous small yellow flowers in the center being greatly assisted in attracting insects by the large white petal-like leaves. On the whole, it appears that these exposed nectar flowers are under a decided handicap, and their success is due, at least in the Carrot Family, to the social arrangements of the flat-topped clusters of many small flowers which are easily pollinated by visitors scrambling across them.

3. PARTIALLY CONCEALED NECTAR FLOWERS. A compromise between the fully exposed and fully concealed nectar flowers. White and yellow is the usual color, as in the preceding class, but the yellows are deeper and a few are magenta and pink. These flowers have an abundance of pollen, and while the nectar may be visible in the bright sunlight, it usually plays hide-and-seek in the recesses of the flowers. Typical flowers of this class are partly closed and cup shaped. They are visited by all the insects of the exposed nectar flowers plus hover flies and bees with short and medium proboscides, including the important honey-bee. This excludes the bumblebees and butterflies. As is so often true with compromises, this class of flowers is well balanced for living. It has wide popularity among different kinds of insects. But we find here the beginnings of true specialization. For example, buttercups and cinquefoils fit so exactly certain small bees with a proboscis about ⅕ inch long, that flower and bee appear to be made for each other. Other examples of this class with partially concealed nectar are the various species of mustard, chickweed, marsh marigold, bugbane (*Cimicifuga*), barberry, bladdernut, apple, cherry, avens, spiraea, hawthorn, strawberry, grass of Parnassus, tear-thumb, rattlesnake plantain (*Epipactis*), and star of Bethlehem.

4. CONCEALED NECTAR FLOWERS. Since the nectar in these flowers is completely hidden, insects visiting them must have instinctive knowledge and special equipment to reach it. The flowers of this group have fanciful variety of form, color and size. Few yellow and white flowers, predominating in the other groups, have concealed nectar. This group has mostly brilliant, rich colors. Red is preferred by butterflies, blue and violet by bees. A few concealed nectar flowers have simple radial symmetry, but for the most part they are irregular in all kinds of fantastic shapes with spurs, sacs and odd shaped petals. These irregularities are external evidence of highly specialized mechanisms for cross-pollination. The long proboscis insects beginning with the ever useful honey-bee (¼ inch proboscis) and ranging through the bumblebees, butterflies and moths are the chief pollinators of this group. The deeper and more inaccessible the nectar, the more exclusive the flower. At the deeper end of this scale are the flowers with nectar buried one to three inches deep which only the hawk-moths can visit profitably.

Although the most striking members of this group require long-proboscis insects to pollinate them, the great Composite Family is a major exception. Daisies, asters, black-eyed Susans and their relatives have concealed nectar but they are social. Their conspicuous aggregations of flowers are pastures for practically every kind of insect. Nectar seeps out on a ridge at the base of the pistil so abundantly that it rises in the tube of the flower and thus becomes available for any length of proboscis.

Other concealed nectar flowers, while more specialized than the preceding classes, may be visited without discrimination by honey-bees, bumblebees or butterflies. Examples are geranium, mallow, loosestrife (*Lythrum*), fireweed, blackberry, Venus' looking-glass, lilac, forsythia, periwinkle, forget-me-not, beard-tongue, and milkweed.

Primarily *bee flowers* are: locust, pea, alfalfa, vetch, mints, butter-and-eggs, corydalis, violets, milkworts, horse-chestnut, blueberry, mountain laurel (a honey-bee flower), gentian, blueweed, foxglove, turtle-head, cow-wheat, wood betony, yellow rattle, bladderwort, butterwort, vervain and lady's-slipper. Clovers, azalea, rhododendron, bearberry, columbine and iris are pollinated almost exclusively by bumblebees.

Primarily *butterfly flowers* are: Deptford pink, firepink, cardinal flower, lilies, phlox, fringed orchis. These are typically red, while *moth flowers*, for example, honeysuckle, hedge bindweed and Jimson weed, are usually white. One exception is the yellow evening primrose, an important hawk-moth flower. Nature's practices are always logical in the long run. Moths are most active at night, hence hawk-moth flowers are white or yellow because these tones are more visible in low illumination.

Odor assists these night flyers also to find their blossoms. Moths have big feathery antennae that they wave in the air to catch the odor of their flowers. These antennae are direction finders as well, for hawk-moths, unlike the whirling butterflies, go straight as an arrow to their flower. Dr. Kerner, one of the first "entomobotanists."* proved how well these antennae work by daubing a hawk-moth with red ink and releasing him after sunset 300 feet from the nearest hawk-moth flower, honeysuckle in this case. The moth waved its feelers a few times and then flew straight to that tiny speck in the distance. Incidentally, hawk-moth flowers are frequently odorless in the daytime, their fragrance mysteriously arising only at evening.

With equal logic, day-flying butterflies are more sensitive to color and less sensitive to odor. They prefer red, but also visit blue and violet flowers. The reverse is true of bees. However, the color discrimination of these insects is limited to only four or five feet, so their course toward the flowers is often zig-zag and uncertain.

The odor of a flower can be compared to radio advertising that calls to customers from a considerable distance, at least in the dimensions of the insect world. The color of a flower is like the store front or neon sign. When the right insect customer

---

*I have coined this word. There should be entomobotanists as insects and flowers belong together.

arrives at the right flower a variety of attractions and devices are provided at the point of sale. These are especially important in the hidden nectar flowers where a visitor must tread in precisely the right places to operate the pollinating gears. Many petals and sepals which act as landing stages have white or yellow streaks, or bright dots, called nectar guides, that converge at the entrance for body or head or proboscis. We find these guides in such flowers as the iris, speedwell, violet, lady's-slipper and countless others. Sometimes the nectar guide is a bright circle, as the red center of certain pinks and mallows and the little yellow circle at the center of bluets and blue-eyed grass. The tall blue lobelia has two white patches at its portal. The tiger lily has red glands that not only converge as nectar guides but also glisten deceptively as though with nectar drops. The lip of the snapdragon is colored red where the bee enters.

These lines, hairs, glands, bumps and dots that act as nectar guides are like gun sights. The action of a bee after pollen is swift. He shoots in his proboscis already extended while he is still in mid-air and the aim is unerring.

Many flowers have a matting of hairs, of exactly the right size and position to give the insect a good footing. Butterflies, whose big wings make them top-heavy, like to take a firm grasp with their feet, and definitely avoid the slippery parts of petals. Members of the Orchid Family always have conspicuous hair mats. These serve both as a foot-hold and to protect the inner mechanism of the flower from raindrops and crawling unwelcome insects.

The most extraordinary example of the way hairs are placed to assist the pollination of a flower is seen in a common native orchid, the grass pink (*Calopogon*). Unlike other species of orchid the stigma of grass pink which is to receive its charge of pollen from the back of a bee is located on the bottom petal of the flower and faces upward. It is as though this flower were upside down. If the bee barged in with pollen on his back in the customary manner, he could not pollinate the flower because the stigma is underneath him. So the grass pink has a matting of hairs held up vertically on the top lip. These hairs offer an inviting foothold, all the more so as they are bright yellow. Thus the bee is induced to land on the top petal in a vertical position, head up, grasping the hairs with his feet. The lip, which is nicely constructed to flex just the right amount under the weight of the bee, bends forward. Look! There he goes into a backward somersault! He is turned upside down with his head pointing outward while the pollen on his back comes into contact with the stigma at the base of the flower.

This backward somersault of the bee on the grass pink is a fine example of flower antics to achieve cross-pollination by insects. These activities are incredibly fascinating, although they are seldom recognized as such. Even scientists devoted little study to this subject until the last half of the 19th century, and information is far from complete to this day. Flower mechanisms and their operations offer a field with many unexplored corners waiting for original research by pioneers of our machine age.

ADDENDUM to CHAPTER FOURTEEN

As indicated in this chapter, there is an intimate relation between flower characteristics and their pollinators. They have evolved together since the Cretaceous period which began about 136 million years ago; there had been a great outburst of insect evolution in the Carboniferous period, some 300 or more million years ago, but this outburst was not associated with flowers in any way. As we look at flowers we are aware that some are constructed on a simple scale, while others are far more elaborate in their design. As a rule of thumb, the more specialized the design of the individual flower the more likely it is that its pollinators will be limited in species number, and that the characteristics of the pollinators will be peculiarly suited to bring about pollination. A number of these instances have been mentioned in this chapter, but here the focus will be on color and its significance.

Color is of primary importance because, to most pollinators, it is the first intimation that a visit to the flower might be worthwhile. Hawk-moths, sometimes called sphinx or clear-winged moths as well, are dusk or night fliers, and understandably are attracted to yellow or white flowers that stand out sharply against a dark background. Hummingbirds are particularly attracted to red flowers such as those of the mimosa or the red trumpet vine, flowers that are generally ignored by most insects. Europe, for example, has no native pure red flowers; neither has it any of the many species of hummingbirds. Bees, on the other hand, respond primarily to blue and yellow flowers; their vision is quite poor in the red region of the spectrum, and virtually absent in the green area; obviously they respond to what they see. This, of course, is true for all pollinators except some small flies and beetles which are attracted by a sense of smell. The bee's apprehension of color, however, is not limited to the visible spectrum that extends from red to violet; the bee can see in the long ultraviolet, that region of the electro-magnetic spectrum between 300 and 400 millimicrons. When photographed in ultraviolet light, many flowers reveal distinctive patterns that to us are invisible, and it is to these patterns that the bee responds. This explains what, at first sight, appears to be an anomaly, to wit, that bees that are red-blind, regularly visit red poppies. It turns out that such poppies have a central pattern that is brightly visible to those pollinators sensitive to the ultraviolet.

An interesting example has recently come to light that indicates how one species of flowering plant can accommodate to two different pollinators whose color preferences also differ. The scarlet gillia, *Ipomosis aggregata*, blooms in mid-summer in the Fern Mountains of Arizona. It inflorescence is an elongated spike, and the individual flowers open over a long period of time. Red or deep pink flowers appear first. These are visited, and pollination brought about, by the broad-tailed and rufous hummingbirds. These birds migrate farther north as summer progresses, and as they leave they are gradually replaced as pollinators by the white-lined sphinx moth. As this change-over occurs, it is paralleled by a change-over in the color of the gillia flowers. The early flowers in red are gradually replaced by those that lighten first to pink and then to white; these, of course, are more visible to the night-flying sphinx moths. One can only wonder at the time and genetic changes that must have occurred for this pattern of coevolution to have been perfected.

—C.P.S.

CHAPTER FIFTEEN

The Precision Tools of Cross-Pollination

We have seen that flowers have odor, color and guides to lead insects toward the pollen and nectar which they seek. We have seen that the size and shape of a flower and the position of its nectary may fit the head, body or proboscis of a certain kind of bee, butterfly, wasp, beetle or fly. So far, so good for the insect. He is well served by these devices. But he has not a single generous impulse. He does not reason that since the flower is so hospitable he should offer to help the flower. The ethics of the insect's behavior are those of the inexorable law of natural balance. Every organism must be brought into line or perish. What do you suppose would become of the flowers if they were preyed upon by predatory insects without compensation? They would be harmed and disappear. Then what would become of the insects? They would migrate or perish. This situation obviously does not exist because flowers and insects flourish year after year together. So the insect is prevented from race suicide by the flower somehow securing compensation ... and the balance of life in the field is maintained. The more you think of it, the more you study it, the more marvelous this beautifully balanced drama seems to be.

It isn't enough for this law of compensation that insects arrive on the scene and simply blunder around, getting stuck up with pollen and then possibly brushing some of it off on a pistil in a hit or miss fashion. This *appears* to be what happens. Because to some accidental extent it does happen, we are easily misled. But species prosper because the law of averages is on their side. A percentage of the plants of a species can fail entirely to set their seeds, provided enough seeds are fertilized to carry on the race. A percentage can fail of cross-breeding and set their seeds from inbreeding (that is, the pistil is pollinated by pollen from its own flower) provided the percentage of cross-breeding is sufficient to maintain the quality of the race as a whole. If the percentage of cross-breeding drops below this critical point, the race languishes and eventually disappears.

What this critical point is for given species of flowers would take life-long experiments in genetics to determine. But it appears to correspond roughly with the position of a species in the scale of evolution. The most primitive flowers such as buttercups and roses mature their stamens and pistils at the same time in the same flower. Moreover these are the flowers whose pollen gets knocked about by indiscriminate visitors like beetles, dragon flies, ants, and worms. It follows that they must get along well with a relatively low percentage of cross-pollinating, as their chances of self-pollinating are high. At the top of the scale the orchids and mints have a foolproof mechanism for 100% cross-pollination. This is circumstantial evidence that cross-pollination promotes progress, at least from our point of view, in the evolution of flower forms.

After all, the critical point for the percentage of cross-breeding to maintain a species is an academic question. The fact stares us in the face that each species which prospers has its own particular mechanism that *never fails to produce enough crossing* for success. It would simplify matters in a book that generalizes as much as this one is doing right now if these mechanics could be summarized. But the fact is that each species has its own individual way of getting compensation from its insects. Let's look at some of the common flowers and see how they contrive to make visiting insects work for them ... how do they extract their compensation for providing pollen and nectar foods?

The magnolia flower (*Magnolia grandiflora*) is pollinated in two curious stages with the aid of beetles. The stigma ripens first and pollen is shed by the stamens of the same flower. In this phase the petals arch over the stigma and form a sun-warmed hideaway with plenty of nectar on exposed juicy glands exactly suited to the beetles (*Cetoniae*). The second phase begins when the anthers of the same flower ripen and immediately afterward the petals open and quickly fall off. With the whole house collapsing about them, the panic-stricken beetles make off to another flower which is in the condition of stage one, but not without carrying along a fresh load of pollen on their backs from the preceding flower. The coordination of ripe stigma enclosed with beetles, followed later by ripening pollen, falling petals and the beetles changing flowers produces cross-pollination to perfection.

The speedwell (*Veronica officinalis*) has a diminutive mechanism delicately balanced, attuned to the visit of the little hover fly. The stigma ripens at the same time that the anthers open and release their sticky pollen. Self-pollination is prevented at this stage by the wide divergence of the two stamens—they project out to the right and left, while the stigma projects forward and downward. Nectar gleams at the base of the pistil where dark streaks on the petals converge. The hover fly charges in. The stigma which projects forward is bent down at exactly the right angle to tickle his stomach just before he settles in. In that fraction of a second the stigma receives its pollen transferred from another flower via the fly's stomach. The only foothold available to the hover fly as he reaches for the nectar is offered by the stems of the projecting stamens. He seizes these stamens and tips forward to thrust his proboscis into the nectar well, almost standing on his head. By this action he draws the stamens together. As they are exactly the right length, their anthers brush his stomach and deposit a fresh load of pollen. In this case flexibility of the stamens must be nicely adjusted so that they will bend inward under the grasp of the hover fly just the right amount to contact his body in the precise spot where the stigma of the next flower will touch. Since the stigma is smaller than a pinhead this is a delicate adjustment.

The stamens of barberry (*Berberis vulgaris*) also project outward at wide angles, protecting against self-pollination. When an insect, either a beetle, bee or fly, treads on the base of the barberry stamens or strikes them with a proboscis, they swing inward like miniature steam shovels bearing a load of pollen at their tips to dump on the insect. This movement of the stamens is not simply a physical pull or push as in the speedwell. The stamens have their own automatic movement that starts at the slightest touch. The touch causes a sudden shifting of water within certain cells so that they curve like a bow and develop spring tension that pulls the stamens toward the insect.

An entirely different sort of stamen performance can be seen in June when the beautiful mountain laurel billows on the hillsides. These flowers, shaped like five-sided bowls, have ten stamens (two to each facet) bent outward and downward with their anther tips caught in little pockets or notches in the petals. If left undisturbed in that position there is no chance of the pollen getting on the pistil which projects well up from the middle of the flower. A bee whizzing in to the nectar concealed in the center of the bowl collides with the projecting stigma and deposits pollen from another flower. Then he bumps against the stamens that radiate across his path, dislodging the anthers from their pockets. The anthers spring up, whip across the bee and fling pollen against his body with the violence of small catapults. This device is nicely calculated to let fly under the weight and speed of a bee. The explosion of the stamens is supposed to

The Bee and the Mountain Laurel

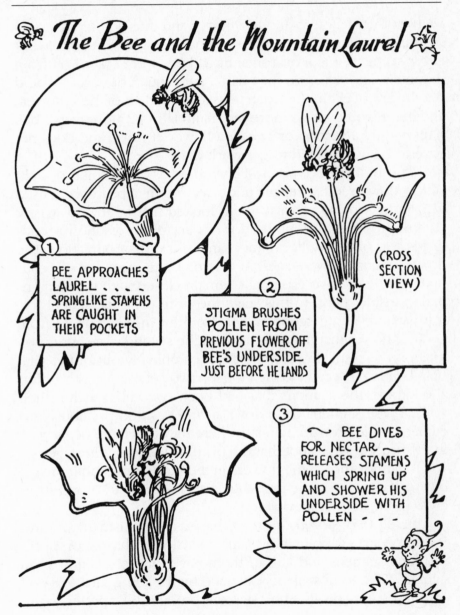

1. BEE APPROACHES LAUREL . . . . SPRINGLIKE STAMENS ARE CAUGHT IN THEIR POCKETS

2. STIGMA BRUSHES POLLEN FROM PREVIOUS FLOWER OFF BEE'S UNDERSIDE JUST BEFORE HE LANDS

(CROSS SECTION VIEW)

3. ~ BEE DIVES FOR NECTAR ~ RELEASES STAMENS WHICH SPRING UP AND SHOWER HIS UNDERSIDE WITH POLLEN - - - -

frighten the bee off to another flower and thus accelerate cross-pollination. This theory of flowers goading their visitors to work faster seems to me a bit romantic. If bees were scared off from mountain laurel before they had a good quaff of nectar, would not the law of evolution teach bees to steer clear of these flowers and there would be no more mountain laurels? Moreover, a bee lingers only a second or two in a flower at most, and does not have to be accelerated to get work done.

The mullein (*Verbascum thapsus*) has a tall spike of light yellow flowers, often ragged and scattered in appearance. I used to wonder why so many of them looked half open and wilted, with the top petals flopping down. Careful observation reveals that is part of the mullein's mechanics for cross-pollination. The flower opens in two stages. At first only the three lower petals open, while the two top petals remain closed with the stamens sealed inside them. In this stage the pistil projects straight forward where it can scoop pollen from an insect arriving from another flower that happens to be in the second stage. After pollination the pistil drops so that it is completely out of the path of in-coming insects, and then the top two petals promptly unfurl and expose the stamens that had been concealed within their folds. These stamens drop down to the position previously occupied by the protruding pistil where they touch the bee's body in the precise same spot that the pistil of a blossom in stage one will touch it. Since some flowers in the same spike and in neighboring spikes are in the first stage and some in the second stage, cross-pollination is inevitable.

Bluets (*Houstonia caerulea*) have a mechanism that insures 100 percent cross-pollination. Half of the flowers have short pistils and long stamens and half of them have long pistils and short stamens. The long stamens produce big pollen grains that will act only on long pistils. Short stamens produce little pollen grains that will act only on short pistils. The bluet appears to have wide open little flowers with sky blue petals and a bright yellow nectar guide that forms a little circle at the base of the petals. Its outward appearance is only the attraction mechanism. Below the yellow

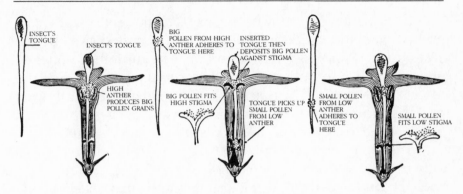

CROSS-POLLINATION OF BLUET. Note that bluets sometimes have high anther and low stigma and sometimes vice versa. This deliberately promotes cross-pollination.

circle the petals are welded together into a long narrow tube enclosing the stamens and pistils, with nectar at the very bottom. As the bee thrusts his proboscis in and out of these tubes it fits so snugly that it comes in contact with the anthers and stigmas unerringly. Going from flower to flower the bee gets small pollen grains sticking to his proboscis near its tip end at exactly the point which the stigma of the short pistil will touch in another flower. And large pollen grains will cling to his proboscis near its base, where they will be brushed off by the long stigma. In case a small pollen grain gets on a long stigma or vice versa nothing happens.

Flowers with mechanisms as foolproof as the bluets are just as efficient for crossing as those trees which produce staminate flowers on one tree and pistillate flowers on another. This bluet mechanism is called "dimorphic," meaning two-formed. The partridge berry (*Mitchella repens*) has the same device. So have some species of primrose and flax. Swamp loosestrife (*Lythrum salicaria*), pickerel weed (*Pontederia*) and wood sorrel (*Oxalis*) have carried the same device a step further. These last three flowers use three different lengths of stamen—short, medium and long—producing small, medium-sized and large pollen grains acting only on short, medium and long stigmas respectively.

In some kinds of flower mechanisms the entire anther or pollen mass, instead of just a few grains, is pulled away by the visiting insect and goes riding on him. The turtle head offers a fine example. This pollen mass adheres to the exact spot on the insect's body that will be touched by the stigmas of other flowers of the same kind. It is as though the insect catches up a torch of life and carries it off to touch one flower after another.

The ladies'-tresses (*Spiranthes*), for example, has its pollen held by a sort of forceps. The handle of the forceps is very sharp and it points out of the flower like a bayonet so that it sticks gently but firmly into a bee's forehead. As she comes away from the flower the forceps go riding off with their pollen held out toward the next stigma. The amazing thing is that until the pollen forceps have been removed the pistil of the same flower is bent down out of the way. As soon as the pollen is carried off the remainder of the stamen turns up out of the way, while the pistil bends up and places its stigma in the exact spot that had been occupied by the anther forceps. As the bee's head bearing the forceps pushes into a flower that has thus swapped the positions of stamens and pistil, cross-pollination is assured.

Bee balm and wild bergamot (*Monarda didyma* and *fistulosa*) have two stamens with their pollen chambers joined together so that they resemble a wishbone. The two stalks (filaments) of this wishbone partially bar the entrance to the flower tubes where nectar is deeply hidden. Only long proboscis bumblebees and butterflies can tap this nectar. To get far enough in, the insect has to force his head between the wishbone. As he pulls away, the stamens are torn out and go riding off, clasping the bumblebee's or butterfly's neck like a little yoke. The beauty of this mechanism is that the pulling away of the stamens releases the pistil, which has been held way up in the roof of the flower. The stigma immediately ripens, becomes sticky to receive pollen and falls down into position to be touched by the anthers which are riding around on other bees or butterflies.

Two of our common native orchids, including the showy and fringed orchis (*Orchis spectabilis* and *Habenaria fimbriata*), are built to receive the impact of bumblebees which ram their heads deep into the flower tubes. Their foreheads strike against two sticky discs which are attached to the butt ends of club-shaped masses of pollen. These clubs of pollen are held in a vertical position under the top petal. That gets the pollen out of the way of contact with its own stigma which is down in the bottom of the flower. After a good sip of nectar the bee jerks back his head and quits the flower. As he zooms off the adhesive discs are sticking to his forehead and their pollen clubs stand up like horns. It's a comical sight. If he entered the next orchis wearing these horns erect, they would get jammed and could not touch the stigma. An astonishing thing happens. A second or two after they are detached the bases of these pollen clubs wilt so as to let them fall forward at right angles. In this position the pollen is aimed straight at the next stigma so as to produce cross-pollination.

The fantastic milkweeds (*Asclepias*) also have club-shaped pollen masses ready to affix to their carriers. Among our common native flowers, the milkweeds (all species are alike in this respect) take first prize for their fancy and complicated mechanism for cross-pollination. Each flower suggests in outline a tiny, beautifully wrought, five-lobed cuspidor. It dangles at the end of a loose stem with twenty or more of these florets, many of them face down in a round cluster. This tumbled condition offers insects no landing stage as most flowers with protruding horizontal petals do. In addition to their more or less upside down position the flowers are a maze of deep pitfalls and complicated recesses. But the diameter of a milkweed flower (about ⅜ inch) is just right for a bee or butterfly to straddle. By hugging the floret insects dangle unconcerned as to whether or not they are upside-down while they explore the depths for nectar which is very abundant in deep curving horns. This position requires quite a struggle to hold on, and the success of the plan depends on a vigorous struggle. While the insect is trying to find a good hold-fast, one of his legs is apt to plunge into the recesses of the flower where it is caught. To pull it out requires such effort that the stamen inside the flower is violently torn away. This is all according to plan. For the stamen consists of a couple of pollen masses that look like tiny chicken croquettes connected by a bow-shaped spring. As it comes away the spring snaps shut on the leg of the insect and away goes the pollen attached to his leg to be thrust into another floret by the struggle of the insect. Perhaps a small number of the florets in a single great ball succeed in getting pollinated in this unique manner. But the great amount of pollen inserted by each croquette when it does reach home can ripen hundreds of seeds in a single pod. When you see the long banana-shaped pods split open in the early fall, and peel off layer after layer of parachute-equipped seeds, you will agree that this complicated mechanism that deposits a pollen *mass*, instead of individual grains, works.

Because of its large size the great blue lobelia offers one of the most vivid demonstrations of floral mechanism to be seen without a lens. If you want a demonstration of the way bees fit exactly into certain flowers, and how petals open and close, and stamens bend in a well coordinated mechanism set in motion by the bee's visit, go find a patch of great blue lobelias. You won't have to wait five minutes. The performance is in full swing wherever these flowers are blooming in late August and early September, and bumblebees are busy on the big blue lobelias. As the bee pushes in head first, the whole flower stiffens and widens; the top two petals fly apart; between them a long curving arm nods up and down like a bee's back-scratcher. Usually this works with a double motion, as the bee makes two lunges into the nectar well. Then out he comes and off he goes for another flower, while this flower resumes its normal position as though nothing had happened.

This lobelia back-scratcher, which projects through the split in the top petals, is a cylinder made by the stamens fused together to form the tube. The tip end curves down so as to contact the bee's back at exactly the same spot for every great blue lobelia. From this tip end pollen grains are forced out by the action of a piston inside the cylinder. The pollen, instead of being discharged on the outside of the anthers, is discharged *inside* the tube. After the pollen is collected inside the cylinder the pistil starts pushing up firmly through the tube. There is no chance of self-pollination because in this stage the stigma is not mature and receptive. It is simply a piston head that pushes out pollen. While this is going on, bees are visiting the flower and the pollen is deposited on their backs. Every time pollen is taken away more is pushed out so that each successive visitor gets a fresh charge on his back. At length, when all the pollen is pushed out and taken away or fallen off, the stigma emerges from the end of the cylinder and suddenly unfurls two fine sticky branches ready to receive pollen from another flower. There is nothing hit or miss in this plan because the stigma of a flower in this second stage is in exactly the same spot formerly occupied by the pollen, so that it touches the bee's back exactly where it will pick up the pollen deposited there from a previously visited flower. Cross-pollination is insured because in any locality where bees are working on lobelias, some flowers are in the first stage, delivering pollen, while others are in the second stage with stigmas unfurled.

The mighty Composite Family (see Chapter 18) also uses the piston and cylinder method for cross-pollination. The greatness of this family—see them sweeping across fields, daisies and dandelions, thistles and Joe Pye weed, black-eyed Susans, goldenrods and asters—is evidence that their mechanism is highly efficient for getting pollen distributed without inbreeding.

Some of the composites have strap-shaped florets, as in the hawkweeds, dandelions and chicory. Others have tiny little tubular-shaped flowers as in the center flowers of daisies and asters, or the pincushions of thistles. But all are alike at heart. Even the strap-shaped florets fold in at their bases to form little tubes. Stamens in these tubes are fused into a cylinder and discharge their pollen inside this cylinder so that the pollen can be pushed out by the pistil acting as a piston. The stigma is dry and not sensitive until all the pollen of its flower is pushed out—when it suddenly blossoms into a beautiful forked stigma with long curving prongs, sticky and ready to receive imported pollen. These silently operating little cylinders are held in a vertical position so that the pollen pushed out at the top adheres to the insect's stomach as he crawls across the top. This is in contrast to pollen adhering to his back as it does in the lobelias, mints, and many other flowers.

A close observer of flower structures might assue that the bittersweet nightshade (*Solanum dulcamara*) has a cylinder and piston. But the operation of this flower is unique. The stamens are fused into a central column and discharge pollen inwardly. It reverses the process just described. The pistil grows out through the tip first, while the pollen is not yet ripe. The stigma projects well out in front to receive pollen from an incoming insect an instant before he alights. Later, after its own pistil is pollinated, the pollen matures inside the cylinder of fused anthers. The insect is attracted by the conspicuous bright yellow color of the whole cylinder (a sort of super nectar guide). As the insect treads on it or hugs it this device operates like a little bellows. Pollen, which has now become dry as dust, puffs out from a pore at the peak of the bellows and is caught among the hairs on the outside of the insect's stomach, where it can go flying off to the next flower.

The iris has a wonderful system all its own. To understand this curious flower requires some modification of ideas as to what pistils and petals look like. In the center three petals stand up vertically. (In horticultural varieties these are often fancy and billowy.) The three big broad petals that flare out and droop (the origin of the name "flag" for this flower) are actually sepals. These generous blue sepals of the native iris offer fine landing fields, marked with bright white and yellow guides. Apparently there are no stamens and pistils. But as the bumblebee scrambles across his landing field, heading toward the heart of the flower where deep wells of nectar await the tip of her long proboscis, she must push under a short overlapping lip that is also blue, and resembles an extra petal. The outer edge of this lip catches on the back of the bee. As she goes forward it curls under and scrapes her back. Although this lip is shaped like a petal it is

The Bee and the Iris

① ATTRACTED BY BRIGHT COLOR BEE APPROACHES IRIS WITH POLLEN ON HIS BACK FROM IRIS JUST VISITED. HE SEES LINES LEADING TO THE NECTAR WELL

② ANTHER   STIGMA   NECTAR WELL
STIGMA IS <u>ON TOP</u> OF LITTLE PETAL THAT ROLLS UNDER AS BEE CRAWLS BENEATH AND SCRAPES OFF POLLEN FROM HIS BACK.

③ ANTHER   STIGMA   NECTAR WELL
AFTER BEE PASSES, STIGMA FLAPS BACK TO ORIGINAL POSITION, WHILE HE SUCKS NECTAR. HIS BACK PICKS UP A FRESH LOAD OF POLLEN.

④ NECTAR WELL
AS BEE BACKS OUT LITTLE PETAL UNROLLS SO STIGMA ON TOP CANNOT TOUCH HIM, THUS PROTECTED FROM ITS OWN POLLEN ～

actually a branch of the pistil. But near its outer lip on the *upper* side, there is a little patch of stickiness. This patch, strangely enough, is the stigma. In order to pick up the pollen on the bee's back it must curl under with the incoming bee. The sticky patch laps up the pollen on her back and the flower is pollinated. But the operation is not complete. The nectar is very deep, and the bee keeps on going. She passes under the anther which is hidden further back under the same petal-like pistil. There she gets a load of pollen. After a couple of lunges at the nectar she backs out. Now the device which had curled under as the bee entered uncurls. So, by this action the stigma which is on its *upper* side is safely removed where it cannot be touched by the pollen of its own flower as the bee backs out. The device has casual simplicity, yet it works perfectly. After pollination the tip of this petal-like stigma remains turned up; it will not curl under for each visitor.

The lady's-slipper (*Cypripedium acaule*) has a unique plan. Its gorgeous bulbous sac has no apparent entrance, no petals to crawl between or under, no stamens and pistil to explore. But the bee's instinct tells her otherwise. On the front of this sac she sees a network of white veins that converge on a vertical slit. The bee and her ancestors for countless years have recognized nectar guides. And those white converging lines on the luscious pink sac are her signal. She strikes unerringly at the slit. Butting with her head and clawing with her feet, she opens it a crack. Her furry oval body is powerful, energetic. She can push into tight places. So in she goes and the slit closes behind her. The bee finds herself in a chamber filled with a soft pink glow from translucent walls. Juicy hairs are scattered around the floor, offering a foothold to a bee's liking. Some of these hairs have little drops of nectar at their bases. Even under these inviting conditions the bee's instinct is to take a few swallows of nectar and be off. But this is not so easy and does not serve the plan of the lady's-slipper. The edges of the sac where the bee entered are inrolled and they closed behind her. The inner surfaces are slippery. She can't push her way out the way she entered. So

The Bee and the Ladyslipper

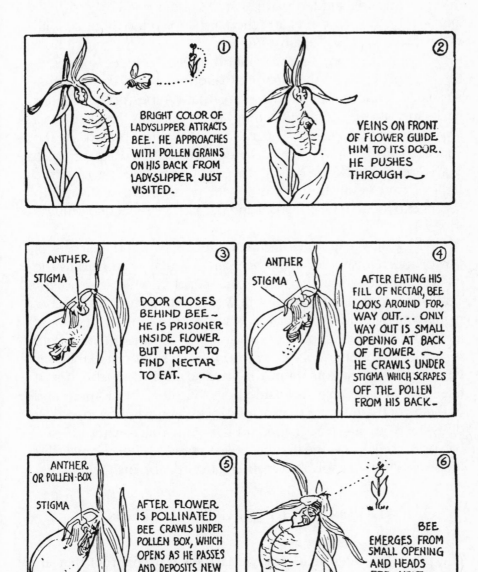

① BRIGHT COLOR OF LADYSLIPPER ATTRACTS BEE. HE APPROACHES WITH POLLEN GRAINS ON HIS BACK FROM LADYSLIPPER JUST VISITED.

② VEINS ON FRONT OF FLOWER GUIDE HIM TO ITS DOOR. HE PUSHES THROUGH —

③ ANTHER
STIGMA
DOOR CLOSES BEHIND BEE — HE IS PRISONER INSIDE. FLOWER BUT HAPPY TO FIND NECTAR TO EAT. —

④ ANTHER
STIGMA
AFTER EATING HIS FILL OF NECTAR, BEE LOOKS AROUND FOR WAY OUT... ONLY WAY OUT IS SMALL OPENING AT BACK OF FLOWER — HE CRAWLS UNDER STIGMA WHICH SCRAPES OFF THE POLLEN FROM HIS BACK —

⑤ ANTHER OR POLLEN-BOX
STIGMA
AFTER FLOWER IS POLLINATED BEE CRAWLS UNDER POLLEN BOX, WHICH OPENS AS HE PASSES AND DEPOSITS NEW LOAD OF POLLEN ON HIS BACK FOR NEXT FLOWER —

⑥ BEE EMERGES FROM SMALL OPENING AND HEADS FOR NEXT LADYSLIPPER.

the bee sets up a great buzzing and commotion inside the lady's-slipper. Bees are thrown into a panic when molested. After a time the buzzing suddenly stops. At the upper end of the slipper a little furry nose appears and then a sheepish looking bee with wings pressed tightly against her body squeezes through a hole that is barely large enough to let her through. To squeeze through this tunnel which is the only exit offered to her, the bee first has to pass under an arching stigma that scrapes pollen off her back. Just above this stigma her way is partially blocked by a swollen mass of pollen. She cannot avoid this pollen so she squeezes under it. This contact deposits a fine load of fresh pollen on her back just before the prisoner escapes into the free light of day. Away she goes and with no sign of fear from her recent experience she seeks out another lady's-slipper and plunges in again.

These few examples point to the variety and marvels of flower mechanisms for cross-breeding. You are referred to the woods and fields for the rest of this chapter, which is endless. You will find that each kind of flower has its own original blueprints and schedules for doing what "all the king's horses and all the king's men" couldn't do. Namely, when the life of a plant is broken asunder and its chromosomes are scattered to the four winds, the flower puts them together again. It does this not of itself but by bringing in outside help. At the right moment and in the right manner the flower interlocks with wind or insects. It does this with such precision and so swiftly that—with the ease of a prestidigitator—the flower "goes to seed." Without any effort it solves almost unsolvable mathematical problems.

ADDENDUM to CHAPTER FIFTEEN

The point has been made in the last several chapters that an intimate relation has evolved between flowers and the pollinators that visit them. An examination of the pollen of these flowers would show that the individual pollen grains are too heavy or too sticky, as well as too limited in amount, to be suited to wind pollination; hence the need for a carrier. The basis of the flower-insect (or bird) interaction may be color or odor, but the end result of this evolved collaboration is a mutual exchange of benefits: for the pollen and nectar received by the pollinator, the plant is enabled to complete its reproductive cycle, largely through cross-pollination.

The question that can legitimately be raised is: Why the necessity of sexual reproduction? That is, why the union of nuclei from a pollen grain with the egg cell in an ovule to bring about the formation of a seed? Is there not some simpler way to accomplish this same end? The answer is yes, but it is an answer in need of considerable qualification; a look into the processes of evolution indicates that while evolution can experiment only with what it has—not with what it wants because it lacks foresight—it usually comes up with solutions to the problems that it encounters that are satisfactory without being too fancy.

Sexual reproduction can be achieved by either self- or cross-pollination, with the latter process having the advantage that from the union of gametes that are genetically dissimilar, offspring are produced that have varying potentials for survival and continued reproduction, with the further probability that those most capable of persisting will carry the species on into future generations. But a large number of species have abandoned, partially or completely, sexual for asexual reproduction. Knowing what we do about evolution, such a change must have taken place because of an advantage gained. This is borne out by the fact that many asexual forms—the common dandelion, introduced from Europe, is one of these—are highly successful competitors.

Asexual reproduction, or *apomixis* to use the botanical term, takes place by a variety of means, and most apomictic species usually are capable of some, if limited, sexual reproduction. In a sense, and without the absolute necessity of mixing of male and female gametes, apomitic species have the best of both kinds of reproduction; through asexual reproduction a highly successful variation can be preserved indefinitely since the offspring, by one means or another, arise from maternal tissue, while the retention of some degree of sexual reproduction continues the formation of individuals exhibiting varied genetic constitutions, the best of which can then be preserved apomictically. This is making the most of a variety of reproductive techniques.

Apomixis embraces a gamut of asexual processes. Several wild species of onion have their flowering heads converted into a cluster of tiny bulblets, and as these fall and take root, new plants of the same genetic constitution are formed. These onions are highly successful in the temperature zone, as anyone knows who has tried to keep a lawn free of them. When occuring in grazing pasture, they are the bane of the farmer, for if eaten by cattle they tend to taint the milk with their oniony taste. Several species of grass—some of the fescues, for example—reproduce in similar fashion.

Many, however, produce seeds, with the embryo arising from some maternal cell in the ovule. Many citrus species behave in this manner, as well as some species of euphorbias, prickly pear (*Opuntia*), August lilies (*Hosta*), onion (*Allium*), cinquefoil (*Potentilla*), blackberries (*Rubus*), apple (*Malus*), hawkweed and Indian paint brush (*Hieracium*), pussy-toes (*Antennaria*), fleabane (*Erigeron*) and Kentucky bluegrass (*Poa pratensis*). Apomixis has a genetic basis similar to that governing self-incompatibility, but it is also quite evident that a great many of the apomicts are hybrids between two related species, and like the hybrid mule, are often sexually sterile. If they are to survive beyond their immediate generation, their sexual sterility can only be compensated for by resorting to some other means of reproduction. Why hybridity brings these different forms of reproduction into being is not fully understood, but it is clearly another example of the flexibility of individuals in coping with life itself, and extending it to future generations.

—C.P.S.

Flower Forms—The Products of Nature's Assembly Line

If wild flowers appear to you as haphazard as a font of pied type, maybe you're missing a point. The conventional way to learn their names is to take a flower guide with pictures and pick them out one at a time. This gives pleasure to enthusiasts but it's probably the chief reason why nine people out of ten don't know many flowers. It's too dull learning them by rote. Flowers not only make more sense than that but also as groups they fit into a pattern of life in a marvelous way. To realize this is to enjoy a fresh point of view—and, I submit, that practical people for whom isolated flower names may hold little lure will find their curiosity and sense of wonder aroused by discovering that all flowers fall into natural groups along their lines of development.

Consider similarities instead of differences! Consider how the buttercup is like the columbine, the apple blossom like the wild strawberry, the similarity of a wake Robin and a lily, of an

Indian pipe and a wintergreen, a Queen Anne's lace and a water hemlock, a black-eyed Susan and a goldenrod, a skunk cabbage and a Jack-in-the-pulpit. How did they get that way? Where does a magnolia stand in the scale as compared with a lady's-slipper?

Do you know what a million years look like? If you come with me across the field, through the woods, and along the brook, we shall see what it looks like. For plants are metaphors of time. The history of the ages is expressed in them. This history of life on this planet is not written in the English language, nor in Latin, but in a sort of picture language. Pictures offer a clear and simple medium of expression. But primitive man was a novice at it. Ages before primitive man began to write by drawing pictures, time was drawing diagrams in the organisms of the plants that tell the story of its forward march. Many of the original diagrams have never been erased. They are recorded in the indelible ink of chromosomes. The story is surprisingly complete from the beginning to the present day. But eloquent as this story is, it was not read even by expert observers until the middle of the nineteenth century. Today many people, even those who specially enjoy trees and flowers and who call them by name, have not the remotest notion about the thrilling history of life that is written in the diagrams of flower forms.

The early botanists observed as keenly as they could without the help of the modern microscope. They had lenses of a kind. In 1664 an English scientist, Robert Hooke, published a book about the structure of cork which he studied through a simple microscope. He used the phrase "little boxes or cells" which is the first reference to the cell as the basic unit in the body of all plants and animals. But it doesn't take a microscope to see structures like stamens and pistils. So the early botanists noted these similarities of flowers and made catalogues out of them. In the light of present-day classifications these early groups appear artificial and static.

Linnaeus (1707–1778) is sometimes called the "father of modern botany" because he invented the method of naming plants with two Latin names, the first for *genus*, the second for *species*. We shall see presently what *genus* and *species* mean. But Latin was the language of science long before Linnaeus. It still enables people in South Africa, or China, or the U.S.A. to talk about the same plant. The Linnaean method of using only two names was a stroke of genius that streamlines plant terminology. His second great invention, proposed in *Systema Naturae*, published in 1735, was a classification of plants according to their stamen counts and the arrangement of pistils. This gave sixty-seven classes. Linnaeus' arrangement is obsolete and all but forgotten—yet it may have been a more important bequest to mankind than his binomial system for plant names. It prepared the way for Darwin. Linnaeus' classifications according to numbers of stamens and positions of pistils contained the elements of natural relationships. But Linnaeus still regarded these features as fixtures. He just missed making the Great Discovery. His successors looked at the sixty-seven groups of flowering plants based on stamens and pistils and the truth began to dawn. Here were facts to conjure with. Why was this true? Were the different kinds of flowers, after all, not separate creations like cakes in a pastry shop? The search for the answer led straight to Darwin.

In his *Origin of Species* (1859) Darwin asserted that different kinds of plants are all evolved from a common ancestor or ancestors. Those that have similarities are more closely related than those that haven't. He asserted that the degree of difference in plants is in proportion to the distance they have travelled down the corridors of time from their common ancestors.

In the ninety years since Darwin, much criticism has been directed at his Theory of Evolution, especially from people who prefer the theory that the Lord created everything all at once. But no scientific evidence has turned up to contradict Darwin. On the contrary, much new evidence supports evolution. Every item in the vegetable kingdom fits into it beautifully. Today, evolution as the explanation for the natural groups of plants is no longer a theory. It is the Great Discovery! It is time for everybody who takes a look around outdoors to appreciate it.

Why do so few people know flower families when they see

them? For one thing, the subject is obscured by scientific jargon. *Ontogeny ingeminates phylogeny*! Before your retreat becomes a rout, I hasten to translate. This is the scientists' way of saying that the life history of an individual plant (the seed-shoot-leaf-flower-seed cycle) repeats the age-long cycle of the *family* of that plant. Everybody can see that an individual plant is dynamic, that it passes through changes of form. The embryo in the seed sprouts, the plant body matures and this is followed by a miraculous form called flowers. Finally the individual goes to seed and the cycle starts all over again. But it took Darwin to prove that the *entire vegetable kingdom* is similarly dynamic.

It is as though eternity had fired off a huge skyrocket—one of those that branch and rebranch as they spread across the sky—which we call the vegetable kingdom. Starting from a single source, the dynamic elements shoot upward through time, branching off this way and that according to the circumstances and obstacles met and overcome. Some of these branches die out, some are short, some are long, some appear to be suspended in mid-air and cut off from their origins, others preserve a long unbroken trail. The pattern is not that of a single line of ascent, it is that of a multitude of many diverging lines.

The Composite Family (see Chapter 18) has elements from at least three distinct sources. The Mint Family stands at the summit of a branch that can be traced back in clear steps through the Figwort, Nightshade, Borage, Phlox, Pink, Saxifrage, to the Buttercup Family! We do not have to know or recognize all these relationships between families. We can leave that to a few specialists. It is enough to know that relationships exist. Family is developed out of family. Flower types are formed from preceding flower types. The radial symmetry of a buttercup has been altered, step by step, through certain families until it ends in the irregularity and fancy specialization of a mint. This gives us a hint as to why some families are more primitive than others. The radial flowers like buttercups and roses are older in the scale of evolution than the irregular and specialized forms like the mints, orchids, peas and figworts.

This demonstrates the plasticity of the vegetable kingdom. The key to evolution is in the flower, because floral designs are more stable than the other parts of a plant. Their changes are gradual over countless years, in accordance with evolution. Roots, stalks and leaves, on the other hand, are more volatile and vary their characters according to local climate and soil conditions, as you can readily see. But the *flower* of a stunted and forlorn little specimen of tree or herb will have the same characteristics as the flower of the same kind of plant in luxurious condition.

The lower plants (algae, liverworts, mosses, ferns, horsetails, club mosses, and fungi) do not have flowers. It may stretch evolution, but certainly not to the breaking point, to claim that the seed-producing or flowering plants were evolved from these spore plants. But that is what is believed to have happened. When flowers that produce seeds finally were achieved, the vegetable kingdom possessed a means for creating fluid symphonies of design similar to the octave of the musical world. Every symphony, jazz number, song, and dance tune is blended out of eight notes and their fractions. All flower forms are created out of four basic components: sepals, petals, stamens and pistils. Other elements like color, fragrance, nectary glands and shape of receptacle (point of attachment of a flower to its stem) are fugitive elements that may be played upon or omitted like the fractional notes of music.

The four basic components (sepals, petals, stamens and pistils) are remolded and changed by evolution in four ways. First, changes of *number*. One or more of the four flower parts may be reduced in number. In fact, sepals and petals may be omitted entirely in their progress up the scale. As the old expression goes, "the higher, the fewer." Second, changes in *relation*. This results in the union of parts. It begins with pistils which become fused together as the flower progresses. Further along on the paths of time its new forms tend to fuse parts more and more, until petals and sepals are merged. Third, changes in *position*. In the more primitive flowers, sepals, petals and stamens are usually attached at the bottom of the pistil—in other words,

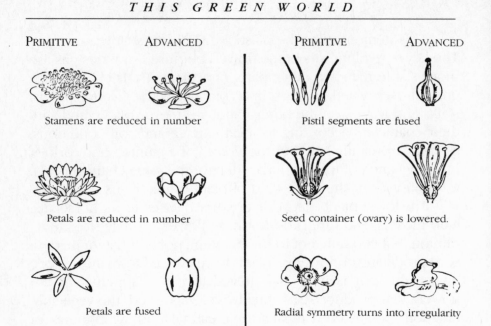

PRIMITIVE ADVANCED PRIMITIVE ADVANCED

Stamens are reduced in number

Pistil segments are fused

Petals are reduced in number

Seed container (ovary) is lowered.

Petals are fused

Radial symmetry turns into irregularity

Mechanical changes in the progress of flower forms

the pistil including its bulbous base, the ovary, is high. It seems to sit on top of the other flower parts. As a flower form goes higher in the scale of evolution the pistil tends to drop lower ... in higher forms the ovary appears *below* the rest of the flower. Fourth, changes in *form*. An example of this is the change previously mentioned from radial symmetry like a sunburst to an irregular form as in a snapdragon. A broader change occurs when one family produces a single flower on a stem, such as a rose, and from that evolution may create a colony of flowers on one stem, such as a wild carrot, or Queen Anne's lace. A result like that becomes the basis of a new family.

These changes may sound a bit technical. It is far easier to see what is meant by a high pistil and a low pistil, for example, than to describe this phenomenon in words. And when you do see it and catch a vision of this drama of movement in flower forms, it's exciting. The point to keep in mind is that these changes are in the direction of greater efficiency in the production of seed.

To say that nature shot off a skyrocket is, of course, sheer hyperbole. The process is the slowest of slow motion movies. Although plant forms are still evolving and moving along their paths of development as rapidly as ever, it takes a cosmic imagination to see that they are moving at all. For practical purposes they *appear* to have arrived at a stopping point in this moment of eternity. Therefore, we can classify them with assurance that buttercups and roses and mints and orchids will be with us tomorrow. In the perspective of evolution, however, our classifications are invested with a meaning and drama lacking in a mere roll call of the flowers and trees. What are these groups based on natural relations?

The narrowest is *species*. Flowers of the same species are as closely related as parent and offspring. Species is the only relationship transmitted through a seed. The seed of a pink lady's-slipper always produces a pink lady's-slipper, never a yellow lady's-slipper. That of the Canada lily always produces a Canada lily, never a Turk's cap.

The next larger classification is that of *genus*. The pink and yellow lady's-slippers and all other lady's-slippers belong to the same genus. The same is true of all lilies, all goldenrods, all asters, or all oak trees. These groups are *genera*, plural for genus. Obviously the species which are members of the same genus are closely related. They are alike, but not alike. Then how did they become different?

Different species must have developed from a common ancestor before our time. This common ancestor bestowed vivid similarities on the species which evolved from itself. But while retaining these similarities they grew different in many ways— by gradually establishing slight changes and not by suddenly leaping the boundaries of a seed. Thus, species suggest the wonder of evolution, and reveal its workings even more than the more complete and thorough differences between genera.

Above species and genera comes a larger classification, *family*. These are spotlighted in the chapters that follow. Family is the most arresting and eloquent relationship of all. When you look at flowers related in families, you are looking through a telescope at the travels of plant life through the ages. A plant family is a group of related genera. Daisies, dandelions, asters, sunflowers are members of the same family. Buttercups, clematis, larkspur, columbine, marsh marigolds and anemones are members of the same family. So are lilies, trilliums, dogtooth violets, tulips. Every tree, vine, shrub and herb wears some family emblem. Often this gives them a family resemblance, but not always. The tall anemone looks like a buttercup except that its petals are white instead of yellow. Asters look like little daisies that come in a variety of colors. The trillium looks like a lily, now that you stop to think of it. On the other hand, a columbine does not look like a larkspur and neither of them looks like a buttercup. In this instance the family resemblance is imprinted in the number of petals and sepals and stamens and their forms, and in the character of the fruit.

Although the flower is most important as the keystone of the family, other features may reveal family characteristics. You can appraise them after seeing them repeatedly, and strike a balance sheet. Even leaves which are variable may be a family earmark. A characteristic of the Pea Family is the compound leaf. This is a leaf made of little segments like the clover leaf, or with segments arranged on each side of a midrib like a locust leaf. A characteristic of the Buttercup Family is a deeply segmented leaf. In this feature the columbine and the buttercup do resemble each other, while the marsh marigold is a remarkable exception. The Maple Family consists entirely of trees. But other families cross the boundaries of herb, shrub and tree forms. All features other than flower forms are collateral comparisons which may or may not be made between members of the same family. If they exist and are recognized they add to the ease of knowing the families.

To run down families when you have only one or two clues

has the makings of a fine detective game. One year in midwinter I found a cluster of little brown pods sticking up through the snow on a withered stalk. No trace of leaves or flower. Out of curiosity I showed this to a taxonomist (plant classifier) at the New York Botanical Garden and asked him whether he could name the plant. Even experts do not profess to identify plants instantly from dry fragments. But if a determining feature happens to be in the fragment the trick is easy. The taxonomist took a single pod about ¼ inch long. He noted how it split open, noted the remnant of pistil still attached to it, and was able to say that this type of pod (a follicle) is produced by the Buttercup Family. Then turning to herbarium sheets of the Buttercup Family, he quickly ran through dried specimens kept on file for reference until he came to black snakeroot (*Cimicifuga racemosa*). It had the same pods! Without herbarium sheets this tiny discarded fragment of a plant could probably not have been run down to its species. But in this instance it was possible to name at least the family from the remnant of its fruit when all other clues were missing.

Have you ever noticed that the veins in the leaves of grass, lilies, orchids, palms and quite a number of other plants pour across the leaves in parallel or radiating lines? They run from the base to the tips of the leaf without crossing. This is in contrast to plants with veins that branch and crisscross so as to make feathered or network patterns. If you carry this observation a step further you will find that the plants with parallel veins have flowers built in multiples of three: three petals, three sepals, six stamens, three pistils. The plants with feathered or network veins have flowers based on multiples of four or five. This is a safe generality although there are exceptions.

These two sets of characteristics reveal two great groups into which all flowering plants are divided. Those with net veins are about four times as numerous in number of species as those with parallel veins; but the latter contains some large and conspicuous families, such as the grasses and orchids.

This simple and conspicuous vertical division of all plants

into two great groups is one of the first ways to see the organization of the landscape. It has been obscured by long and mysterious names given to the two groups. The parallel veined group built on a plan of three is called the *monocotyledons*. The net veined group, with their flowers designed usually with four or five petals, is called the *dicotyledons*. There is no small English word to use in place of these two words, and since they are the labels for the two major categories of all flowering plants they are worth knowing. They can be translated as "one cotyledon" and "two cotyledons." What does that mean?

Every plant begins as a tiny embryo embedded in the seed. This embryo is a sort of pre-view of the herb, tree, or shrub to come. It is equipped, as we saw in an early chapter, with a more or less complete set of organs: root, stem, and leaf. In other words, the unorganized protoplasm in the first cells has divided and divided until various kinds of cells have formed the organs of a plant—all this while it is imprisoned in a minute seed. At this point the embryonic plant ceases to grow and goes to sleep inside its seed. When the time comes to burst the seed and begin to sprout, this plantlet is already equipped with a leaf. In fact, it had *one* or *two* leaves tucked away inside the seed. This leaf is just large enough to snare a bit of air and sunlight and make food for the plant until it can grow regular leaves. The name of this interesting embryonic leaf is *cotyledon*. The *di*cotyledons have two of these leaves. The *mono*cotyledons have one.

Botanists say that the dicotyledons came first in the scale of evolution and the monocotyledons branched off from primitive buttercups. But this is getting in deep. The point is interesting only to show how fundamental features once they get established run up through a stream of evolution without much change if they work well in facilitating the life cycle.

The parallel veins and criss-cross veins are outward and visible signs of two sets of blueprints used in laying out the plumbing systems of plants. A plumbing system consists of the pipelines and their associated valves and structures that bring water from the soil, up through the roots and stems to every leaf and tip of the plant, as well as the vessels which convey food manufactured in the leaves back through the plant down to the most remote root. In herbs and very young trees water travels in one direction, food in the reverse direction, in conveyors that are bunched together like the strands of a cable. When a stem is cut clearly across, the ends of these cables may be seen under a lens. If these cable ends, when cut in cross-section, make a circular pattern just inside the outer edge of the stem, the plant is a *dicotyledon*. If the cables are scattered through the stem, the plant is a *monocotyledon*.

Let your imagination roam over the face of the earth, from where the grasses and stunted heaths edge the polar ice fields, to the "steaming stillness of an orchid-scented glade" in an equatorial jungle, across continents, through rich valleys, lush forests, across prairies, and up mountain sides—everywhere, flowering plants. All of them have been organized and classified by the flow of time. Since man discovered this amazing fact he has recorded 200,000 species, and 300 families—divided into the two groups of dicotyledons and monocotyledons.

If there are only 300 families of flowering plants in the whole world how many families would be found in any one locality? An inventory made by Dr. Moldenke, a curator of the New York Botanical Garden, for a few square miles in northern New Jersey gives a total of around 100 families of plants in that area. Of these, about fifty include all the familiar wild flowers of the area. To find these fifty would require a year-round search by an expert observer. On any given day you and I would not see more than about twenty families in flower.

Nature did not deal out the species to be members of the genera, or the genera to be members of the families, as from a pack of cards. The number of members of each category varies enormously. The largest family, the Composites, has a thousand genera and some twenty thousand species; the smallest has but one genus and one species. The Ginkgo is an example of one species that constitutes its whole family. A family should not be evaluated by its size alone. From an economic standpoint the most important family of flowering plants is that of the Grasses, which gives man his cereals. From the standpoint of the wild-flower enthusiast the most important families, or at least those most interesting to recognize, are the families which are most colorful, most often seen, and usually have the loveliest flowers. If you know the features of only a score of families, you can place in its family almost every plant you commonly see. In the two following chapters some of these leading families are summarized.

ADDENDUM to CHAPTER SIXTEEN

The flower forms discussed in this chapter are not, as rightly indicated, a haphazard array of shapes. Rather, they, like all else in this universe, are the present "residues of change" of an on-going process of evolution, and among the diversities of form that plants exhibit, relationships, or natural affinities, are detectable. Among flowers the trends are clear: from many floral parts to few; from radially symmetrical flowers to those that are bilaterally arranged; from single flowers to clusters of various types; from simply branched inflorescences to umbels, corymbs to composite heads. On a subtler scale at the cellular and molecular level, the same thing is evident: in the pathways of reactions; in DNA, the basic source of hereditary information; and in the proteins, carbohydrates and lipids (fats) that are involved in the structure and behavior of cells, organs and individuals; in the water-conducting cells of wood which may be simple in structure and wall sculpturing to those that are highly complex and interlaced with several kinds of cells.

Trends are discernible in those parts of the plant which are readily visible. In Chapter 5, for example, the leaves go from the simple, smooth-edged form found among the poplars to the deeply incised ones characteristic of the oaks and maples, and from single leaves to compound ones made up of three of more leaflets. On a larger scale of plant form, the evolutionary trend has been from trees as the most primitive of forms among the flowering plants, to shrubs, to herbaceous perennials, and finally, to herbaceous annuals. In terms of floral primitiveness, the magnolias and the tulip poplar (*Liriodendron*) are among the most ancient of our northern trees: their wood is soft and consists of relatively uniform and simply constructed cells, their leaves are single and simple in shape although the tulip poplar is slightly sinuous and truncated at the tip, and their flowers have many petals, stamens and unattached capsules (fruits).

Ancestry and patterns of natural affinity are, therefore, not based on a single character, as was suggested by the stamen-based Linnean system, but rather embrace arrays of traits, thus bringing the science of comparative anatomy to bear on questions of origin and relationships. Similarly, our view of evolution and its modes of operation have undergone change, and we view the past with altered pairs of scientific spectacles. The Darwinian theory of evolution through natural selection, the most significant biological idea ever advanced since it bound all of biological thought into a common web of relations, viewed biological change as the result of many small alterations in the hereditary structure, accumulating over long periods of time. We now know that these small changes do occur in the DNA; we call them mutations. Undoubtedly such slowly moving change does occur under some circumstances, but it now seems that evolution is not always a slow and inexorable process, grinding out new species as one era of time succeeds another. Evolution can also be abrupt, but abrupt in geological, not human, terms. Great groups of organisms, for example, discernible most clearly among the fossil remains of animals of the past, have disappeared from the fossil record, and were replaced in the following geological ages by newly evolved arrays of related species. In addition, and related to these geologically sudden appearances and disappearances, evolution seems to have been a process during which periods of relatively little change were punctuated by singular bursts of new forms—the appearance of flowering plants and the coevolution of insects for pollination can be interpreted in this manner.

It is obvious, then, that there is still much to learn about the process and rates of evolution, but such a statement should in nowise be thought to cast doubt on the existence of evolution as the process that has provided this earth—and the universe as well—with the wealth of diversity and beauty that abounds. Evolution is a fact, and an indisputable one, even if we are still trying to understand the basis of all of its manifestations.

—C.P.S.

From Buttercups To Figworts

If, in prosperous days, you bought a new car, the old one soon became obsolete and ended up as scrap. Anybody who has to do with airplanes, radios, machinery of all kinds, knows obsolescence. But on nature's assembly line where startling new models and drastic innovations evolve, some with accessories never dreamed of by horsetails, the law of obsolescence does not necessarily retire obsolete models. In fact, there's no such thing as obsolete flower forms. Because flowers renew themselves every time they put a generation through a seed, the forms that survive the struggle for existence are fresh and young. You have ancestral types and later types—or primitive and modern types.

In almost any few square feet of field, woods or mountain side representatives from the bottom to the top of the scale are doing business side by side. This makes the progressive story of flower forms all the more vivid and interesting. You don't have to suppose, like an archaeologist; you don't have to conjure with fossils to see what the ancestors of a mint looked like. Just pick a buttercup—and there's the ancestor. Even back of the buttercup this living diagram continues through pine cones, horsetails, club mosses. The model T's are in operation along with the latest streamlined models. The countryside is an exposition, not a museum.

The milestones in this parade of time are plant families. You can have much enjoyment recognizing the leading families. It puts individual flowers into perspective, gives them relationship and meaning. If, in addition, you see the broader relation between families, the whole wonderful pattern of the landscape comes into focus. You stand on a mountain peak of time and see eternal order unfold before your eyes.

Keep this in mind when referring to the summaries of flower families that follow. The Buttercup Family is the oldest, and considered the basic family of flowering plants. Therefore, we shall examine them in ascending order from Buttercups to Orchids. In addition to the physical features by which a family may be recognized, you will find clues that help explain the position of the family in the scale, showing how these various forms have been modified by time in the four ways mentioned on page 189.

THE BUTTERCUP FAMILY is also called the Crowfoot Family because so many members have leaves with deeply cleft segments suggesting the toes of a crow's foot. The scientific name of the Buttercup Family is *Ranunculaceae*.* This word comes from *Ranunculus*, the genus of the family's most prominent member, the common field buttercup. It is Latin for "little frog." Because Pliny, the Roman botanical writer of antiquity, saw buttercups growing in damp places where frogs abounded, he named buttercups for the frogs.

The buttercups are famous as the ancestors of all other common wild flowers. A clear sign of antiquity is the fact that all

---

*Family names usually end in *-eae*. This is pronounced *ee-ee*.

buttercup flower parts are separate. Pistils, stamens, petals and sepals become welded together as flowers advance up the scale. Also buttercup pistils are arranged in a spiral on a cone-shaped structure suggestive of pine cones from which buttercups evolved. The Pine Family with its characteristic cones is a transitional stage from the lower spore bearing plants like horsetails and club mosses to our "modern" seed plants. Another primitive feature of buttercups is the indefinite number of stamens and pistils. As flowers advance these parts are reduced in number and become fixed at five or ten or whatever the count is for the species.

The Buttercup Family happens to be herbaceous so that fact can be considered a family feature. You never see buttercup relatives growing as trees or shrubs. Besides the various species

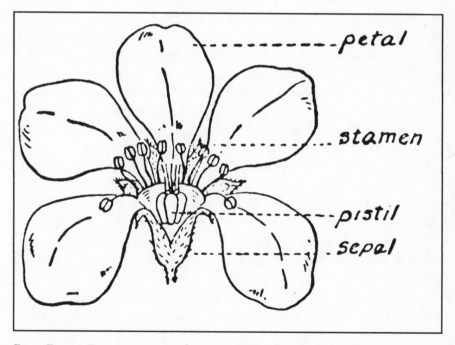

ROSE FAMILY DIAGRAM. 5 sepals, 5 petals, many stamens in multiples of 5. (In cultivated roses the stamen and petal counts are confusing because stamens are turned into petals by breeding.)

of buttercups, the family includes meadow rue, hepatica, anemone, clematis, marsh marigold, columbine, larkspur and baneberry. This is a handsome and distinguished group, vigorous
and fresh, even if they are the ancestors of all flowers.

Mechanical features of the Buttercup Family, easily seen,
are: five petals, five sepals, numerous and separate stamens and
pistils attached in a spiral arrangement on a conical receptacle
in the center of the flower.

THE ROSE FAMILY is called the *Rosaceae*. This name is derived
from one of its most familiar members, the genus *Rosa*, the wild
rose. The family is obviously primitive because, like the buttercups, the parts of the flower are all separate. But it is a step above
the Buttercup Family in the scale of evolution because of the
more or less definite number of stamens—five or multiples of
five. And the pistils do not sit high up on a cone-shaped structure,
but they are partially sunken into a cup-shaped receptacle. The
petals and stamens in a whorl are attached to the rim of this
cup. We have noted that one of the changes in the progress of
evolution is in the position of the parts of a flower. For example,
in a primitive flower the stamens, petals and sepals are attached
at the *bottom* of the pistil. This makes the whole pistil including
its bulbous base (the ovary) seem to sit up on top of the flower.
In advanced flowers this position is reversed. The stamens, petals
and sepals are attached at the top of the ovary which projects
below the rest of the flower. This may sound like a fine point, but
it is very interesting and easy to detect. Here in the Rose Family
we see the beginning of this process of lowering of the ovary
with the use of the cup-shaped receptacle. It is partly lowered
—a transitional stage.

The Rose Family may be called the fruit tree family since
most of our orchard fruits belong to it. These include apple,
cherry, quince, pear, peach. Other members are hawthorn, rose,
cinquefoil, strawberry, blackberry, raspberry, and the spiraeas.

Mechanical features are: five sepals, five petals, many stamens but in multiples of five. Thorns are frequent but not always

present. The compound leaf is also characteristic. This often consists of five leaflets as in the rose and cinquefoil, but the strawberry has three leaflets, and fruit trees have simple leaves. The type of fruit varies but the most famous fruit of the Rose Family is the *pome*. This is a delicious botanical word for a fat juicy fruit like an apple or pear; it is used also for rose and hawthorn hips, although they are not good to eat.

THE MUSTARD FAMILY has the scientific name *Cruciferae*. This appropriate label refers to the pattern of the petals which resembles a Maltese cross or crucifix. The Mustard Family is at the primitive end of flower progress, as shown by the separate stamens, petals and sepals, and the fact that these are attached at the bottom of the pistil so that the ovary rides high.

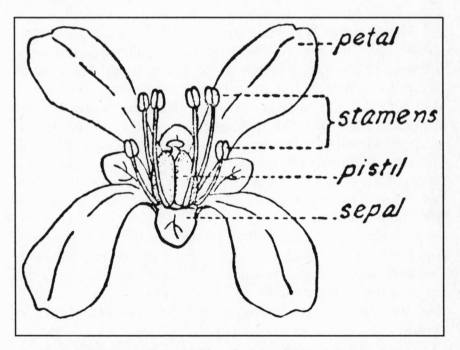

MUSTARD FAMILY DIAGRAM. 4 petals, broader at tips than at base suggesting a Maltese cross. 6 stamens, of which 4 are long and 2 are short.

On the other hand, the family shows progress in the reduced number of floral parts, and the fusion of the two pistils. The fruit of this family is unique and efficient for its purpose and therefore considered a sign of progress. The fused base of the pistil makes a double ovary that turns into a pod, like a bivalve, or clam. This is not necessarily shaped like a clam but is separated into two valves. When separated, each half of the pod is covered with a membrane that holds in the seeds until the pod has been knocked about a bit, insuring better distribution.

The mustards open their flowers progressively, beginning with the lower flowers on an individual plant. The pods form so swiftly that one plant usually has full grown pods below at the same time that its top flowers are in full bloom. Typical also is the acrid juice and strong flavor and odors of the mustards. They are never poisonous, in fact, this family gives us some of our finest vegetables.

We eat the leaves of mustards: cabbage and watercress. We eat the buds: Brussels sprouts; the flowers: cauliflower; the roots: radishes. This is also the leading condiment family: horseradish and mustard. Winter cress is one of the most prolific wild flowers, painting fields and banks of streams with creamy yellow in early spring. In June the wild radishes bring similar flowers to the fields. Black mustard lays a yellow carpet in August. Unless you know the differences in leaves and some fine points about the shape of the pods all these mustards look much alike. The shepherd's purse is a common weed with a unique pod that gives it the whimsical name.

Mechanical features of the Mustard Family are: four sepals, four petals, six stamens of which four are long and two are short. The two pistils are joined together so they look like one. The petals of the Mustard Family are usually yellow, but occasionally they are white or rose-colored as in the rock cress and cuckoo flower.

THE PEA FAMILY is also called the Pulse Family. A pulse is the esculent seed produced by the family. This was celebrated by

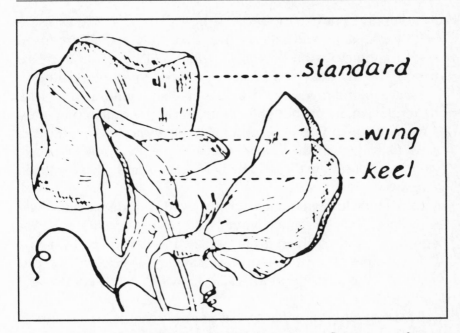

PEA FAMILY DIAGRAM. 5 petals, of which upper one flares up to form a standard, two petals flare out sidewise (wings), and the two lowest petals are fused to form a keel.

Milton in *Paradise Regained:* "With Elijah he partook, or as guest with Daniel at his pulse." No one who enjoys a steaming dish of fresh garden peas will doubt they are esculent. The scientific name of the family is *Leguminosae.* This is derived from the characteristic fruit of the family which is a pod called a legume (think of a string bean).

The Pea Family illustrates definite progress in evolution. You can see partial fusion of petals, sepals and stamens. Another progressive sign is that these parts are attached at the top of the ovary which appears below the rest of the flower. The irregular, flamboyant type of flower marks a radical change from the more primitive radial types of flowers. The sweet pea typifies the flowers of the family. Their flaring form is described as *papilionaceous,* from the Latin *papilio,* meaning butterfly. One big showy petal, called the standard, makes a roof for the flower. This is often turned up in front like the broad brim of a gay hat. The two side petals are separate and called wings. Two lower petals are fused except at their tips and are called the keel petals as they are formed like the keel of a boat. There are ten stamens, nine of which are joined together, making a tube surrounding the pistil. The tenth stamen, as though evolution had not quite completed its work at this point, is separate. All this indicates that the Pea Family is caught in the act of evolving and, in a cosmic sense, is in a state of flux with partially fused petals and partially fused stamens.

It's a little known but interesting fact that floral parts evolved from leaves. Pistils, stamens, petals, sepals are modified leaves. You can see this easily in green sepals. In the Pea Family a ripe pistil becomes the fruit or pod. Consider how clearly the two halves of a green pea pod look like leaves in color, texture and veining.

This up and doing family has another characteristic important to farmers and gardeners. For some unexplained reason the roots of the members of the Pea Family have an affinity for bacteria with the peculiar ability to collect free nitrogen from the soil and store up this nitrogen in their bodies. These are known as nitrogen fixing bacteria. They bunch together into bumps or nodules that you can see on the roots of legumes. Nitrogen, one of the chief constituents of protein, is a vital plant chemical. One of the best ways to enrich soil is to plow under crops of clover or soy beans or some herb of the Pea Family that has bacteria knobs on its roots. In this way you can put a good supply of nitrogen into the soil with the bodies of the bacteria contained in the knobs on the roots.

The Pea Family is second only to the Grass Family in its value for producing food. Peas, beans, peanuts are cultivated species. Everywhere in summer you see native or naturalized members: vetch, wild peas and beans, trefoil and clover. The last named may seem not to resemble the description of the flower given above; but if you examine a clover closely, you will discover that it is a compact head of tiny flowers, each of which has the standard-wings-keel form. This big family also includes trees. The most familiar are the black locust, honey locust, Judas or redbud, and the Kentucky coffee tree.

To summarize these characteristics of the Pea Family: five sepals, five petals, ten stamens, one pistil. The type of flower is called papilionaceous (like a butterfly). The fruit is a legume (green pea or bean pod). Frequently, but not always, a compound leaf, as, for example, the three leaflets of a clover, or the many little leaflets arranged in two rows along an axis as in a locust leaf.

THE CARROT FAMILY is also called the Parsley Family. Its scientific name is expressive: *Umbelliferae*. This means "bearing umbels." An umbel is a flat-topped or curved-topped circular

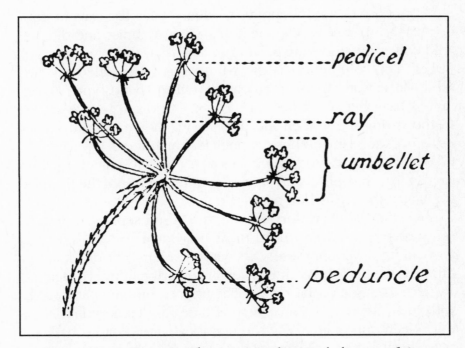

CARROT FAMILY DIAGRAM. Flat- or curved-topped clusters of tiny flowers constructed like an umbrella. The large umbrella is compounded out of small umbrellas.

2 0 7

cluster of little flowers on radiating spokes like an umbrella. When you examine the flower cluster of a single plant of the Carrot Family you find that it is put together like a compound umbrella. The spokes radiate from the same height on the stem, the outer spokes being longer, and then these in turn break into smaller spokes, each with a tiny flower at its end.

This family is midway between the most primitive and the most advanced. The sepals are fused except for five little teeth. The petals are separate and usually curved over the five separate stamens. An advanced feature is the low position of the ovary; the bulbous base of the pistil appears below the sepals and petals. Also the umbel formation is considered progressive. Here we have a fine example of a colony formation of flowers. Many little flowers in a cluster are more efficient for pollen transfer when an insect walks over them.

The Carrot Family supplies garden vegetables: carrots, celery, parsley, parsnips. Also the herbs, caraway, anise and dill. Its wild flower members are prolific and so hardy they live in waste places. The commonest is the wild carrot, also called Queen Anne's lace. Water hemlock resembles tall and handsome Queen Anne's lace, but water hemlock is deadly poison to live stock. In the spring the golden Alexander with the wonderful name *Zizia* is exquisite. Another member is the wild parsnip (*Pastinaca sativa*) that rears its green-yellow flat top clusters on mighty stems three or four feet tall in early summer. Most of the flowers of this family have white petals.

Mechanical characteristics are: five fused sepals, five separate petals and stamens, one pistil. An individual flower is so small you can hardly count these parts without a lens. For quick identification the flat form of the flower cluster is the thing. The leaves are characteristic of the family. They are commonly cut-leaved, with many segments. For example, note the feathery leaves of the Queen Anne's lace. The stem of a leaf spreads at its base so as to sheathe the main stem of the plant, and this stem is usually hollow.

THE HEATH FAMILY bears the scientific name *Ericaceae*, derived from *Erica*, the genus name of heather. In Europe, Africa and Asia heather covers the downs (heaths) of large areas. In the United States, strangely enough, we do not find heather except where it has been introduced. Nantucket has a few patches of true heather that probably arrived somehow from overseas, years ago in the days of whaling ships.

Although the family bellwether is lacking in the United States, other members of the Heath Family are among the aristocrats of our native flora. Unlike other families in this summary which have a predominance of herbaceous flowers thought of as typical wild flowers, the Heath Family consists mostly of woody shrubs. The diagram of their flowers shows that they are midway in the scale of evolution. This family gives us a vivid example of progress in the fusion of petals. The fused petals are usually white or pink and form exquisite little bell-shaped or urn-shaped flowers with small triangular scallops around their brims; these scallops represent the tip ends of the individual petals. The sepals, fused except for their tips, are usually like little green or blue saucers that hold the white cup of the petals. Separate stamens is a primitive note. The pistil shows transition. Sometimes it is in a high position, sometimes a low position.

The Heath Family inhabits colder places—rocky mountain sides among spruces and hemlocks—and damp shady woods where it makes luxuriant ground cover of rhododendron, mountain laurel, and wild azaleas. Trailing arbutus, the State Flower of Massachusetts and a pioneer among spring flowers, is no exception to the fact that this is mostly a family of shrubs. Even though trailing arbutus creeps on the ground it has woody stems and technically rates as a shrub. Blueberries and huckleberries have great masses of the white bells characteristic of the family. Exactly the same type of flower can be seen on the shrubs of aromatic wintergreen, although these plants are dwarfs only a few inches high. (Small boys chew the leaves for their strong wintergreen flavor.) The other wintergreen, *Pyrola*, is also a member of this family. The *Pyrola* flower is shallow like the hemisphere of the old-fashioned electric bell, and its pistil protrudes like a long clapper. It is shiny and wavy as though made of paraffin. The weird little Indian pipe is often included in the Heath Family, although it is so unusual in one respect that some botanists put it in a family all its own called the Indian Pipe Family. This is one of the few flowering plants that has no green chlorophyll. It grows in the decayed leaves on the floor of the woods, and because of its whiteness might be mistaken for a fungus instead of a family connection of the gorgeous rhododendrons. The Indian pipe plant is translucent and often looks bluish as though it were made of ice. The scope of the family is shown by the fact that a full sized tree, the sourwood (*Oxydendrum*) of the Middle West and South also belongs among the Heaths.

Mechanical features of the Heath Family are: five fused sepals and petals, ten stamens, and one pistil. Leathery, oval evergreen leaves are characteristic, although not invariable. The typical flower is a little bell or cup half an inch or so in length. Petals are usually white, but some of the showiest rhododendrons, mountain laurels, and azaleas are pink, flame or rose-colored.

THE FIGWORT FAMILY is also called the Snapdragon Family, or the Foxglove Family. Its scientific name is *Scrophulariaceae*, which comes from a prominent genus of the family, Scrophularia, supposed by the ancient herbalists to have curative properties for scrofula. The swollen throat or neck of the flower gives the impression that it is itself the victim of swollen glands, a malady which it took away from human victims.

The Figwort Family is well up the scale of progress. Its characteristic flower is so fancy and so colorful that gardeners and florists know its members well. Progress is evident not only in the fusion of petals but also in the specialization of their form like the puffy, nearly closed, mouth of a dragon. The pistil is double, but still retains an ancestral touch because the base of the pistil, the ovary, is in a high position. The four stamens are separate, but this is an even break for progress since their number is reduced. One member of the family actually exhibits evolution in the very act of reducing the number of stamens. The beard-tongue, or pentstemon, has a fifth stamen that is sterile and obsolete. That's how it gets the name pentstemon, meaning "fifth stamen."

Prominent members of the family are butter-and-eggs (as beautiful as a yellow and orange snapdragon but spreads like a rampant weed), painted cup, monkey flower, turtlehead, mullein, gerardia, speedwell. A slender sky blue figwort (*Linaria canadensis*) colors the fields of South Carolina and other southern states in April. Among the cultivated members are foxglove or digitalis (source of the heart tonic) and snapdragon.

The mechanical features of the Figwort Family are: five fused petals, five sepals fused into a tube except for their five points, four stamens, and one double pistil. To speak of five petals is technically correct. But they are so fused as hardly to be counted separately, and the quickest recognition lies in the general form of the flower with the swollen tube and the puffy lips. The features of the Figwort Family are similar to the Mint Family, so one other characteristic might be mentioned which supplies a sure check. If you look straight into a figwort flower so as to get a cross-section view of the base of the pistil, you will see that the ovary is two lobed. Viewed from above it makes a figure eight ∞. This is easy to see and it's a foolproof test of a Figwort as compared with a Mint that will be described in the next chapter.

CHAPTER EIGHTEEN

From Mints To Orchids

In the preceding chapter seven leading families stood up to be counted one after the other in the sequence in which their types were evolved. Does this mobility stir you? Does a dimly defined reality begin to emerge? The fact that all plant forms are plastic and connected one to another not only gives the landscape a pattern into which every tree and flower fits beautifully, but also reveals the most arresting fact about plants in this green world. *Trees and flowers have a visible fourth dimension!*

Philosophers and physicists have conjured with a fourth dimension, but it has always been intangible, elusive. Einstein figured out a theory of relativity which, I understand, only six people in the world have brains enough to comprehend. Here in the flowers of the fields and woods is a kind of relativity all of us can see. These flowers and trees exist in our three-dimensional world in the height, width, and thickness of their physical substance. But to these three dimensions is added—*time*. They have height, width, thickness—and duration! This is visible in butter-cups and lilies, magnolias and asters. It is seen in the changes from one family to the next; in the comparison of similarities of plants within a family. This graph of time written in living plants extends as far beyond the narrow limits of our historic age as the electromagnetic spectrum extends beyond the limits of our visi-ble spectrum. We can see it running back through the eons; we can only imagine it extending forward into the future.

Because of an emotional attitude toward the words primitive and advanced, it is hard not to consider some flower forms as "better" than others. This is a sort of pathetic fallacy. The butter-and-eggs of the Snapdragons is no better than a wild strawberry of the Roses, just because it has responded more vividly to the influence of time. In evolution's code the "best" flower forms are those that survive and the "worst" have disappeared. The fact that the mechanics of advanced forms are more complicated, precise, and more to be marvelled at, still does not make them better. It only makes them different. And having become different what then? Time will tell. The plant may survive in its present form endlessly while at the same time offering a stepping stone to some still more advanced design. Or a change of conditions may cause it to migrate or perish. The landscape is nicely bal-anced. When its equilibrium is disturbed a redistribution of its plant and animal life must be made.

Darwin in his *Origin of Species* suggests (in an unaccus-tomed anecdotal mood) that the more cats in a neighborhood the more red clovers. The cats destroy the nests of field mice which in turn prey on the combs and hives of bumblebees. Red clovers can be pollinated only by bumblebees. This is why Dar-win saw more red clovers around villages and small towns than out in the countryside beyond the cat zone. This is a local instance of what may happen to a progressive form that has attuned its life to one kind of insect, when the balance is upset.

And now back to our summaries of leading plant families.

In our last chapter we progressed to the Figworts. From here on the families are well-advanced, highly distinctive.

THE MINT FAMILY—scientific name, *Labiatae*, comes from the Latin labium, meaning lip, and refers to the fact that the flower resembles two lips. These are smooth and graceful and wide open, as compared with the puffy almost closed lips of the Figworts. The family has scope. Some of its members inhabit damp, marshy places, others exceedingly dry, virtually waterless spots. Some of the flowers are inconspicuous, in closely compact clusters in the axils of leaves; others are trumpets several inches long at the top of the plant.

The high rating of this family is earned by the fusion of sepals and petals, the reduced number of stamens, the double pistil, and the irregular form of the flower. This last feature, found in most of the higher families, is considered to be more efficient in attracting the right kind of insect for cross-pollination than the primitive radial symmetry. But the Mints, like the Figworts, with all their progressiveness own up to a primitive note in that their petals and sepals are attached below the pistil.

This family is a big producer of volatile oils used in candy, chewing gum and medicines. Some of its leading members are peppermint, spearmint, catnip, hoarhound, horsemint, thyme, rosemary and pennyroyal.

One of the most ubiquitous wild flowers in the world belongs in this family, the heal-all or self-heal (*Prunella vulgaris*). Other prominent wild members are bee-balm, motherwort, bugleweed, ground ivy. The elegant salvia and sages of the garden are Mints.

Mechanical features are: five petals, united and forming two lips with two lobes above and three lobes on the tips of the lower lip. Five sepals fused into a tube except at their tips. Four stamens attached to the petals. For the close observer who isn't sure whether he is looking at a Figwort or a Mint, the final test is the lobes on the ovary. In the Mints there are four lobes which appear like this ✛ in cross section. Another interesting mechanical feature of the Mints, occasionally of the Figworts, is the four-sided stem (square in cross-section) with leaves in pairs, opposite each other on the stem. If you find a pretty little blue flower that grows out horizontally on an aromatic plant with square stem and opposite leaves you can be pretty sure it's a Mint.

The scientific name of THE COMPOSITE FAMILY is *Compositae*, a most appropriate title for the World's Leading Flower Family. Its flower heads are composite in the sense that they are a close aggregation of tiny flowers.

So efficient is this great family in the production and distribution of seeds that its members cover the face of the earth more than any family of the small herbaceous flowering plants except those of the Grass Family. To understand the Composite Family it is necessary to have a new viewpoint about what a flower is like, and then to recognize three types of composites.

What is usually considered as a single flower, such as *a* daisy, *a* thistle, *a* dandelion, must now be considered as a compact head of many tiny flowers. For example, a single dandelion head will be composed of around 200 separate little flowers. Beneath these flowers like a saucer or cup to contain them are little overlapping green leaves. These may resemble the green sepals of large single flowers of other families. But sepals are organs of individual flowers. These green leaves, known as bracts, are actually specialized leaves for the protection of the flower head. This general formation is found in all the composites—compact flowers in a saucer of tiny green leaves.

The daisy, thistle and dandelion are typical of three types of Composites as follows:

1. *Radiate Composites,* like the daisy, have a central disc composed of little tube-shaped flowers, surrounded by rays. Each of these rays is tubular at its base but this tube unrolls to become a long strap-shaped affair. This form makes the ray flower resemble a petal, with which it is so often confused. The fact is, how-

ever, that each ray consists of five petals fused together, as you can see by the ridges if you peer closely. This formation of disc flowers surrounded by ray flowers resembles a sunburst. Prominent members of this group, besides the daisy, are: aster, sunflower, yarrow, black-eyed Susan, ragwort and goldenrod. To understand goldenrod you have to change focus three times, so to speak. First there is the whole plant as people commonly see it; then there are the individual heads indicating the radiate type of composite with disc flowers and ray flowers; and smaller still, requiring a lens to examine in detail, are the individual florets of each head.

2. *Discoid Composites*, like the thistle, have only the disc flowers, that is only tubular flowers. Besides thistles others of this type are: iron-weed, snakeroot, thoroughwort, Joe Pye weed, everlasting, tansy. In the case of the thistle the tube is very long, its lobes are slender and elongated, giving the pin-cushion formation a certain openness and fluffiness, but these thistle flowers are nevertheless disc flowers. Ragweed (hay fever!) and cocklebur are also discoid composites but their tube flowers lack white or colored petals, and so we scorn to call them wild flowers.

3. *Ligulate Composites*. The term comes from the Latin *ligula*, meaning tongue, and refers to the strap-shaped flowers. This type of composite has no central disc, but consists entirely of rays. These are numerous and bunched together so that they tend to lose the radiating pattern. The commonest member is the dandelion. Lettuce, chicory, hawkweed, Robin's plantain and rattlesnake root are also ligulate Composites.

To appreciate the remarkable efficiency of these three types for seed production and dispersal, examine an individual floret by breaking apart the head of a dandelion or the disc of a daisy. Each flower is a very slender tube, perhaps a half inch long, at the bottom of which is the egg-shaped ovary. From the crest of this ovary grows a circle of white hairs. This, strange to say, is the equivalent of a calyx, only the "sepals" instead of being green leaf-like structures as in more conventional flowers are white hairs. This white hair calyx of the Composites goes by the name of *pappus*, from the Greek word for "grandfather" who was always a gray-beard in those days. The tube of the flower, consisting of five petals fused together, rises up inside the circle of the pappus hairs. Out of the tube projects a little structure as delicate and handsomely wrought as a part in a Sperry gyroscope. This is the stalk of the pistil with a forked crest for a stigma. Just below its crest a sort of jacket makes a cylinder surrounding the style or stalk of the pistil; this cylinder has five segments. These segments are the fused anthers, that is, the pollen producing organs of the stamen.

It would be hard to imagine a more compact and simple little gadget, beautifully designed for its function of seed production.

The arrangement of the florets into heads builds up breadth and color so that little flowers become as conspicuous as big flowers for attracting insects in the competition of the field. This compact formation results in a kind of cross-pollination between individual flowers of the same plant. However, the abundance of daisies and dandelions proves that this partial cross-fertilization can make healthy seeds. The pappus form of calyx is not merely nature's whim but plays an important part in seed dispersal. For example, in the dandelion as the seed ripens, the circle of white hairs raised aloft on its stem becomes the familiar little parachute which carries the seed. Most of the members of this astonishing family have variations of this device and use the pappus to good advantage in seed dispersal.

Even the green bracts of the flower head may play a definite part in this all-important job of getting the seeds manufactured and dispersed. For example, after the flowers in the head of a dandelion are pollinated, the bracts turn upward and inward and compress the head. It's as though a bud, once open, were suddenly to close up again. For several days it remains pressed together while the petals disintegrate, the seed is being set, and the pappus is growing into a parachute. These things accomplished, the bracts open again and away go the seeds.

The Composite Family stands at the summit of flower forms. Its high place is seen in the fusion of petals and stamens, the reduced numbers of floral parts, the low position of the ovary, and organization of the head for attracting insects of all sorts and in that way speeding up seed-making and vigor.

The nine families described so far are listed roughly in the order of their progress in the scale of evolution from the most primitive to the most advanced. These families are the largest of the dicotyledons. Their members are so widespread and numerous, and they have so many genera that if you recognize these nine families you can enjoy the family relationships of a large percentage of the wild flowers you see, perhaps more than half of them.

It is important to distinguish between a family with many genera and a family with many individuals. It happens that these nine families are large in both respects. But there are also a number of families, containing a small number of genera, which are nevertheless conspicuous for one reason or another. The members of these small families are rugged individualists. Family features are stamped on them so strongly that they need no detailed description, and in some a single genus is practically a whole family in itself. Here are a few of these exclusive, highly distinctive families.

All members of THE VIOLET FAMILY look like violets, whether blue, white or yellow. The family imprint is clear and constant. The cultivated garden pansy and Johnny-jump-up belong in this family.

THE MILKWEED FAMILY is dramatic. It has big round clusters of unique flowers, rubber-plant-like leaves, creamy sap, and enormous pods from a single one of which seeds pour out by the hundreds like parachute troops. The small flowers are highly characteristic with their fantastic designs built around some of the most complicated gearing for cross-pollination possessed by flowers (see Chapter 15). The common milkweed (*Asclepias syriaca*) has been despised as a pesky weed but now research scientists are on the trail of hidden assets. Milkweed may supply fibers for making jute bags, soft silky fillings for dolls and pillows, sap derivatives for rubber, paper, and oil like soy-bean. The plant needs no coddling; it will grow in inhospitable places. This family has a future.

THE DOGWOOD FAMILY is best recognized by its member, the popular flowering dogwood, which illustrates the characteristic floral formation of the family. The flowers are small and green but these are surrounded with big showy white bracts or leaves usually taken for petals. Some of our finest native shrubs, famous for their red twigs, are Dogwoods. The little bunchberry (*Cornus canadensis*) of the northern woods is a member of this family.

THE CACTUS FAMILY, which always has prickly stems and showy flowers, is one of the most distinctive and well-known of our native flowering plant families. The gorgeous colorful flowers make sandy spots of the South and arid places of the Southwest famous for their displays of yellows and reds and other rich colors. The plants bear few or no leaves. The stems, wrongly referred to as leaves, expand and become green, performing the function of leaves.

THE GENTIAN FAMILY is made famous by the rich deep blue of the treasured closed and fringed gentians. The rose-colored sabatia of the pine barrens along the Atlantic Coast also belongs in this select family. The gentians are so choosy in their soil requirements and the company they keep (it takes a certain kind of fungus growing in collaboration with the roots of a fringed gentian to make that flower flourish) that they are considered elusive. The fringed gentian likes soil in limestone areas, where I have found it localized in abundance. But generally it is rare, and because of its exquisite beauty, it is a prize example of a flower needing protection.

One genus of THE LOBELIA FAMILY contains three species of our choicest wild flowers of late summer. The small light blue spiked lobelia makes a straight wand, standing a foot tall in the grass of a dry meadow. The cardinal flower takes a pure red band out of the spectrum and stands about two feet tall in wetter places. The tall lobelia is about three feet tall and deep blue. All have the characteristic lobelia type of flower with a split upper petal through which the fused stamens project, and three lobes of the lower petals hang below.

THE GERANIUM FAMILY has as its type the dependable wild geranium with its rose purple flowers about an inch across and its handsome, deeply cleft leaves. This flower is called wild cranesbill, because of the long sharp fruit. When this fruit ripens it splits into four steel blue springs that coil up violently, flinging out seeds contained in little boxes at the ends of each spring. The slender herb Robert grows in great abundance in woods and looks like a small replica of the wild geranium. It has such long sharp sepals that they are arresting and worth looking for. The fluidity of flower parts is seen when horticulture can turn stamens into petals by tricks of breeding. This is what happened to the geranium that stands in a flower pot on city window sills so that it bears no resemblance to its native prototype with five petals.

Two members of THE WATER LILY FAMILY are commonly seen, a white and a yellow water lily. They have the family almost to themselves. Everybody knows them with their round floating leaves that give such pictorial quality. No photographic salon is complete without a picture of a water lily.

THE PITCHER PLANT FAMILY has two northern species, often seen in peat-bogs, one with red flowers, the other with yellow. Unusual as the flowers are, the leaves are stranger, forming deep wells of water in which to drown insects. The pitcher plants may be considered the most individualistic of all families. None other uses its leaves to drown animal life for food. The pitchers vary in contour and markings. I have seen one species in a remote spot near Pensacola, Florida, with slender erect pitchers six feet long. Another southern species has transparent spots just above the well of the leaf that act as windows, holding insects by their light so that they don't scurry away so fast, and the chances are thereby increased of their falling into the well. This subject of carnivorous plants is so large and fascinating that it must be left for another time.

The foregoing families, big and little, all belong to the great division of the flowering plants called *dicotyledons* (the double seed-leafers). As we have said, nature built four times as many species from dicotyledon blueprints as from monocotyledon (the single seed-leafers). However, the latter group is a powerful minority with its streamlined families and unusual efficient flower forms. If we can say any form is more "unusual" than another in a kingdom where novelty and incessant invention are the order of the day!

The four families that follow are conspicuous representatives of the monocotyledons. These are listed in the order of evolution, although it is somewhat misleading to show them in single file. The Arums and Grasses are on sidetracks that branched off from the Lilies.

THE CAT-TAIL FAMILY is one of the smallest families of flowering plants with but a single genus named *Typha*, from which the family gets its scientific name, *Typhaceae*. Everybody knows the cat-tails, those curious tall plants that look like sausages on top of wands growing in marshes. Their long and narrow leaves, like oversized grass, have parallel veins typical of the monocotyledons. Two kinds of flowers grow on the same wand elevated above the leaves. The topmost few inches are occupied by a compact mass of flowers composed of two to seven stamens each. The fact that these are separate and vary in number is a primitive sign. There are no sepals and petals. After these stamens have discharged their pollen they wither and fall off, leaving the familiar bare spike at the top.

Just below these staminate flowers the blooms which contain pistils make the densely crowded cylinder that you think of as the cat-tail. Each flower has one pistil. The ovary is elevated on a stalk, another sign of the primitive. Again there are no petals or sepals, but long hairs are attached to the stalk of the pistil. These hairs are so numerous that they give the appearance of felt to the cat-tail. When the fruit ripens this felt turns to a rich dark brown.

THE LILY FAMILY. Both the popular name and the scientific name, *Liliaceae*, stem from the great genus, *Lilium*. Although famous for some of the aristocrats among decorative plants, the Lily Family gives us the garden vegetables, onions and asparagus. Prized among wild flowers are the red, Canada, and Turk's cap lilies. Other prominent members are hyacinth, star of Bethlehem, tulip, smilax, Solomon's seal, trillium, bellwort and the misnamed dog's-tooth violet, better called the trout lily as this lily is by no means a violet.

The mechanical features of the Lily Family are: three sepals, three petals, six stamens and the pistil with three lobes. As the family belongs to the monocotyledons the leaves have parallel veins. (Two exceptions should be noted. The catbrier and the trillium, despite their membership in the Lily Family, have net-veined leaves.) When checking the numbers of petals and sepals you must remember that the sepals are colored like the petals and are as large as the petals so that the observer would say at first glance that the flower has six petals and no sepals, instead of three and three.

The scientific name of THE ARUM FAMILY is *Araceae* from *Arum*, the keynote genus of the family. Most of the family members are tropical. The huge curiosity *Monstera* is a greenhouse immigrant from the tropics, which illustrates how variable are the leaves of the family. The Monstera has large holes in the leaves indicating the transition of a primitive family from simple to compound leaf formations. The Calla lily of the Easter florist trade is another tropical import.

Some of our most famous spring flowers are Arums. The skunk cabbage and Jack-in-the-pulpit are beautiful examples of the flower structure that makes this family so interesting. The most conspicuous feature of the petal-less flowers is a canopy-like arrangement called a spathe—often colored with purple spots or stripes—which encloses a club-shaped formation called a spadix. The spadix is a spike of tiny flowers; the canopy is simply a leaf that is modified in such a way as to give protection to the flowers and keep off the rain. The spadix flowers have no sepals and petals; they are closely compact florets with stamens or pistils, not both. They are so crowded that they may give a fuzzy appearance to the club. However, it is easy to see the two kinds. As with the cat-tails, the upper part of the spadix, occupying most of its length, has stamen-bearing flowers. Those with pistils are at the bottom of the spadix.

THE GRASS FAMILY. The scientific name of this teeming family is *Gramineae*, from the Latin word *gramina*, meaning grass. The English word "grain" comes from the same source. An individual of the Grass Family is the humblest, most inconspicuous of flowering plants. Indeed, it may come as a surprise to some people to think that grass *is* a flowering plant. The flowers have no sepals, no petals, no brightly tinted anthers and stigmas, no colorful accessories. Yet these smooth-running, rapid-fire little spark plugs mature their seeds in such astronomical numbers that the family covers the face of the earth and gives man his chief source of food. See Chapter 12.

The cereals are all members of this family: corn, wheat, oats, barley, rice, rye. It also includes the forage crops: timothy, Kentucky bluegrass, millet, sorghum. Sugar-cane is a member. And the family can even boast a tree member—bamboo.

Golfers and suburbanites with lawnmowers think they know grass when they see it, but if you and I are going to take an interest in the mechanics of a grass flower we need a lens. The flowers grow in compact little spikes. There are no sepals or petals, but instead of that each flower has a little drab papery scale, the "chaff" of the grain. Behind this scale three tiny stamens are inserted and one pistil, which waves a fancy branching stigma above the flower like a feathery insect feeler. This type of stigma is designed to catch the pollen grains that blow around in the breeze. The Grasses have no insect collaborators. The fruit is a grain. Only one grain is produced in each flower. Since there are a number of flowers in each spikelet and many spikelets in the whole floral assemblage of a single plant, the number of grains produced is enormous.

An important physical feature of grass is, of course, the ribbon-like leaf with its parallel veins. This is attached to the stem by a long sheathing base that is split open on the side opposite the projection of the leaf blade! The stem is cylindrical, round in cross-section, and hollow (old-fashioned soda straws!).

A word of caution is needed if you think that you can quickly recognize a member of the Grass Family. An entirely different family of monocotyledons, the Sedge Family, can easily be mistaken for grass. Because of its slight interest to the layman (although every other botanist seems to specialize in sedges) I shall only mention how a detective can instantly tell the difference between a sedge and a grass. The sheath of the sedge (that is, the lower part of the blade that embraces the stem) is not split; the stem is three-sided, triangular in cross-section while the stem of grass is cylindrical; and the stem of a sedge is usually filled with pith, instead of being hollow as are grass stems.

THE ORCHID FAMILY. The scientific name *Orchidaceae* is from an old Greek word *orchis*, implying that this aristocrat family

2 2 5

has a long history. On the other hand, the Orchid Family probably has more new species yet to be discovered than any other family. One of its homes is in the jungles of the tropics where there is much exploring still to be done. However, many members of the family are among the most prized wild flowers in almost every lush habitat in the United States. There are about forty different kinds of orchids in every state from Illinois to New England. Nowhere are these abundant in the sense that social flowers like daisies are abundant. They grow as individuals. But anyone can find them if he has his mind and eyes in focus. Some of our commonest native orchids are the lady's-slipper, orchis, pogonia, grass pink, arethusa, rattlesnake plantain, coral root and twayblade. Ladies' tresses are perhaps the most numerous as orchids go, dotting upland pastures in September with their little spirals of white flowers on wands a few inches tall. The comparative scarcity of all individuals of the Orchid Family gives them greater value than other wild flowers. They are definitely on the list of flowers needing protection—unless you pick only a few ladies' tresses, if you find a healthy patch.

The outstanding physical feature of all orchids is the fantastic form of the flower. This represents a high degree of specialization, as the orchids are exceedingly particular as to which insects shall help them transfer pollen. The flower has three sepals, usually green but sometimes brightly colored like the petals. There are three petals, two of which might be considered normal forms of petals. These two flare out at the sides and are called wings. The third petal is the crux of the situation, creating the variety and unique appearance of this family flower. The third petal may have flamboyant wavy or fringed edges; it may end in a long spur; it may be formed like a trumpet, or perhaps a bulbous sac as in the lady's-slipper. This showy petal takes a surprising range of colors, pink, yellow, lavender, purple, rose, brown—never red. (If anybody ever breeds a red orchid it will be as wonderful as a black tulip.) The showy petal is called the lip. Three stamens are welded together with the pistil to form a column. Some orchids have a curious practice of taking a sterile stamen, one that produces no pollen, and separating this from the other stamens, give it an original shape and color with all the appearance of a petal. The little hood of the lady's-slipper is an example of this aberration. This colorful hood can easily be taken for a beautiful petal, but it is in fact a stamen performing as an individualist. The variety of detail in an orchid is puzzling, but on the whole its mechanics fit into the foregoing plan of the flower.

The high place of the orchids is seen in the fusion of stamens and pistil into a column, in the reduced numbers of floral parts, and above all in the extraordinary specialization of the flower forms.

With the Composite Family at the apex of the dicotyledons and the Orchid Family at the head of the monocotyledons we have two climaxes of flower forms in our day. What flower forms and families are to come next? To answer this question the philosopher will have to take over from the botanist.

How to be a TREE DETECTIVE
in WINTER

Here's a way to enjoy naming trees from small clues. You can pick a couple of twigs and bring them into the house for this purpose. Only the commonest trees are included in this key. It can serve as a stepping stone for the more complete and scientific keys mentioned in the bibliography.

Directions

First look for the buds. Note their arrangement, shape, size, and scales. Pay special attention to buds at end of the twig.

Second look for the leaf scar. Note its shape and the dots in it.

Third look for other clues. These may or may not be present; bright colors, thorns, catkins, peculiarities of pith, sap, twig, or bark.

Answer questions below as though "true or false." If the first A does not fit, go on to the next A. When A fits, then take B under the A that fits and so on, until you reach the answer.

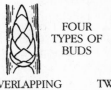

FOUR
TYPES OF
BUDS

OVERLAPPING
SCALES

TWO SCALES
LIKE A VALVE

SINGLE SCALE
COVERING BUD

NAKED
(NO SCALES)

EXPLANATION OF CERTAIN WORDS

Leaf Scar: Mark on twig where last season's leaf fell from stem. Usually found just below bud.

Bud Scales: The hard outer covering of buds.

Pith Partitions: The pith is the core of a twig. When sliced lengthwise you sometimes see partitions like the rounds of a ladder.

BUDS
ALTERNATE

BUDS
OPPOSITE

Catkins: These are little stiff tassels (often 1 or 2 inches long) that hang on some trees. Frequently found on the birches.

Witches' Brooms: Seen on the hackberry, like a dark brunch or tangle of twigs.

(A) BUDS OPPOSITE

(**B**) **Buds Large** (½ to 1 inch or longer) blunt, oval .... HORSE CHESTNUT

(**B**) **Buds Small** (½ inch or less)

(**C**) **Scales Meeting at Edges,** bud on end of twig like a silver-gray shoe-button with 4 scales .... FLOWERING DOGWOOD

(**C**) **Scales Overlapping**

(D) Buds oval, those at end of twig in threes with middle one much longer. Leaf scars narrow, triangular with 3 dots............................ MAPLE

(D) Buds fatter, dark brown. Buds at end of twig close together making fancy design. Leaf scars shield shape, or almost circular, with many dots forming a horseshoe .... ASH

(A) Buds in Whorls of Three

Tiny fat buds. Leaf scars round, standing out on platforms; two large scars and one small scar in each whorl .... CATALPA

(A) Buds Alternate

(**B**) **Sap Milky**

1. Buds triangular with 2 or 3 red brown scales .... MULBERRY
2. Tiny brown buds and powerful thorns .... OSAGE ORANGE
3. Pith orange, small tree or shrub ......
SUMAC

WHITE OAK

ELM

HICKORY

(B) Sap Not Milky

(C) Twigs With Thorns

1. Buds sunken out of sight in bark, thorns slender, *branched* .... HONEY LOCUST
2. Buds sunken out of sight in barks, thorns thick, unbranched, *in pairs* at leaf scars .... BLACK LOCUST
3. Single thorns, from side of twig; buds minute .... HAWTHORN
4. Single heavy thorn from end of short branch .... PEAR

POPLAR

N.H.D.

(C) Twigs Without Thorns

(D) Pith With Partitions

1. Spaces between partitions empty. No scales on buds .... WALNUT
2. Pith white, buds light brown with 2 scales like a duck's bill ..... TULIP TREE
3. Pith partitions unequally spaced. Buds dark red-brown with about 4 scales... TUPELO
4. Pith partitions unequally spaced. Buds dark, triangular. Bark in square chunks PERSIMMON
5. Partitions close together. Bark warty. "Witches' brooms" often visible....... HACKBERRY

SYCAMORE

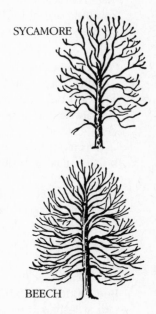

(D) Pith Without Partitions

(E) With Catkins

1. Bark smooth, or papery and curly BIRCH
2. Bark in narrow, ragged vertical strips .... HOP HORNBEAM

(E) Without Catkins

(F) Buds Usually Clustered Toward Tip of Twig .... OAK

(F) Buds Not Usually Clustered Toward Tip of Twig

BEECH

(G) With Distinctive Twigs

1. Twigs green with spicy taste ....
    SASSAFRAS
2. Older twigs with corky ridges. Buds mahogany brown, shiny .....
    SWEET GUM
3. Young twigs red above, green beneath .... PEACH
4. Twigs with bitter taste like cherry pits. (Young bark smooth like birch)
    CHERRY

BLACK WILLOW

(G) Without Distinctive Twigs

(H) No Scales on Buds. Tiny folded leaves of buds sulphur yellow ...
    BITTERNUT HICKORY

(H) One Scale Showing on Buds.

1. End bud big, sometimes an inch long, oval, hairy .... MAGNOLIA
2. Buds like light brown conical hats. Leaf scar makes narrow circle around base of bud .... SYCAMORE
3. Buds red, pressed against twig
    WILLOW

(H) Two Scales Showing on Bud

1. Little round buds set into the top of a big oval leaf scar. About 9 dots just inside edge of leaf scar .... AILANTHUS
2. Green or red scales, one of which bulges, making bud lopsided. ....
    LINDEN
3. End bud fat, wide oval. Scales soft, light gray, or tan. (Note: the tough outside scales fall off early)
    MOCKERNUT HICKORY OR PIGNUT
    HICKORY

APPLE

(H) Three Scales Showing on Bud—Buds smooth, oval, brown. Pith star shaped in cross-section.

    CHESTNUT

(H) More than Three Scales Showing on Bud

1. Inner scales soft gray. Outer scales with long points. . . . .
SHAGBARK HICKORY

2. Light brown. Longest, sharpest of all buds. (Often ¾-in. long) . . .
BEECH

3. About 6 scales arranged in two vertical rows. Bud usually tipped and on one side of leaf scar. . ELM

4. Long sharp buds often shiny as though varnished and pressed close to twig. Pith star shaped in cross-section. . . . . POPLAR

5. Blunt, woolly, so that scales may not show clearly. Squatty tree. Trunk often leaning . . . . APPLE

Pictorial Key to Native Evergreens

Evergreen names are often confused although the different kinds can be easily identified.

The trees commonly known as evergreens are members of the Pine Family. Their leaves are needles, and they produce cones. A few trees in other families with broad leaves are also evergreen. This is true of the live oak, magnolia, and rhododendron. On the other hand, two members of the Pine Family are not evergreens: the larch and the bald cypress shed their needles in winter.

The six shown here cover most of the common evergreens, except cultivated kinds and some that are restricted in their distribution.

Pine
Long needles held together at the base by a sheath of papery bark. The number of needles in each cluster tells you the kind of Pine. For example: White Pine, 5 needles; Red Pine, 2 needles; Pitch Pine, 3 needles.

Fir

The only native Fir east of the Rockies is the Balsam. Needles in two ranks make a flat design. Pluck off needle and you see on the twig a little round scar with a dot in the center.

Hemlock

Needles in two ranks like the Fir, but shorter, flatter, and blunt. Dark green and shiny above, pale below with 2 parallel dotted lines. Along top of twig you see little upside-down needles.

Juniper

Common tree form called Red Cedar whose red heartwood scares off moths. Two kinds of needles often grow on same shoot: sharp awl-shaped projecting at angles; and flat overlapping scales that hug the twig.

Spruce

Needles are short, four-sided (awl-shaped), arranged in spirals on the twig. Pluck off needles and you see their stems left on the twig like little hooks or projections.

White Cedar

Common form called arbor-vitae. Needles in four ranks, flat, shiny and overlapping closely, forming geometric design. Center needles with dots. (Drawing magnified about 6 diameters.)

How to be a TREE DETECTIVE in SUMMER

Directions

Note points about leaves in this order:
 1. Arrangement whorled, opposite, or alternate.
 2. Simple or compound.
 3. Edges entire or toothed.
 4. Texture leathery or soft.

5. Shiny or dull.
6. Average size if full grown.
7. Proportions.

For additional clues as called for in key you may have to note thorns, pith (split twig lengthwise with sharp knife), sap, bark, taste of twig.

Answer questions below as though "true or false." If the first A does not fit, go on to the next A. When A fits, then take B under the A that fits, and so on, until you reach the answer.

For explanation of words see diagrams.

LEAVES
OPPOSITE

(A) Leaves in Whorls of 3
Leaves large, 6 to 12 inches ...... CATALPA

(A) Leaves Opposite
(B) Leaves Compound
(C) Plamately Compound (like the fingers on your hand) ....
HORSECHESTNUT and BUCKEYE

(C) Pinnately Compound (like a feather)
3 or 5 leaflets ....BOX ELDER
5 to 11 leaflets ....ASH

(B) Leaves Simple
1. Large, heart-shaped, edge entire, 5 to 15 inches. .... PAULOWNIA
2. Three major lobes (smaller lobes also) .... MAPLE
3. Smooth ovals, edges entire ....
DOGWOOD

LEAVES
ALTERNATE

(A) Leaves Alternate
(B) Leaves Pinnately Compound
(C) Twigs With Thorns
1. Thorns in pairs on each side of leaf stem .... BLACK LOCUST

LEAF
PINNATELY
COMPOUND

2. Thorns single, often branched like daggers, leaves often doubly compound like a fern .... HONEY LOCUST

(C) Twigs Without Thorns

(D) Edges of Leaflets Entire or Slightly Toothed

1. 7 to 13 leaflets, flowers or berries white, tree or shrub of swamps (DON'T TOUCH THIS) ....POISON SUMAC

2. 9 to 21 or more leaflets, midrib between leaflets has wings, yellowish flowers or red berries, tree or shrub of drier locations .... DWARF SUMAC

3. One or two teeth at base of leaflet tipped with shiny gland, often seen in cities .... AILANTHUS

4. Leaves doubly compound like a fern .... KENTUCKY COFFEE TREE

(D) Edges of Leaflets Definitely Toothed

(E) Small Tree or Shrub, Sap Milky; Flowers, If Present, Yellowish; Berries Deep Red ....STAGHORN and SMOOTH SUMAC

(E) Larger Tree, Sap Not Milky

(F) Pith of Twigs Has Partitions With Spaces Between Empty ..... WALNUT

(F) Pith Without Partitions

(G) Leaflets Large, 3 to 7 inches, and usually fewer than on walnut HICKORY

(G) Leaflets Small, ¾ to 4 inches, 9 to 17 on a leaf ... MOUNTAIN ASH

(B) Leaves Simple

(C) Sap Milky, leaves variable, heart-shaped, unlobed or 2 or 3 lobes ....
MULBERRY

(C) Sap Not Milky

(D) Twig With Thorns

1. Thorns attached at base of leaf stalk,

LOBE
SHARP

LOBE
ROUNDED

SINUS
ROUNDED

SINUS
SHARP

BASE
HEART
SHAPED

BASE
LOPSIDED

leaves small, oval and heavily toothed
or with lobes, fruit like a little apple
HAWTHORN
2. Thorns from end of twigs or spurs.
Leaves medium ovals, 2 to 4 inches,
shining .... PEAR

(D) Twigs Without Thorns

(E) Leaf as Broad or Nearly as Broad as it is Long

1. Leaf heart-shaped, 3 to 5 inches,
edge entire .... REDBUD
2. Leaf lobed like a maple, bark with
white patches .... SYCAMORE
3. Leaf triangular, edge with fine teeth
or scalloped .... POPLAR
4. Base lopsided, heart-shaped, fine
teeth .... LINDEN
5. Leaves squared off at top. Trunk a
tall straight cylinder .... TULIP TREE

(E) Leaf Oval, Longer Than Broad

(F) Edges Entire or Almost

1. Small leaves, 2 to 3 inches, leathery, shining dark green on top, whit-
ish below .... LIVE OAK
2. Large leaves, 6 to 20 inches, leathery, highly polished, very dark
green .... MAGNOLIA
3. Leaves 4 to 6 inches, not leathery.
Bark in square chunks. Occasional
teeth .... PERSIMMON

(F) Edges of Leaves Scalloped or Wavy

1. With prickles, dark, leathery,
polished .... HOLLY
2. Leaves 3 to 6 inches, long, oval,
bark smooth, silver-gray ..... BEECH
3. Leaves with wavy edges, bark dark
and deeply sculptured ....
CHESTNUT OAK

(**Note:** Do not confuse chestnut oak
with American chestnut. The latter

LEAF SIMPLE
EDGE TOOTHED

LEAF SIMPLE
EDGE ENTIRE

LEAF
LOBED

has been killed by a blight. You often see shrubby forms or suckers of the true chestnut. They have handsome slender oval leaves, 6 to 10 inches, with scalloped edges and sharp teeth.)

(F) Edges of Leaves with Teeth
1. Teeth sharp and double, leaf leathery, base lopsided .... ELM
2. Leaf tapering, curved, soft texture, base lopsided .... HACKBERRY
3. Fine teeth, broad oval 2½ to 4 inches, twigs slightly hairy, small, stocky tree, often a shrub ....
SHADBLOW
4. Leaf broad oval, dull, woolly beneath, 3 to 5 inches .... APPLE
5. Symmetrical oval leaf, shiny green, 2 to 5 inches, upper bark and twigs smooth deep red with prominent raised dots .... CHERRY
6. Teeth small and crowded, leaf soft, slightly hairy on both sides, bark shredded in vertical strips ....
HOP-HORNBEAM
7. Leaf smooth and soft similar to preceding, bark dark gray, smooth, muscular ridges .... BLUE BEECH
8. Leaf similar to preceding but smooth bark, sometimes peeling off in horizontal strips, white, yellow, or dark red .... BIRCH

(F) Leaves Lobed .... OAK
(Note that certain oaks without lobes are keyed out elsewhere.)

(E) Tree With Broken Twigs and Suckers, Leaf Very Long and Narrow. Heavy tree in wet places, leaves 3 to 6 inches long .... WILLOW

Bibliography

Any good library will have its shelves stocked with a great many volumes dealing with plants and gardens, so that what are listed here are but a few among a wealth of others. Some have aged very well, and have not outgrown their usefulness or charm, or been outdated by new advances. Others, however, deal with the science of plants that has grown explosively since *This Green World* saw the light of day in 1942; the reader can judge these newer volumes from their publication date.

TREES

The Audubon Society Field Guide to North American Trees   (two volumes divided into eastern and western regions).   Alfred A. Knopf, N. Y. The dividing line between East and West runs from southwest Texas up the eastern edge of the Rockies to the Arctic tree line. This book lacks the tropical species inhabiting some of our southeastern states, but 364 eastern and 314 western species are included, with each categorized as to leaves, flowers, fruits and autumn foliage. The species are arranged taxonomically, and are illustrated with many colored photographs. An excellent field guide with accompanying range maps and mature silhouettes.

A Field Guide to Trees and Shrubs. Roger Tory Peterson Field Guide Series. Houghton, Mifflin, Boston.
Covers an area from Newfoundland south to South Carolina, and west to Kansas and the Dakotas. Divided into five sections, based on leaf shape and arrangement, and accompanied by black and white illustrations of leaf, twig and bud characteristics. It lacks range maps and the listing of species is artificial, presumably for convenience, rather than by natural affinities. A quite usable field guide, nonetheless.

Trees and Shrubs in Eastern North America, by B. Blackburn. Oxford University Press, N. Y. 1952.
A readable and easy to use key to both wild and cultivated woody plants growing in temperate regions. It does not include the conifers.

The Adaptive Geometry of Trees (2nd edition) by H. S. Horn. Princeton University Press, Princeton.
Why do trees have the shapes that come to characterize them? Why are some canopy trees, others undergrowth species? What strategies are used to maximize their interception of light? The author deals with these topics in a most intriguing and enlightening way.

Physiology of Woody Plants, by P. J. Kramer and T. T. Koslowski. Academic Press, N. Y. 1979.
A well-documented and comprehensive textbook dealing with the growth, nutrition and water relations of a variety of tree species.

The Growing Tree, by B. F. Wilson. University of Massachusetts Press, Amherst. 1970.
A small volume dealing, in non-technical language, with all of the aspects of tree growth: leaves, roots, trunk, branches and buds.

Xylem Structure and the Ascent of Sap, by M. H. Zimmerman. Springer-Verlag, N. Y. 1983.
A popular account of the movement of water in woody plants by one who has contributed a good deal to our understanding of this subject.

Trees: Structure and Function, by M. H. Zimmerman and J. Cracraft.   Springer-Verlag, N. Y. 1975.

The physiology of woody plants differs in many ways from that of their herbaceous cousins, and it is to this topic that the authors go in this rather sophisticated volume.

A First Book of Tree Identification, by M. Rogers, with photographs by Wynn Hammer.   Random House, N. Y.

A beginner's volume dealing with 31 species of common American trees. Divided into several sections: Branches and leaves; How they grow; Barks—distinctive; and Barks—miscellaneous. The illustrations are excellent.

The Book of Trees, by Alfred C. Hottes.   The A. T. De La Mare Company, N. Y.

A fine handbook on the home uses of trees: What kind grow best in certain locations; feeding; pruning; transplanting; etc. Even the history and romance of trees. Illustrated with rather out-of-date photographs and some excellent diagrams.

Tree Flowers, by Walter E. Rogers, with drawings by Olga A. Smith. Published by the author at Appleton, Wisconsin.

A large artistic volume with remarkable full page, magnified photographs of tree flowers. These photographs of a subject seldom found elsewhere more than offset some minor defects of the book, such as a confusing arrangement.

Winter Botany, by William Trelease.   Published by the author at Urbana, Illinois.

A unique book with its accurate, eloquent line drawings of winter buds. In a small, pocket-size volume it gives winter characteristics of most trees and shrub species throughout the United States. The book also features a key for winter identification. If you are willing to learn some technical words and want *all* winter buds, this is the book.

FLOWERS

How We Got Our Flowers, by A. W. Anderson.   Dover Publications, N. Y. (in paperback).

A popular treatment of the plant hunters in bringing many plants into our gardens.

The Audubon Society Field Guide to North American Wildflowers (in two volumes divided into eastern and western regions). Alfred A. Knopf, N. Y.

> Beautifully illustrated volumes, with the colored photographs grouped at the front of the volumes, and with numbered references to comprehensive species descriptions in the text. Identification usually, but not always, relatively easy.

A Field Guide to Wildflowers of Northeastern and North-central North America. Roger Tory Peterson Field Guide Series. Houghton, Mifflin, Boston.

> A companion to three other volumes covering the rest of North America (the Southeast excepted). Species are grouped by color, and as with other Peterson volumes, illustrations and descriptions face each, and are reinforced with other details of lead and flower to aid in identification. A good and most useful guide.

A Guide to Enjoying Wildflowers, by D. and L. Stokes. Little Brown & Co., Boston.

> This is not a comprehensive text since it covers only about fifty widely distributed genera, but it has other virtues. It is well illustrated, with discussions that include medicinal properties (if any), cultivated varieties, life histories and pollination strategies.

Helpful Hints on Conserving Wild Flowers. A leaflet giving lists of wild flowers that must be protected—never picked; those that may be picked in moderation; and those that may be picked freely. Everybody interested in preserving our wild flowers should have this list. Enclose return, stamped envelope when applying to: Conservation Committee, The Garden Club of America, 598 Madison Avenue, New York, N. Y.

EVOLUTION AND GENETICS

Biological studies of the past quarter century and more have been dominated by the molecular biologists, geneticists and evolutionists almost to the point of overshadowing all other facets of plant and animal science. The volumes below are included to aid in placing the more descriptive features of plant studies in a more modern context.

Molecular Biology of the Gene, by B. Albert, *et al.* Garden Publishing Co., N. Y. 1983.

A sophisticated volume dealing with the enormous strides made in our understanding of the nature and function of DNA.

The Theory and Process of Organic Evolution, by F. J. Ayala and J. W. Valentine. Benjamin, Cummings Publishing Co., Menlo Park, Calif. 1979.
An excellent treatment of evolution in all of its varied aspects.

Evolution and Plants of the Past, by H. P. Banks. Wadsworth, Belmost, Calif. 1970.
A short text on fossil plants, evolutionary relations, and the possible origins of the flowering species.

Phylogenetic Patterns and the Evolutionary Process, by N. Eldredge and J. Cracraft. Columbia University Press, N. Y. 1980.
A solid treatment of evolution by two of the advocates of punctuated evolution as opposed to the Darwinian view of slow and undramatic changes taking place through long periods of time.

Plant Speciation, by V. Grant. Columbia University Press, N. Y. 1971.
All aspects of plant evolution are covered by the author who is an authority on the genus Phlox and other western North American plants.

Dimensions of Darwinism: Themes and Counterthemes in Twentieth-Century Evolutionary Theory, by M. Grene (ed.). Cambridge University Press, N. Y. 1983.
A series of articles by those who adhere to the various points of view that have been advanced to explain evolution as a process.

Beyond New-Darwinism: An Introduction to the New Evolutionary Paradigm, by M. H. Ho and P. T. Saunders. Academic Press, N. Y. 1984.
A difficult text but worthwhile for those interested in keeping up with modern trends in the biological sciences.

The Eighth Day of Creation, by H. Judson. Simon and Schuster, N. Y. 1979.
A semi-popular treatment of the fascinating history of the rise of modern genetics and the discovery of the nature and function of DNA.

The Path to the Double Helix, by R. Olby. Macmillan, London. 1974.
Another readable history of the discovery of the molecular basis of inheritance, and of the investigators who were involved in this search.

The Mode and Tempo of Evolution, by G. G. Simpson.   Yale University Press, New Haven. 1951. (Revised and abridged paperback.)
This and the volume listed below are thoroughly readable presentations of evolution in the Darwinian tradition, and in the context of modern genetic discoveries.

The Meaning of Evolution, by G. G. Simpson.   Yale University Press, New Haven. 1967. (Revised paperback.)

POLLINATION

Insects and Flowers, by F. C. Barth.   Princeton University Press, Princeton. 1985.
An excellent and up-to-date volume on pollination biology, and the exciting research being done in that field.

Cellular Recognition Systems in Plants, by J. Heslop-Harrison. University Park Press, Baltimore. 1978.
A slender volume of sixty pages by the former director of Kew Gardens on pollen-stigma and style interactions, self-incompatibility, and interspecific incompatibility systems.

The Story of Pollination, by B. J. D. Meeuse.   Ronald Press, N. Y. 1961.
This very readable volume ranks as one of the finest books not only on pollination, but in the whole field of plant science; it is the basis of an excellent film on pollination. The significance and meaning of pollination is well handled, as are insect-flower interactions, and the role of the wind. Contains a good bibliography.

The Golden Throng, by E. W. Teale.   Dodd, Mead & Co., N. Y.
A fascinating book about bees and the dramatic lives of these pollinators of flowers. Superb, close-up photographs by an entomologist who is also an expert photographer set a fresh and higher standard for a natural history book.

Pollen Grains, by R. P. Wodehouse.   McGraw-Hill Book Company, N. Y.
This book, by the outstanding authority in the field, stands alone for its readable, carefully edited text and its remarkable drawings of pollen grains. The painstaking index and bibliography make it also the top book of reference for students.

GENERAL BOOKS

How Plants Got Their Names, by L. H. Bailey.   Macmillan, N. Y.
A charming volume dealing with the origin and meaning of the Latin names given to plants; written by one of the great American horticulturists.

La Plante, by C. Brossfeldt.   Verlag Ernst Wasmuth, A. G., Berlin.
This is a rare and beautiful volume. The brief 5-page text is in French, but the 120 full-page, 9½ by 12 inch photographs of buds, leaves, fronds, leaf scars, fruits, tendrils, flowers and growing shoots are among the most remarkable and exquisite available in any language. Should be read in relation to the contents of Chapters 6 and 9.

The Life of the Green Plant, by A. W. Galston, *et al.*   Prentice-Hall, Englewood Cliffs. 1980. (Paperback.)
A well-written and illustrated introductory text covering most aspects of the physiology and growth of plants.

Seed to Civilization by C. B. Heiser, Jr. The Story of Man's Food. W. H. Freeman & Co., San Francisco. 1973.
A fascinating story of man's dependence on plants, how he has domesticated them, and then exploited them to feed the increasing number of people of the world.

New Concepts in Flowering-Plant Taxonomy, by J. Heslop-Harrison. Harvard University Press, Cambridge. 1960.
A brief but excellent review of the basis of plant classification as judged by modern techniques, and with an understanding of hereditary and ecological discoveries. This is prefaced by a comparison of "classical" versus "modern" classification systems.

Botany: An Ecological Approach, by W. A. Jensen and F. B. Salisbury.   Wadsworth, Belmost, Calif. 1972.
A good general text written from an evolutionary as well as an ecological point of view.

Photochrome and Plant Growth, by R. E. Kendrich, and H. Frankland. Studies in Biology Series, #68 (2nd edition).   Edward Arnold Publishers, London. 1983.
An excellent, if elementary, treatment of the chemical basis of photoperiodism.

Taxonomy of Vascular Plants, by G. H. M. Lawrence.   Macmillan, N. Y. 1951.
>A sound treatise on plant classification, with good family descriptions; includes a history of taxonomy.

Introductory Plant Physiology, by G. R. Noggle and G. Fritz. (2nd edition).   Prentice-Hall, Englewood Cliffs. 1985.
>A good text, but requires some knowledge of elementary botany and chemistry to make use of it.

Biology of Plants, by P. H. Raven, *et al.* (4th edition.)   Worth Publishers, N. Y. 1986.
>A widely used, well-written and excellent text touching on virtually all aspects of plant science.

The Biology of Flowering, by F. B. Salisbury.   Natural History Press, N. Y. 1971.
>A semi-popular volume on photoperiodism, with an emphasis on the short-day species, Xanthium.

Patterns in Plant Development, by T. A. Steeves and I. M. Sussex.   Prentice-Hall, Englewood Cliffs. 1972. (Paperback.)
>A sound and comprehensive text dealing with the elusive and complex problems of plant growth.

The Cell, by C. P. Swanson and P. L. Webster. (5th edition.)   Prentice-Hall, Englewood Cliffs. 1985. (Paperback.)
>An introduction to cell biology, covering the structure and function of membranes, organelles, and hereditary apparatus, bioenergetics, and the role of the cell in development, inheritance, evolution and death.

Humanistic Botany, by O. Tippo and W. L. Stern.   Norton, N. Y. 1977.
>A superbly written and illustrated, essentially non-technical textbook dealing with the interrelations of plants and people.

DARWINIANA

Many of us are accustomed to thinking of the influence of Charles Darwin as stemming from two books: *Journal of Researches into the Geology and Natural History of the Various Countries Visited during the Voyage of the H. M. S. Beagle*, a splendid but rather typical early Victorian travelogue published soon after his return in 1836 from his

5-year trip, and his *On the Origin of Species by Means of Natural Selection, or the Preservation of Favored Races in the Struggle for Life*, published in 1859, and without doubt the most significant volume ever written on a biological subject. But Darwin was an excellent writer and a well-versed botanist in his own right, experimenting with a number of species in his own garden at Downs, and corresponding widely with many of the plant breeders in England. The list below indicates that he published extensively in the plant field, and made contributions in several fields.

Fertilization in Orchids. 1861.

Variation of Animals and Plants under Domestication. 1868.

Climbing and Insectivorous Plants. 1875.

Effects of Cross- and Self-Pollination in the Vegetable Kingdom. 1876.

The Power of Movement in Plants. 1881.

The Different Forms of Flowers on Plants of the Same Species. 1897.

INDEX